Ezra Pound's Early Verse and Lyric Tradition

Ezra Pound's Early Verse and Lyric Tradition

A Jargoner's Apprenticeship

Robert Stark

EDINBURGH
University Press

© Robert Stark, 2012

Edinburgh University Press Ltd
22 George Square, Edinburgh EH8 9LF

www.euppublishing.com

Typeset in 10.5/13 Sabon
by Servis Filmsetting Ltd, Stockport, Cheshire, and
printed and bound in Great Britain by
CPI Group (UK) Ltd, Croydon CR0 4YY

A CIP record for this book is available from the British Library

ISBN 978 0 7486 4617 3 (hardback)
ISBN 978 0 7486 4618 0 (webready PDF)
ISBN 978 0 7486 7459 6 (epub)
ISBN 978 0 7486 7460 2 (Amazon ebook)

The right of Robert Stark
to be identified as author of this work
has been asserted in accordance with
the Copyright, Designs and Patents Act 1988.

Every effort has been made to trace the copyright holders,
but if any have been inadvertently overlooked, the publisher
will be pleased to make the necessary arrangements at the
first opportunity.

Contents

Acknowledgements

This book was written in sometimes extraordinary, sometimes farcical circumstances, and quite simply could not have been completed without the sustenance of many friends and accomplices: Yasser Abu Elmakarem Abdelrahim, Matt Boris, Clayton Hanson, Rob Hilken, Garrett Hill, Tatiana Komarova, Dmitri Kotik, James McDougal, Malek Hardan Mohammad, Hans and Lucia in Oaxaca, Matthew Schum, Gary Watson and M. Colleen Willenbring most especially, and spectacularly. I owe a unique debt to my wonderful, baffled family, especially my Dad, Arthur, for whom this endeavour has meant my being too far and too long away – but much more than this, as well.

The project began as a comparative study of what I then termed 'picture-thinking' in Hegel, Heidegger and Gadamer, mutated into a contextualisation of epistemology and symbolism in W. B. Yeats's verse, reimagined itself as an epic philological history of jargon from Aristophanes to Auden, before settling tentatively into its present form: my PhD advisors – Peter Firchow, Tom Clayton, Brian Goldberg and Jørn Erslev Andersen responded sympathetically, thoughtfully and carefully to all of this. It scarcely occurred to me at the University of Minnesota between 2000 and 2007 that the sedentary toiling of a graduate student could be the most stimulating and rewarding part of a career; but with such teachers it has proved to be so many times over. I am grateful especially to Tom and Brian for their endless support in the dark backward and abysm that has followed graduation.

Real thanks are also due to Jackie Jones of Edinburgh University Press for soliciting four brilliant readings of my preliminary text. I hope these anonymous readers will recognise substantial improvements here. Demetres Triphonopoulos was kind enough to go through the manuscript more than once and his rich comments could easily have resulted in another such volume; as it is, I have utilised as much of his learned advice as my hampered circumstances would allow.

I am grateful also to a number of subtile editors who have, often unbeknown to me, feelingly improved this nascent text: portions of the book have appeared in earlier forms in *Paideuma: Modern and Contemporary Poetry and Poetics* 36, the *Journal of Modern Literature* 32.2 and *Textual Practice* 25.6.

In memory of
Peter Edgerly Firchow (1937–2008)

You are young in my only photograph
in love & in a foreign country drawn
to that long unvisited familiar place
wherever it is, the traveler's skyey home

that world of well-made cars & mountain pass
-es that might as well have never been
being so far gone: ah the camera cheats
us into memory
                & if the students ask
you were a bug, you were a nightingale,
you were even dust when Hardy put to task
Shelley on the count of loss, a realist
in this if nothing else, vital
& sensitive & undeceived at last
that same traveler, that same, that high path.

Birds were made by transformation: growing feathers in place of hair, they derived from harmless but light-witted men who studied the heavens but imagined in their simplicity that most reliable evidence in such matter is obtained through the eye.

Plato, *Timaeus*

Nor doth it follow, that they cannot speake, because we cannot heare, or that they want language, because we want understanding.

Thomas Fuller, *Ornitho-logie; or The Speech of Birds*

You shall know a bird by his cry, and great birds cry loud, but sing not. The eagle screams when the sun is high, the peacock screams at the dawn, rooks call at evening, when the nightingale sings. And all birds have their voices, each means a different thing.

D. H. Lawrence, 'Birds'

They had changed their throats and had the throats of birds.

W. B. Yeats, 'Cuchulain Comforted'

Introduction

Headless Statues

Music and poetry enjoyed a kind of association in ancient literature that is now difficult to imagine. Nietzsche put it best in *The Birth of Tragedy*: 'the most important phenomenon of ancient poetry', he says, is 'that union – nay identity – everywhere considered natural, between musician and poet (alongside which our modern poetry appears as the statue of a god without a head)'.[1] The emblem is still more apt for twentieth-century poetry in English than for the poetry of Nietzsche's time. On the one hand, the advent of free verse has resulted in a neglect of the traditional prosodic aspects of the art. On the other hand, some of the most noted poets of the century have consistently shown how the musical features of poetry continue to have a vital role to play in the present. Ironically, the same poets have usually been responsible for both tendencies.

Ezra Pound is precisely such a figure. As Wyndham Lewis once remarked, Pound 'would teach *anybody* to be Dante, *technically*'.[2] At the same time, however, Pound's attempt to 'break the pentameter' line, his scepticism about ready-made poetic forms (such as the sonnet, which he considered to be obsolete by the twentieth century), his promotion of precise visual presentation, and many other aspects of his poetry and teaching, mean that he is perhaps as responsible for the neglect of the musical aspect of the art as any other single figure.[3] Pound was, like Nietzsche, a breaker of statues and idols, a decapitator of convention. He is as responsible for the acephalisis of the ancient statue as any modern poet; yet he was always committed to erecting as completely embodied a poetic artefact as his talents, and his era, would allow.

'It is impossible to read Pound's poetry or prose criticism without realizing the important role music plays in his thought and writing,' Ellen Stauder remarks. The poet's attention to auditory matters was intense and acute at every stage of his career.[4] Musical emblems of poetic art fascinated him as an apprentice poet in Pennsylvania: figures like the aeolian harp (which he found in Coleridge) led him to consider poetic inspiration from a pneumatic and aural perspective. At the same time, the outlandish qualities of traditional and regional poetic diction ensured that the young poet responded keenly to the sounds and rhythms of poetry; sometimes, in this early verse, to the neglect of meaning. In his first published volumes he became, on the one hand, an avid makar (the traditional Scots term for the poet as craftsman), refashioning and redeploying such 'cantabile value' as he discovered in Villon and Cavalcanti. On the other hand, he stood heavily indentured to the comparatively decivilising influence of Whitman and Browning and, as a result, he learned to exult in the redemptive barbarity of his own rough and ready native tongue. These influences combine in the stark, sensual language of his greatest early achievement: his translation of the Old English 'Seafarer', which succeeds in estranging a modern reader from the language of his protagonist through a rare command of the intense phonics of alliterative verse. His lifelong study of the troubadours culminates in a series of masterful modern translations and the critical emphasis on what he terms 'melopoeia' – an ideal of perfectly musical arrangement of language. In *The Cantos*, finally, the immediate datum of interpretation is often acoustic. The poem contains many passages of pure sound and foreign languages that conspire to bewilder the most polyglot reader and to force his audience to consider human meaning in the process of its emergence from mere noise. Pound's epic articulates sounds in new and unique ways, foregrounding the process of selection and arrangement of theme and sound that is, from one perspective, the essence of the modern poetry. *The Cantos* encapsulate the lessons learned in each earlier phase of Pound's career, so that its difficulties are best understood as the direct result of his frantic early pursuit of lyricism and musicality.

Each of his early influences, in one way or another, contributes to the lesson that discursive difficulty, far from constituting a fault, often attends genuinely lyrical poetry and contributes to its success as musical utterance.[5] This lesson was well known to the poets of the *fin de siècle* largely due to the influence of Walter Pater, for whom 'all art constantly aspires towards the condition of music'. For Pater,

> Lyrical poetry, precisely because in it we are least able to detach the matter from the form . . . is, at least artistically, the highest and most complete form of poetry. And the very perfection of such poetry often appears to depend, in part, on a certain suppression or vagueness of mere subject, so that meaning reaches us through ways not distinctly traceable by the understanding.[6]

Although Pater's aesthetic was attractive to Pound, muting a 'mere subject' for the sake of a mellifluous expression, to pleasantly circumvent intellection, or for any reason, was unacceptable, and became synonymous with the excesses of Victorian poetry for him. The modern poet needed to present the thing as he saw it. The problem with Pater's formulation of musical aesthetics was that it flaunted an oblique attitude towards its subject matter; lyrical technique obfuscated and complicated the presentation. In a crucial swerve away from Paterian aesthetics, Pound insisted that the gamut of lyrical techniques he wrested from tradition would not abstract language from its object or thwart the 'understanding' but, on the contrary, allow a more authentic relationship between language and its object to emerge by a process of defamiliarisation. Pound shared this basic approach to poetry with his contemporaries. T. S. Eliot, for example, famously proclaimed that the modern poet would have 'to force, to dislocate if necessary, language into meaning'.[7] For Pound, this exertion is not exceptional; it is basic to the way that poetry *makes* meaning. When the prose meaning of a poetic utterance is not immediately apparent, the acoustic and traditional and associative properties of the language, for example, prevail upon the reader, and hopefully result in a fresher, firmer purchase on the object of contemplation. Although Pater claims that poetry strives towards the condition of music and that, in lyric poetry, it comes closest to identity with music, this understanding nevertheless assumes the a priori separation of the two. Pound's melopoeia is founded upon a much more Platonic understanding of language and its operation, wherein the sound of language is irremediably part of its signifying apparatus, arguably the most decisive part. Lyric poetry, that is to say, does not end in the unification of language and sound, but rather begins there: melopoeia, music 'as if it were just bursting into speech', captures human meaning in its precarious emergence from ordinary sound, sense in its marvellous materialisation from non-sense.[8]

Pound began his career very much under the sway of Pater and the Pre-Raphaelite Brotherhood. He learned the craft of poetry and modelled his verse on that of his immediate predecessors, with the important difference that, for him, lyrical and auditory devices were not extrinsic and extensive effects but a substantial part of meaning. Rather than write for the sake of musical arrangement and the abstraction that it brings, Pound increasingly sought to use musicality as a means of intensifying his art. He was initially drawn to conventional poetic strategies, but he found a different level of significance in these strategies than his predecessors. In etymology, for instance, something that Pound was always alert to, he discovered the innate attachments of language prior to the impositions of habit, laziness and spin. In rhyme – the rhyme, for example, of Arnaut Daniel – he professed to discover a way not of padding out discourse and slavishly reiterating, but of probing the subtle associations and reverberations of vast and often barely conscious structures of meaning. He supposes that, properly handled, rhyme is intensive rather than extensive. With barbarism and onomatopoeia he found that he could appeal to pre-linguistic and acoustic forms of communication and understanding, and make the sensual, animalistic basis of his writing stand out in donative relief. In rhythm, in the repetition of sounds, he discovered the emotional and human dimension of language.

In order, therefore, to capitate Nietzsche's 'statue of a god without a head' once more, the poet needed, first, to look to the example of poetic tradition.[9] Mastery of poetic technique, Pound hoped, would enable a rich and pliant tongue capable of squaring up to the social and aesthetic challenges of the modern world. This would, from one perspective, lead to an obscure kind of poetry – one, at any rate, that did not resemble the language spoken in any metropolis or province – but it would be founded on the ancient prerogative of musicality that appeared to Nietzsche to be the essence of the art.

The Warp of Melody

Ezra Pound appears to have been convinced of the need for a prolonged literary apprenticeship from about the age of fifteen.[10] That such a youngster might harbour such ambition is surprising, but less surprising than the apparently orderly and unrelenting pursuit of this aim that the mature poet would have us believe he then undertook. His plan largely comprised of the systematic exposure to – and imitation of – a variety of foreign literatures, with varying degrees of formal academic success.[11] It is almost impossible to conceive of a pre-poetic Ezra Pound: his own personality and voice emerge in the milieu of his literary studies, after the decadent fashion.[12] In Thomas Jackson's diagnosis,

> Pound's problem with style was the same as his problem with 'identity' . . . he could deal with experiences in a satisfactory manner mainly by assuming the mask of an identity other than his own, so in his first collection he can speak in a satisfactory voice only by the wholesale adoption of someone else's verbal manner.[13]

His earliest verse is valuable, first, because of its constitutive function for the man and for the poetry he would go on to produce. This, at least, is how the sage of St. Elizabeths rationalised his beginnings, and it has proved a boon for biographers and for the occasional critic, like Jackson, who has returned to the pre-cantos volumes for clues about the early life and the later work respectively.

T. S. Eliot was first to plot this line of inquiry with, one suspects, the author's collusion. On at least seven occasions, he emphasises the importance of certain early influences: the Pre-Raphaelites, the Decadent and Aesthetic poets of the 1890s (Ernest Dowson especially), Browning, Swinburne and Yeats, as well as 'the influence of Provençal and Italian' authors.[14] Eliot's provocation has yielded three excellent studies of Pound's early verse from N. Christoph de Nagy (1960), Thomas H. Jackson (1968) and, more recently, Thomas F. Grieve (1997). Each of these studies ably ruminates among these early influences and reveals a conscientious and meticulous apprentice poet at the task of discovering his niche and his voice. At their best, these monographs demonstrate how discerning a reader of post-Romantic poetry the young Ezra Pound could be: de Nagy's encounter with Dowson makes a compelling case for Pound as the last of the Aesthetes; Jackson's study foregrounds the foundational aspects of the medievalism of William Morris and Dante Rossetti; Grieve offers an especially shrewd analysis of Pound's meeting with Yeats and the Celtic Twilight. Each unveils an Ezra Pound that is in some ways a product of the individual critic's time and predilection, but essentially Pound nonetheless; a poet we are no longer much accustomed to thinking about, in addition to the poet of consensus: the disciple of Browning who brought the dramatic monologue into the twentieth century, the purist who conveyed a consecrated art unto the confessional poets of the 1950s and 1960s, the arch-modernist experimenter and mad scientist of St. Elizabeths, etc.

Nevertheless, studies of Pound's early verse have tended on the whole to compartmentalise the poet's development according to the authors he studied and championed, and the result is that we sometimes end up with a generalised recipe for the post-Romantic type of poet. Such criticism can amount to little more than a (however detailed and illuminating) taxonomy of constituents, an inert list of ingredients. This book aims for something different. Picking up on the more active encounters in each of my predecessors' work, I hope to offer a sort of narrative of method, rather than a list of ingredients, that situates these authors as evanescent stations appointed in advance upon Pound's dialectical journey toward becoming a sovereign poet. Each offers something different, acoustically, and enables an especially rounded development and understanding of the lyrical aspects of his art. Like the shades that Dante meets in Hell, Purgatory and Paradise, the authors Pound discourses with have, each of them, something to teach the poetic pilgrim; but his fate is different from theirs and he must shrewdly discriminate among the cacophony of their voices and claims to his attention. The poet's path is not the way of the critic: he or she cannot afford to adopt a passive, neutral point of view towards the accomplishments of the past and must decide, and decide again: What is good poetry? What is good art?

Rather than narrowly compartmentalise the authors Pound encountered on his way, and the lessons they impart, I will focus resolutely upon a set of evolving concerns that occupy him throughout his career, and try to witness their unfolding. This model derives from Hegel's description of the ephemeral formations of consciousness striving towards Spiritual realisation in the *Phenomenology of Spirit*. In what is perhaps the most poetic passage in his seminal work, Hegel describes how spiritual growth is accomplished:

> Just as the first breath drawn by a child after its long, quiet, nourishment breaks the gradualness of merely quantitative growth—there is a qualitative leap, and the child is born—so likewise the Spirit in its formation matures slowly and quietly into its new shape, dissolving bit by bit the structure of the previous world, whose tottering state is only hinted at by isolated symptoms. The frivolity and boredom which unsettle the established order, the vague foreboding of something unknown, these are the heralds of approaching change. The gradual crumbling that left unaltered the face of the whole is cut short by a sunburst which, in one flash, illuminates the features of the new world.[15]

I suppose something like this quantitative and qualitative heave-ho for the advent of Pound's mature style or styles, for the genesis of *The Cantos* and for the birth of lyrical modernism. This has the advantage of substantially coinciding with Pound's career-long advocacy of a method of 'luminous detail', first outlined in 'I Gather the Limbs of Osiris', wherein 'certain facts or points . . . govern . . . knowledge as the switchboard the electric circuit'.[16] In this pursuit of tangible Poundian truth, the reader will have to grant a few speculative indulgencies, bear with a number of hazardous detours, and risk several dead ends, accordingly; only to discover that, in the end, Pound's poetry becomes what it already was.

A youthful Ezra Pound writes in an abandoned essay in the San Trovaso Notebook:

> All art . . . begins in the physical discontent (or torture) of loneliness and partiality . . . it was to fill this lack that man first spun shapes out of the void. And with the intensifying of this longing gradually came into him power, power over the essences of the dawn, over the filaments of light and the warp of melody.[17]

He looks for art to unleash formidable, preternatural forces, and music seems to him, like many of his generation, to be the elemental, the most perfectly mysterious art. This 'warp of melody' is a uniquely telling description of its strange capacity and signature. Pound refers, among other things, to the stupendous ability of music – and, by extension, of lyrical poetry – to project through space, to cast, throw; to fling open; to drive out, expel, reject or renounce; to plunge; to utter or pronounce; to bend, twist, curve; to turn aside, to divert or deflect; to weave, twine; to tow, to move gradually forward; and finally, to run aground.[18] Pound's interest in melody encompasses the totality of its thaumaturgical action: its uncanny ability to transport the poet and his or her audience, or its aptitude to immovably fix poet and audience both; its facility in accessing and organising new perceptions and experiences, and its propensity to smother and thwart the same; its fervent foraging for meaning and its consorting in sham, lies, deceit; its making – and unmaking – of 'kulchur' and civilisation. 'Melody', Pound says elsewhere, is 'the creation of the human intelligence standing up against nature' with all the ambivalence and ambiguity that this entails.[19] In what follows, I propose to listen in to this 'warp of melody', trying to discern and accommodate the plethora of meanings and the contradictory forces it often comprehends.

Pound inculcates the decadent habit of thinking about poetry in musical terms from his first enthusiasm for the literature of the *fin de siècle*: 'the poetic language of the nineties was his natural speech', suggests Thomas Jackson; meaning, I think, that it was the first euphonious assemblage of sound that he would attempt to master, once having determined to be a poet.[20] The elusiveness of the task seems to have struck Pound almost immediately; he subsequently wrote that 'one [cannot] learn English, one can only learn a series of Englishes', and by the time of his first extant collection of verse, the unpublished 'Hilda's Book', he is already haltingly conversant in a number of idiolects – none of which come over quite distinctly. His music phase-shifts across poems, between lines and among words themselves. I have tried to trace these essential confusions, modulations and transpositions rather than to isolate and attribute the singular 'effects' of individual authors (their 'tricks', as Pound will have it). No single poetic source, no original, is the subject of any chapter here. What will be most apparent by the end of this study will be the fundamental opacity of all talk about sources and originals where Pound is concerned. This is a point that Pound himself is always pained to convey – in his muddling of En Arnaut and Bishop Douglas, de Gourmont and Fenollosa, Homer and Andreas Divus. At some risk, I will stake out a similarly dialectical terrain. Thus

Robert Burns's brogue, we shall see, is experienced by Pound via the intermediacy of James Whitcomb Riley; Swinburne's most authentic music becomes, paradoxically, his translation of Villon and his worrying over Greek Choruses; Browning ventriloquises the uncouth eloquence of Shakespeare's Caliban. The ensuing mélange will listen in for other voices too, whose undertones, it may be, are of moment to Pound's evolving art but that have not, as yet, been considered integral to the warp of his melody: Allan Ramsay and Aristophanes, Samuel Taylor Coleridge, Gorgias and Gower, George Santayana and Robert Louis Stevenson chief among them. Pound's explicit translations are further overlaid in harmony and contrapunto: his Seafarer intermediates an already archaic, urgent and yet vanished poetic register; his troubadours harken to Greek myth; and his Chinese verse – his Chinese verse is Japanised and Anglicised by a hybrid translator-poet of no fixable identity in a language with no obvious means of seizing its pictographic essence – but 'the warp of melody'.

The Total Organisation of Sound

Some of this is incipient in previous studies of Pound's early verse. The methodological framework these readings provide also yields some important clues for dealing systematically with this early body of work, and my efforts are particularly in tune, I hope, with N. Christoph de Nagy's advice at the outset of his trailblazing two-volume close and sensitive reading of Pound's earliest verse and criticism. He considers that

> Any study of Pound up to 'Mauberley' . . . will naturally be concerned primarily with the relationship between Pound and the various kinds of poetry that influenced his verse; it is also obvious that this influence will primarily be of a formal character. Pound says quite explicitly that the purpose behind most of his early poetry is experimenting with verse forms, conscious undergoing of a multiplicity of formal influences. Thus form must always be our point of departure . . . this alone necessitates that one should examine a great number of the most representative poems individually.[21]

Pound's poetry has benefited from the sound formal analysis of several subsequent critics, most notably Stephen J. Adams and Ellen Keck Stauder, but their readings – and listenings – restrict themselves almost exclusively to Pound's mature work. Nevertheless, these authors have broadened the aperture and lexicon of a traditionally esoteric field of criticism by considering Pound's experiments in quantitative verse, and by ascertaining that an overarching interest in musicality insistently informs his writing. More recently, Robert Hughes and Margaret Fisher have enabled readers of *The Cantos* to consider Pound's often-simultaneous composition of two radio operas and other miscellaneous musical works. My reading of Pound's lyrical apprenticeship complements these studies of his later musical form and hopes to suggest, not how or where his views and practices originate, but how foundational Pound's ideas about music always are to his approach to literature. The more lyrical a composition, the more will readers and listeners benefit alike from such an expanded understanding of poetic form: this is my general persuasion, and it emerges from Pound's own consideration of poetic form, Eliot's suggestive promptings and a cogent – but sometimes derelict – line of Pound criticism.

The Romantics and Walter Pater, Swinburne and the Decadents celebrated lyric poetry as the supremely musical literary form. N. Christoph de Nagy discerns a steady trend towards this position in the last half of the nineteenth century: that 'in English poetry from 1850 to the end of the century a gradual dissolution of "meaning", a slow diminution of rationalisable content, of anything that can be rendered in prose', is apparent, along with a concomitant pursuit of what he terms 'pure form'.[22] For Pound, this means drawing upon an assortment of musical influences from the first moments he conceived of himself as a poetic aspirant. In a startling short essay packaged with the compact disc *Ego Scriptor Cantilenae: The Music of Ezra Pound*, Margaret Fisher presents the fullest picture yet of the poet's embrasure of music. Detail after detail casts the poet's whole career in a new light: his 'earliest musical training', for instance, came from his parents, who were both amateur musicians; his 'musical career' – and, I would add, his poetical career – began 'as a transcriber of medieval song in the archives of the great libraries of Europe while on his doctoral research fellowship the summer of 1906'; his employment as a music critic for *The New Age* and an estimated '300 consecutive days or ten months of writing music on paper' for his second opera reveal that Pound was fully justified in considering himself as a 'poet and composer' at the onset of his poetic maturity.[23] Fisher's conclusion is as irresistible as it is perhaps surprising: Pound's 'venture into music for literary reasons – poetic analysis, preservation, and, ultimately, popularization (the goal of all scholarship for Pound) – is unparalleled'.[24]

When Pound arrived in London, therefore, 'the synapses were already in place' to make the most of a publication climate in which music was already the natural province of the lyrical postulant.[25] As A. David Moody shows in the first volume of his superb critical biography, literary London was identically predisposed to the prevailing notion of poetry and music being – not sister arts – but a single, indissoluble aesthetic endeavour:

> Pound was concerned much more with the musical than with the imagistic powers of words, and with the auditory rather than with the visual imagination. That was the dimension in which his work had been thus far most inventive and advanced . . . In April 1909 Elkin Mathews had just published [Florence] Farr's book, *The Music of Poetry*, in which she set out her method for bringing out the full music of words. This would have been of immediate interest to Pound [and have] given him a start on the technique of discovering and realizing the music latent in vowels and consonants and their combinations, a technique which would be the basis of his mature verse, and of his first opera.[26]

Moody goes on to establish how Pound's collaboration with Walter Rummel developed this interest in 'the relation of words and music in the song of the troubadours' still further, again with the explicit aim of publication – of making public – this still-neglected corpus of work.[27] He concludes that Ezra Pound's 'basic observation was that music is "pure rhythm; rhythm and nothing else, for the variation of pitch is the variation in rhythms of the individual notes, and harmony the blending of these varied rhythms"'.[28] The critic's task, in this context, is abundantly clear.

This book aims to approach Pound's poetry from a prosodic point of view. I mean to take account of what Pound terms 'the articulation of the total organization of sound' in some of Pound's lesser-known poems. Prosody, on this total understanding, is hardly a question of syllable and stress, of line length, stanza and form alone. Rather, the ordinary aural and auditory aspects of language must be understood to exert a priority in Pound's melodic and rhythmic sensibility: a fact that is as true of his earliest discarded sonnets as of *The Cantos*. This usage admittedly extends the scope of the term as it is conventionally understood in literary studies, but it does so in a way that is germane to the word's origin and consonant with recent developments in Pound Studies: the Greek etymon originally signified 'a song sung to music, an accompaniment': it articulates the word for 'song' and the word for 'ode'.[29] Pound was undoubtedly inspired by this broader conception of prosody and his practice seems designed to highlight the rigor mortis of contemporary prosodic tracts like Robert Bridges' *Milton's Prosody* (1893) that secured a sound, if unlikely, foundation for staid Georgian versifiers. He complains in his 'Introduction' to *The Sonnets and Ballate of Guido Cavalcanti* that 'the science of the music of words and the knowledge of their magical powers has fallen away': I hope to remedy this in part.[30] Pound's consideration of *le mot juste* – one might even say his contribution to theories about *le mot juste* – begins with the insight that the *sound* of words is often instrumental in meaning, and in a direct, intrinsic way. Since prosody cannot, therefore, be separated from questions of diction, it must also involve, and be involved in, the themes and discursive issues that this diction raises.

I will examine the complex of musicality, obscurity and meaningless-ness that is so central to Pound's poetry without transforming it into what Pound calls 'an onomatopoeic paste'.[31] The problem of writing criticism that remains responsive to genre and ontology, to the fact of a poem's being a poem, is an acute one in the twentieth century. Recent critics have begun to develop a more refined, if less colourful, critical apparatus than that suggested by Pound's comment. For Amittai F. Aviram, for example,

> Poetry may be thought of as a kind of utterance opposed to prose, and there-fore as a principal end point on a spectrum opposite prose, with various texts falling between the two principles. What distinguishes poetry in the abstract sense is the tendency toward opacity of language. Actual poems divide the focus of the reader's or listener's attention between the communicative content of their language and the physical features and effects of that same language. What contributes most to this focus on the physical, nonmeaning substance of language in poetry is rhythm. For the interpreter of poetry who wishes to preserve a sense of distinctness of poetry from prose – who wishes to avoid letting his or her interpretation obviate the whole point of the poem being a poem – the question will be, how can these opposing sides of the poem, the meaningful and the rhythmic, the transparent and the opaque, be related to each other? How can they form a unity, without one of them, especially the opaque side, disappearing into triviality?[32]

I shall assume something like the continuum posited here, and focus my attention on the rhythmical, opaque end of the spectrum.

Pound operates on precisely such an acoustic gradient in his mature work, as prosodists have not infrequently observed. Stephen Adams – one of the best – affirms that

> the prosodic range of *The Cantos* is not just more or less tightly control-led free verse, but a full spectrum from prose through degrees of free verse through the disciplined form of Cavalcanti's canzone, and even, ultimately, to wordless music itself in Canto LXXV.[33]

Pound's poetic media in *The Cantos* – and the plural is obviously appro-priate if Adams's analysis is correct – is vibrant and spectral: the tautness and strain, the phase-shifting of the versification is itself significant, not in spite of its modulation or its scrambling of the message, but precisely because of it. This warp of melody bears invisibly upon every aspect of Pound's epic communication, but it remains to be seen whether, or how, this foundational understanding informs even his earliest poetry. Despite Pound's caveat, then, I hope to show that the 'physical, non-meaning substance' of a poem – what de Nagy might term the non-rationalisable content – often proves as sensible (if not as meaningful) as the more transparent, prosaic aspects of his early poems.

Notes

1. Nietzsche, *Birth of Tragedy*, p. 38.
2. Lewis, *Men Without Art*, p. 67.
3. Pound, *The Cantos*, p. 538.
4. Stauder, 'Towards a Grammar of Relationships', p. 45.
5. This study will not consider the reasons for this vogue for difficulty or its cultural and intellectual significance in any detail (Leonard Diepeveen's *The Difficulties of Modernism* examines these matters thoroughly). By understanding Pound's difficulty as a function of his interest in poetic jargon (in the manifold sense I will explain shortly), I hope to establish only what this difficulty consists of in its most characteristic forms.
6. Pater, *The Renaissance*, p. 156; p. 157.
7. Eliot, *Sacred Wood*, p. 128. Eliot also concluded that 'the music of poetry is not something which exists apart from the meaning' (*On Poetry and Poets*, p. 21).
8. Pound, *Gaudier Brzeska*, p. 82.
9. Nietzsche, *Birth of Tragedy*, p. 38.
10. Cf. Moody, *Ezra Pound: Poet*, p. 13.
11. Ibid. pp. 14–16.
12. As Rosette says of Chevalier d'Albert in Théophile Gautier's archetypal decadent novel, 'his real poem is himself and I doubt if he will ever write another' (*Mademoiselle de Maupin*, p. 146).
13. Jackson, *Early Poetry*, p. 120.
14. Eliot, 'Introduction' to Pound, *Selected Poems*.
15. Hegel, *Phenomenology of Spirit*, pp. 6–7.
16. Pound, *Selected Prose*, p. 24. For Pound, 'the Arts work on life as history works on the development of civilisation and literature'. Moreover, the properly '"donative" author' 'seems to draw down into the art something which was not in the art of his predecessors. If he also draws from the air about him, he draws latent forces, or things present but unnoticed, or things perhaps taken for granted but never examined.

    Non e mai tarde per tentar l'ignoto. His forbears may have led up to him; he is never a disconnected phenomenon, but he does take some step further. He discovers, or, better, "he discriminates". We advance by discriminations, by discerning that things hitherto deemed identical or similar are dissimilar; that things hitherto deemed dissimilar, mutually foreign, antagonistic, are similar and harmonic' (ibid. p. 25).
17. Qtd in Moody, *Ezra Pound: Poet*, p. 64.
18. 'Warp', *Oxford English Dictionary*.

19. Qtd in Stauder, 'The Rhetoric of Music', p. 48.
20. Jackson, *Early Poetry*, p. 176.
21. De Nagy, *Pre-Imagist Stage*, p. 23.
22. De Nagy, *Pre-Imagist Stage*, p. 82. For de Nagy, W. B. Yeats is the best exemplar of this aesthetic, but Ernest Dowson is surely a close second. In a letter to Arthur Moore, for example, Dowson remarks that he has 'been writing verses, in the manner of the French "symbolists": verses making for mere sound, and music, with just a suggestion of sense, or hardly that; a vague, Verlainesque emotion' (Dowson, *Letters*, p. 120).
23. Fisher, 'Ezra Pound: Composer', p. 14; p. 15; p. 24.
24. Ibid. p. 15.
25. Ibid. p. 14.
26. Moody, *Ezra Pound: Poet*, p. 98.
27. Ibid. p. 154.
28. Ibid. p. 154. Cf. Pound, *Poems and Translations*, p. 193.
29. 'Prosody', *Oxford English Dictionary*.
30. Pound, *Poems and Translations*, p. 194.
31. Pound, *Literary Essays*, p. 437.
32. Aviram, *Telling Rhythm*, p. 109.
33. Adams, 'The Metrical Contract of *The Cantos*', p. 67.

Chapter 1

Poetic Jargon

Since prosody, even in the total Poundian sense, has usually been reckoned an extrinsic or superficial matter largely unrelated to the meaning of poetry, despite the many entreaties of poets themselves, it is vital to avoid subjecting it to an a priori, artificial and ill-suited terminology. Instead, I will concentrate on a symbol that incorporates poetry's tendency towards music, on the one hand, and towards opacity and obscurity, on the other hand. This symbol has the merit of being incipient in the poetic tradition itself, and of being an explicit and lifelong concern of Ezra Pound. I mean to focus, that is to say, on birds and their song. As Derek Walcott notes,

> poets' real biographies . . . are like those of the birds . . . their real data are in the way they sound. A poet's biography is in his vowels and sibilants, in his meters, rhymes and metaphors . . . with poets, the choice of words is invariably more telling than the story they tell.[1]

I aim to take this advice as literally as I can in the following pages. Pound is drawn to the archetypal symbol of birdsong not because it presents a theme to his imagination, but because it offers a methodological principle to guide his art. He is forced in the process to reassess the role and importance of bird symbolism in modern literature.[2]

By considering poetry as a special kind of jargon, I aim to demonstrate a necessary relationship between 'the meaningful and the rhythmic, the transparent and the opaque' in Ezra Pound's poetry and, by implication, in poetry more generally.[3] The word 'jargon' has an impressive range of meanings that make it uniquely suited to this task. Most obviously, the word refers to arcane and specialised diction typically employed by a community of experts. When we think of this kind of language we tend to be sceptical: 'jargon is a species of crime against language and clear thinking, typically described by such adjectives as "incomprehensible", "pretentious", and "dreary"', writes Walter Nash, author of

Jargon: Its Uses and Abuses, and a representative 'expert' on the subject. Nonetheless, we have not always been so disposed to jargon. The word originally meant 'birdsong' and was not thought of as meaningless gibberish at all, but as a powerful and eloquent natural language bespeaking the disposition of the gods and proscribing, therefore, the lives of mortals. Subsequently, the significance prized by augurs and poets came to be disregarded, and the word came simply to designate 'the inarticulate utterance of birds'.[4] Although these two basic meanings are in some respect antithetical, since they cater to the unambiguous verifiable truth and ambiguous symbolic truth respectively, the issue of difficulty and its adjacency to knowledge is consistent. Both principal meanings are evidenced throughout English literature, as we shall see in a moment.

The word 'jargon' has additional meanings and associations that are also fundamental to the application to poetry that I wish to make here. It has been used to refer directly to poetic devices that, by virtue of their musical qualities, resemble birdsong, and especially to 'a jingle, or assonance of rimes'. This association has more often been used to censure 'ornamental', or incidental, rhyme than to extol the associative and incisive qualities of rhyme. The general use of the term for 'unintelligent, meaningless talk; nonsense, gibberish', is similarly deprecating. 'Jargon' was also contemptuously applied to language deemed 'barbarous, rude or debased'. Language described in this way is usually foreign and is often of hybrid or polyglot form, a lingo or a patois. From this usage, the term has been extended to any heterogeneous utterance, any 'medley or babel of sound'. Finally, the word can also refer to 'a conventional method of writing or conversing by means of symbols otherwise meaningless; a cipher, or other system of characters or signs having an arbitrary meaning'.[5] Each of these meanings describe an aspect of Pound's poetic style and offer a means of thinking, in their various ways, about any poetry in which questions of lyrical form, musicality, obscurity and difficulty are central interpretative data.

Much of the most recent criticism on Pound and modernism has been heuristic in nature. Daniel Albright and Daniel Tiffany, for example, have offered metaphors that allow a modern reader to approach Pound's difficult poetry in (it is hoped) productive, speculative ways. For Albright, the language of quantum physics (and especially the competing notions of particle and wave) explains the modern conception of the poem, and the unbounded radiance, as it were, of the Imagist's Image. For Tiffany, Maurice Blanchot's discussion of the cadaver serves as an important paradigm for the cryptic aspects of the Image.[6] 'Jargon', it may be readily supposed, offers just this kind of heuristic device for understanding poetry: it describes the contours and peripheral regions of lyrical art in a speculative way. In this heuristic capacity, certainly, the word is more or less apt for any poem or poet one cares to approach, difficult or not. In Ezra Pound's corpus, however, poetic 'jargon' offers more than a heuristic metaphor. Pound himself uses the term literally and surely in his own verse and critical writing, in direct response to traditional literary usages. The concept stands as an intrinsic aesthetic concept, helpful (and, I will argue, indispensable) for appreciating and unifying the two most vital aspects of modern lyric composition.

This critical vocabulary, then, is part of the language that poets including Pound use to understand their job. The original sense of the term has been enshrined in poetic usage and Pound would have made its acquaintance via several of the authors he championed. He would certainly have been familiar with the original sense from Coleridge's *Rime of the Ancient Mariner*, where the word appears in a nautical context that parallels Pound's own usage in 'The Seafarer'. Coleridge uses the word at a magical moment in the poem – the sort of moment that captured the young Pound's imagination. Coleridge, describing the spirits who inspire the mariner's dead crewmates, compares their sound to birdsong:

Around, around, flew each sweet sound,
Then darted to the Sun;
Slowly the sounds came back again,
Now mixed, now one by one.

Sometimes a-dropping from the sky
I heard the sky-lark sing;
Sometimes all little birds that are,
How they seemed to fill the sea and air
With their sweet jargoning!

And now 'twas like all instruments,
Now like a lonely flute;
And now it is an angel's song,
That makes the heavens be mute.[7]

Strange, sublime sounds like these often serve as analogues for poetic speech in Coleridge's poetry, as we shall see in Chapter 2. Pound responds strongly to this mysterious conception of poetry, and it serves as the point of departure for his own jargonish verse.

Ultimately, however, modern poetry would not acquiesce in these 'sweet', mellifluous airs. Pound's own jargoning, in particular, is typically more uncouth, more medieval. His primary source for this rougher conception of jargon appears to have been the early modern usage of the term that Coleridge harkens toward in these lines. In fact, John Gower, along with the author of the *Romaunt of the Rose* (1366), appears to be responsible for bringing the word over into English from the Middle French.[8] Pound professed a strong admiration for Shakespeare's *Pericles*, which features a strange, antiqued narration by Gower, and he singles out the first two scenes of the play for special praise.[9] He also mentions the play in the first of his initial 'Three Cantos of a Poem of Some Length' in 1917.[10]

Gower's *Confessio Amantis* (1390) is especially significant for this study because it offers the first comprehensive, and the most compelling, account of the Tereus, Procne and Philomel myth in English. This myth is archetypal in poetic treatments of birdsong in Western literature, as the Appendix to the present volume explains at some length. The French word *jargoun* – alien and shrill – helps the author to articulate the acute agonies of Philomel's rape and glossectomy, and the outlandish horror of her tongueless speech. He uses the term at the climactic moment, just after the glossectomy and just prior to the announcement of her imprisonment:

> And out he clippeth also faste
> Hire tongue with a peire of scheres,
> So what with blod and what with teres
> Out of hire yhe and of hir mouth,
> He made hire faire face uncouth:
> Sche lay swounende unto the deth,
> Ther was unnethes eny breth;
> Bot yit whan he hire tunge refte,
> A litel part thereof belefte,
> Bot sche with al no word mai soune,
> Bot chitre and as a brid jargoune.[11]

Tereus's barbarity literally hastens Philomel's metamorphosis into the nightingale by mutilating her tongue and rending her capacity for communication: she becomes capable only of stricken, plaintive, evocative, pitiable sounds. Pound uses the term in something like this sense in 'The Seafarer'.

The term also occurs just prior to this, as Gower relates the story of Medea. Ovid, a likely source for Gower's poem, describes 'the music chanted in her spells'.[12] Gower takes this image a step further by comparing Medea's weird music to the sound of a catalogue of birds:

> Sche made many a wonder soun
> Somtime lich unto the cock,
> Somtime unto the Laverock,[13]

Somtime kacleth as an hen,
Somtime spekth as don the men.
And riht so as hir jargoun strangeth
In sondri wise hir forme changeth.[14]

Medea's language is described as a weird jargon composed of the same strange sounds that appealed to Coleridge. Again, the feeling inarticulacy, and the suggestion that her speech resembles that of the birds, accompanies her metamorphosis.[15] As these usages of 'jargon' attest, birdsong appeared to early modern English writers very much as it had to ancient Greek writers: as a weird, inscrutable and sensual language, and their poetry very often aspired above all to this very condition. Pound seems to adopt this sense of the term quite explicitly in the 'Seafarer' (with, perhaps, additional nuance provided by Gavin Douglas's *Eneaidos*, where the word refers to a harsh, grating, creaking noise).[16]

The word 'jargon', then, entered the English language from the French in something like this way. In the earliest usage, the harsh sound, the foreignness and incomprehensibility of birds' chatter, are the salient features secured by the word, which readily lend themselves to Philomel's hampered speech, Medea's incantations and analogous utterances. The term is simply a means of describing strange, uncanny speech, and it remains so exclusively until the eighteenth century. When, in the course of the later Enlightenment, philosophers become preoccupied by the ideal that each object should be made known by a single word, and that word alone, the word 'jargon' undergoes a conceptual transformation. It still refers to an utterance whose sound alights upon the hearer before its meaning, but rather than a sensual, donative expression, it comes to signify listless, hampered, opaque – and above all, overly specialised – language. This ideal quickly becomes a problem for philosophers: the more they seek for the single, unambiguous concept, the more esoteric and arcane their language becomes, and the more distrusting becomes their readership.[17]

The conceptual transformation of 'jargon' in the eighteenth century leads to the systematic opposition of philosophic language, which behaves like a code in the strongest sense, and whose object is knowledge, and literary language, which behaves . . . more speculatively. Jargon, in the modern sense, governs the former, while jargon, in the ancient sense, governs the latter. The term is still used to arraign philosophers for being abstruse, then, but it is admitted that philosophy has a certain right to behave in this way, and jargon is welcomed provided it does not contravene the taxonomic method that is in a sense based upon it. Jargon is not to be avoided and it is not, in itself, an obstacle to truth.

The staunch determination of the philosopher to preserve the *structure* of language and to employ particularised concepts self-consciously and consistently is what guarantees the happy result of philosophic inquiry.

Ironically enough, the word 'jargon' becomes common in poetry around this time. Poets seem to have followed philosophers in their usage, and demanded that their fellowship also pursue truth in verse, rather than ornament or fad. Jonathan Swift, for example, uses the term to denounce inferior poets who approach the art of verse in a hackneyed fashion. In a representative passage from 'On Poetry: A RHAPSODY', he writes:

> But, if you think this trade too base
> (Which seldom is the dunce's case),
> Put on the critic's brow, and sit
> At Will's, the puny judge of wit.
> A nod, a shrug, a scornful smile,
> With caution used, may serve awhile.
> Proceed no further in your part,
> Before you learn the terms of art
> (For you can never be too far gone,
> In all our modern critics' jargon).
> Then talk with more authentic face,
> Of *unities, in time and place.*
> Get scraps of Horace from your friends,
> And have them at your fingers' ends.
> Learn Aristotle's rules by rote,
> And at all hazards boldly quote;
> Judicious Rymer oft review:
> With Dennis, and profound Bossu.
> Read all the prefaces of Dryden,
> For these our critics much confide in,
> (Though merely writ at first for filling,
> To raise the volume's price, a shilling).[18]

Swift takes issue with the superficial accoutrements of literary style here. He is seemingly unaware of the earlier meaning of the term 'jargon', and deploys the word in its now-current sense as an erudite code. He laments the advent of a hyper-critical scientific age and its encroachment upon the imaginative domain of verse-writing in this passage, which takes these phony devices for the essence of the art of poesy. The preponderant deference to public opinion, and the dissection of poetic craft that these lines advertise, lampoons the shallow understanding of contemporary critical scientificism. For Swift, poetry cannot be pursued by systematic and solely rational means, nor can it be composed in a precisely analytical fashion. Neither memorising the formal stipulations of the ancients, nor committing the classics to memory by rote, nor any supercilious concern with contemporary tastes can transform a shoddy imitator into an authentic poet. Modern literary criticism has taxonomised the aspects of successful verse without considering that the components it has identified and analysed are only the means of the art. Critical jargon leads to derivative, inauthentic and incoherent literature. Stupidly analytical treatment of the poet's art and sloppy iteration of what is presumed thereby to be poetic: both lead to botched work. This is why the subject of his satire is, in this instance, 'A Rhapsody', or a 'miscellaneous collection; a medley or confused mass (of things)' – itself one of the cardinal meanings of 'jargon' underwriting this study.[19]

This double objection to hyper-critical and uninspired poetry was useful and popular. The Scots poet Allan Ramsay (considered in detail in Chapter 2) appears to have had this passage of Swift's 'Rhapsody' in mind when he attempted to distinguish his own vernacular verse from that of the 'Grub Street hacks' of his day. For Ramsay, the problem was how to exonerate himself from the charge of writing in an indecipherable (for the metropolitan literati) code. His solution was to distinguish his Scots dialect, for which he claims an intimate and inalienable relationship with the local objects it comprehends by virtue of its aural rather than alphabetic basis, from the language of hack writers who haphazardly appropriate the bits and bobs of others' poems. For Ramsay, like Swift, the poet who is more concerned with stylistic propriety than with authenticity of subject and legitimacy of treatment is no poet whatsoever.

As this example implies, the tendency of poetic language to approach the condition of jargon in the manifold sense is far from a purely philological or aesthetic matter: social and anthropological dimensions complicate the discourse and often add to the viability of jargon as an aesthetic construct in the eighteenth century. Crucially, this debate occurs in a period of rapid expansion of British colonialism, and notably within the context of the 1707 Act of Union. If these circumstances decisively inform Ramsay's aesthetic critique, they are hardly an exclusively parochial concern. Indeed, in 1755, Samuel Johnson places great emphasis on the role of empire, cultural and linguistic exchange in the formation of language, ordinary and poetic. He contends that

> total and sudden transformations of a language seldom happen; conquests and migrations are now very rare: but there are other causes of change, which, though slow in their operation, and invisible in their progress, are perhaps as much superior to human resistance, as the revolutions of the sky, or intumescence of the tide. Commerce, however necessary, however lucrative, as it depraves the manners, corrupts the language; they that have

frequent intercourse with strangers, to whom they endeavour to accommodate themselves, must in time learn a mingled dialect, like the jargon which
serves the traffickers on the Mediterranean and Indian coasts. This will not
always be confined to the exchange, the warehouse, or the port, but will
be communicated by degrees to other ranks of the people, and be at last
incorporated with the current speech.[20]

Johnson here suggests that jargon – in the sense of a heterogeneous
dialect or patois – is the unfortunate but inevitable result of mercan-
tile activity and colonial expansion. It manifests itself first in marginal
regions, before gradually contaminating the English of the metropolis
and of the aristocracy, which was felt to be inherently superior to such
'mingled' strains. Ezra Pound became fanatic about the negative effects
of capitalism on language almost two hundred years later, but for
different reasons altogether.

A dichotomy between official literary language and a more marginal
kind of speech is offered by each of the preceding authors. The allegiance
of the commentator varies in these examples, and 'jargon' is, in each
instance, used to denigrate the supposed indecipherability, inauthentic-
ity or uninspired nature of language that does not meet the author's
particular literary bent. Two important points emerge here: first,
the eighteenth century supposed that inter-linguistic exchange could
meaningfully impact what it conceived to be the health of language; it
discovered that language was not fixed, but constantly changing according to the practice of its users. It could thereby become better or worse,
depending on the facility and the inclination of those who wielded it.
Second, this led to the desire to improve language in several directions:
for Swift, this meant allowing poets to practise their art without subjecting their imagination to the taxonomising reason of scientific and critical
inquiry; for Ramsay, this meant insisting on the prerogatives of regional
knowledges and languages; for Johnson this meant fixing the meaning
of words in a *dictio*nary.[21]

Poets of the eighteenth and nineteenth century continued to make a
case for the adjacency of poetry and other forms of jargon. In addition
to the examples I have already given and shall give in Chapter 2, the
word appears in poems by John Gay ('Wine' and 'Wings in the Dark'),
Robert Burns (*'Epistle to J. Lapraik*: An Old Scotch Bard, April 1, 1785'
and 'To James Tennant of Glenconner'), William Cowper ('Truth')
and William Motherwell ('The Sword Chant of Thorstein Raudi'). In
the context of Pound's appropriation of the term in 'The Seafarer', it is
worth noting that several of these usages associate jargon with the sea;
a usage that was possibly suggested by Gavin Douglas. Gay writes, for
example, that 'passing fishers through the darkness call, / Deep greeting,

in the jargon of the sea.' More recently, Browning (in *Aristophanes' Apology*), Francis Thompson (in 'Her Portrait') and Lionel Johnson (in 'A Sad Morality') may have reminded the metropolitan literati of the scope of poetic jargoning.

But of all the eminent authors who respond to the various meanings of the term 'jargon', the modernists do so most thoroughly and satisfyingly. Even fairly traditional poets like Robert Graves are quite convinced of the centrality of secret code to poetic endeavour. Ancient poets, he contends, made use of secret bardic alphabets whose surreptitious knowledge was guarded and passed on to succeeding generations. According to Graves,

> a large part of poetic education, to judge from the Irish *Book of Ballymote*, which contains manuals of cryptography, was concerned with making the language as difficult as possible in order to keep the secret close; in the first three years of his educational course, the Irish student for the Ollavship [i.e., the master-poet] had to master one hundred and fifty cipher-alphabets.[22]

These were not the only secret poetic languages known to the modernists. Victorian interest in François Villon, for example, revealed that the Coquillards (a group of truant and petty criminals that Villon is said to have belonged to largely on the evidence of his *Ballades en Jargon*) conversed among themselves in a fraternal dialect that made its way into both criminal and literary argot of the time. This jargon was often related to birds.

Yeats presents another example. He never mastered the Irish language, although he succumbed to its phonological charms in his early verse to an extent that poses very real challenges to English readers. What can be said about his notorious symbology in this regard? As he readily admitted, it comprises 'an arbitrary, harsh, difficult symbolism', a cryptic, personal jargon to rival any other.[23] His poems are filled with birds and bird sounds, more than any other poet I am aware of, and his dying comfort, like that of his character Cuchulain, was that he should find himself again among spirits 'who had changed their throats and had the throats of birds'.[24]

James Joyce, on the other hand, apparently began his life with this same fantasy. Richard Ellmann writes that

> Joyce longed to sing; a dream of his youth was to be a bird, both in its song and in its flight; and his unassuming lyrics, which he was to disparage and to cherish, were spurts of his lost, birdlike aspirations.[25]

Joyce frequently defended his works in terms of music, and he has become forever synonymous with the development of twentieth-century jargon because of the following extended bird-passage from *Finnegans Wake*:

> *– Three quarks for Muster Mark!*
> *Sure he hasn't got much of a bark*
> *And sure any he has it's all beside the mark.*
> *But O, Wreneagle Almighty, wouldn't un be a sky of a lark*
> *To see that old buzzard whooping about for uns in the dark*
> *And he hunting round for uns speckled trousers around by Palmerstown*
>   *Park?*
> *Hohohoho, moulty Mark!*
> *You're the rummest old rooster ever flopped out of a Noah's ark*
> *And you think you're cock of the wark.*
> *Fowls, up! Tristy's the spry young spark*
> *That'll tread her and wed her and bed her and red her*
> *Without ever winking the tail of a feather*
> *And that's how the chap's going to make his money and mark!*

Overhoved, shrillgleescreaming. That song sang seaswans. The winging ones. Seahawk, seagull, curlew and plover, kestrel and capercallzie. All the birds of the sea they trolled out rightbold when they smacked the big kuss of Trustan with Usolde.[26]

This passage resembles little in Western literature except, perhaps, that archetypal adaptation of birds' jargon – the hoopoe's rousing (in the sense that Joyce invites with the phrase 'Fowls, up!') solo in Aristophanes' *Birds*, discussed at length in the Appendix.

A 'quark', needless to say, came to be known as 'any of a group of sub-atomic particles (orig. three in number) conceived of as having a fractional electric charge and making up in different combinations the hadrons, but not detected in the free state'. The term's originator, M. Gell-Mann, cites the above passage in a letter to the editor of the *Oxford English Dictionary*, given in the word's etymology there. The term does have one less-cited antecedent, however: the (highly Aristophanic) verb 'quark', which means 'to croak'. The *Oxford English Dictionary* provides two nineteenth-century examples to illustrate this usage, but it is understandable, in the context I have been developing, that physicists tend to prefer the Joycean derivation. Literature draws upon jargon and, in this instance, jargon draws upon literature. It has become part of the epistemological and cultural apparatus of the twentieth century, and the lore surrounding this particular example, well known beyond the worlds of physics and of literature, illustrates its pervasiveness.

We may finally gauge the legitimacy and utility of describing modernism in terms of jargon by deferring to an entity that was in the end immovable by poetry or by aesthetics (although producing both by the score) or by the songs of birds: the Fascist authorities for which Pound broadcast during the Second World War became concerned on several occasions that he was airing some kind of code.[27] Pound felt the need to repudiate the same charge to his American censors, writing that 'The Cantos contain nothing in the nature of cypher or intended obscurity.'[28] The same charge was levelled at Joyce's *Ulysses*.[29]

If these examples may be considered representative, it would appear that a new relationship between language and knowledge, especially technical and scientific forms of knowledge, arises in the twentieth century and helps ensure that an aesthetic of jargon, which was always implicit in the lyric tradition, becomes a dominant literary and modernist mode. Part of the reason for this change seems to be that a greater proportion of the population began to have personal experience of the results of formerly esoteric knowledges. The Victorians, to be sure, had their technologies: the railroad, for example; however, as H. C. G. Matthew notes,

> the opening years of the twentieth century . . . brought the widespread use by the better-off of its characteristic appliances, available in the 1890s but slow to find markets because of technical inadequacies – electric light in the houses, telephones, typewriters, gramophones, automobiles – and, soon, wireless and aeroplanes. The first building in the world specially designed as a cinema was opened in Colne, Lancashire, in 1907. Quite suddenly, the Victorian years and their preoccupations began to seem worlds away.[30]

Victorian 'science' – for the first time designating the exclusively 'natural and physical . . . the phenomena of the material universe and their laws' – was perfected and applied; efficiency was improved, markets found.[31] Although the technology underpinning these new devices was becoming more complex, the results were becoming more pervasive. This trend was true not only of technological development but of abstract concepts: Darwin, for example, was socialised, and the result was a popular 'facile assumption of racial superiority, linked to imperialism'.[32] Psychology, and even physics, would have their celebrities too.

In an ironic, and prophetic, passage from his 'Preface' to *Lyrical Ballads*, William Wordsworth in essence prepared the way for poets of succeeding generations to accommodate precisely this eventuality. He supposed that

> the remotest discoveries of the Chemist, the Botanist, or Mineralogist, will be as proper objects of the Poet's art as any upon which it can be employed, if the time should ever come when these things shall be familiar to us, and the relations under which they are contemplated by the followers of these respective

sciences shall be manifestly and palpably material to us as enjoying and suffering beings. If the time should ever come when what is now called science, thus familiarized to men, shall be ready to put on, as it were, a form of flesh and blood, the poet will lend his divine spirit to aid the transfiguration.[33]

Probably, the general public in the twentieth century was no better informed about chemical, botanical or mineralogical matters than their ancestors a hundred years ago; the implications of these emerging disciplines impinged increasingly upon ordinary people's lives, however, and their jargons were increasingly the language of the everyday life. As Pound later put it in one of his radio speeches, 'people learned that bacilli can kill. Prophylaxis entered the general mind': by virtue of its many applications, which had to be utilised and spoken of, science *was* in a way 'familiarized to men'.[34] Indeed, it is crucial to realise that these branches of knowledge became 'science' in the modern, accepted sense only when their languages became ubiquitous; their hieratic ciphers were admitted into ordinary conversation precisely on the precondition that they did not too readily discover their austere knowledges unto the masses. Nietzsche, who drolly observes that 'one does not only wish to be understood when one writes; one wishes just as surely not to be understood', grasps the thoroughgoing ambivalence of the emerging relationship between language and knowledge towards the end of the nineteenth century.[35]

'Science', in its now familiar sense, always promises a sort of miracle. As Harriet Monroe observed in *Poetry* magazine, in an essay provocatively titled 'Wanted – a Theme', poets became concerned with 'knowledge which brings the mysterious forces of nature to our service and presents to us every day a new miracle – knowledge which annihilates distance, unveils the invisible and the illimitable, which conquers disease and postpones death', subjects which, she goes on to claim, are endemic to the twentieth century.[36] In many ways, the old Platonic ideal of an authentic, supercharged language with the capacity to penetrate the increasingly perplexing enigmas of day-to-day existence is required to accomplish the routine miracle. A cursory examination of the *Oxford English Dictionary* reveals many examples of Victorian scientific jargon becoming ordinary modern idiom. Words like 'analysis', 'calibrate', 'carbohydrate', 'egocentric' and 'genetic', for example, are all words that attained scientific currency in the Victorian era and became much more common in the twentieth century. Prefixes illustrate this trend still more forcefully: *aero-*, *auto-*, *electro-*, *hetero-*, etc. were highly favoured by Victorian scientists, but would become fundamental to ordinary expression in the English language only in the twentieth century.

Another telling example of Victorian scientific jargon becoming indispensably apt to the modern condition is the word 'expertise', a twentieth-century phenomenon if ever there was one. This word alone testifies to the abundance of scientific applications in the marketplace and the technical knowledge that necessarily underwrites them. It illustrates that this knowledge was increasingly beyond the limits of the laity, who tended more and more to defer to various classes of priestly specialist. At the same time, the word forcibly demonstrates how the very process of scientisation peppered the ordinary language with jargon. One of the most fundamental reasons that a new aesthetic emerged in the modern era, therefore, was epistemological. The increasing specialisation and fragmentation of scientific discourse made it obvious how linguistic specialisation configures language into outlandish acoustic structures; its very oddness bearing the brunt of its purportedly direct relationship with knowledge.

For F. R. Leavis, it was clear that 'not only poetry, but literature and art in general' were 'becoming more specialized'. He reasoned that 'the process is implicit in the process of modern civilization'.[37] Leavis makes two arguments here that help explain the preponderance of miscellaneous jargon in twentieth-century aesthetics: increased specialisation, on the one hand, and some unspecified peculiarity about 'modern civilization', on the other hand. Pound was in agreement with the first and, like Harriet Monroe, sometimes associated this new-fangled terminology directly with modern literature, as in the following announcement:

> I take pleasure in welcoming, in Monsieur Jouve, a contemporary. He writes the new jargon and I have not the slightest doubt that he is a poet. Whatever may be said against automobiles and aeroplanes and of the modernist way of speaking of them . . . still it is indisputable that the vitality of the time exists in such work.[38]

This may be the first explicit association between the emerging modernist aesthetic and literary 'jargon'. Pound departs from the censorious usage of the term that governs eighteenth-century critical usage, and yet does not precisely return to the original sense either. Jargon represents a special literary language devised to accommodate specific historical circumstances, Villon providing the impetus.

Leavis's second point was familiar too, and is rudimentary to theories of literary modernity beginning with Pound's beloved Decadents. In his 1868 'notice' to *Fleurs du Mal*, for example, Théophile Gautier is keenly aware that the new barbaric style epitomised by Charles Baudelaire is occasioned by specific historical and cultural forces: 'Decadent style . . . is simply art that has reached the extreme point of maturity which marks the setting of ancient civilisations', says Gautier, offering a parallel:

In connection with this style may be recalled the speech of the Lower Empire, that was already veined with the greenish streaking of decomposition, and the complex refinement of the Byzantine school, the ultimate form of decadent Greek art. Such, however, is the necessary, the inevitable speech of nations and civilizations when factitious life has taken the place of natural life.[39]

A decadent style invariably arises during the deliquescence of 'civilization'; civilisation ultimately manifests itself in its ancient opposite, barbarism, in a kind of grotesque pastiche of itself (hinting at Pound's splendid bastardisation of kulchur). Considered in the abstract, decadent style has all the trappings of the modernist jargonings of Pound, Eliot and Joyce. When Gautier describes it as 'the final expression of the Word' and delights in 'the solecisms and barbarisms of that marvelous tongue [that] reveals the charming unskillfulness of the Northern barbarian kneeling before his Roman Beauty', he seems to take the word 'barbarian' in the original – auditory – sense.[40] He emphasises the borrowings and novel, exotic insights that the new style is capable of: 'it is an ingenious, complex, learned style, full of shades and refinements of meaning, ever extending the bounds of language, borrowing from every technical vocabulary, taking colours from all palettes, notes from all keyboards . . .'[41]

With a few notable exceptions (especially Arthur Symons and Lionel Jonson), the English metropolitan literary establishment of the 1890s preferred to focus on the personality capable of producing this kind of art than to investigate the necessity or inevitability that a moribund culture might invariably produce such a diffuse aesthetic response, and, as a result, one aspect of the relationship between Anglo-American modernism and its roots in the collapse of the British Empire has been obscured. In fact, however, the erosion and decline of the British Empire must be reckoned among the chief determinants of Pound's poetics of jargon, just as the decline of French colonial power was critical to the emergence of French Décadence. According to standard historical accounts such as H. C. G. Matthew's, 'in the last third of the [nineteenth] century, imperial issues became much more of a public preoccupation'.[42] One feature of this preoccupation was a serious challenge to the assumption that colonials were brutish barbarians and that colonisers were civilised, beneficent, godlike. By the Nineties, the British were resorting to conspicuous, ingenious and quite unprecedented forms of barbarism themselves, culminating in the notorious concentration camps of the Boer War (the most expensive of Britain's imperial exploits by far).[43] The rhetoricians of the *fin de siècle* responded to this ambivalence by intensifying their colonial discourse and by grudgingly including

America and other European nations among what they acknowledged to be the 'advanced races'. The result, therefore, was an ambiguously Eurocentric internationalism. Once more, the English language itself provides ample testimony to this cultural and epistemological habit: the term 'Anglophone' became current only in the twentieth century, at more or less the same time as 'Francophobia'.

London then seemed to many, including Pound, to be the cultural capital of the civilised world in the same way as Athens or Rome had been in ancient times. This was complicated, to be sure, by a grave distrust of British colonial motives, which Pound's early writings sometimes criticise directly. Writing in *The New Age* in 1912, for example, he insists that

> If Turkey had been maintained in the 'unspeakable' status quo, I should like to know by what force if not by the force of the allied monopolies of Europe? If it had not been to the interest of European capital to maintain the Turk, why has he persisted?
>
> If an oriental despotism is not lock, stock and barrel of our matter with the industrial tyrannies of Europe, to what is it allied? . . . [W]e wish we could throw off the subtle strands of the hidden tyranny of the monopolists as swiftly and cleanly as you are throwing off the yoke of a tyranny of arms.
>
> Uncivilised Montenegrins, Servians, decadent Greeks, pestilent Bulgarians, I wish you well, and I pray that you conserve your ideal of freedom better than men have done in my own 'free' country or in constitutional England.[44]

As the archness of this passage suggests, Pound was always sceptical of terms like 'civilisation' and 'culture', largely because they saturated the propaganda and reportage of the period. As we shall see in Chapter 4, Pound's aesthetic receives a decisive impulse from his discovery of, and sympathy with, a certain class of margin-alien that culture and civilisation had long maligned; but he inherited this scepticism in part from the literary tradition.[45]

It has long been recognised that modernism takes its bearings from the city and the cosmopolitanism it enables. Raymond Williams famously contends that 'the most important general element of the innovations in form is the fact of immigration to the metropolis, and it cannot too often be emphasized how many of the major innovators were, in this precise sense, immigrants'.[46] The semantic innovations of the modernists, no less than their formal innovations, can be traced to Empire and its centripetal urging towards the capital. They clearly sought something similar to the ethnographic and anthropological savvy of the ancient Greek poets and dramatists: from their cosmopolitan, metropolitan environs, their curiosity reached out to variously remote cultures and languages and tried to assimilate their outlandish lore.[47] In Eliot's version, this exchange was restricted to ancient and European languages; Pound aspired to be more inclusive still; and Joyce seemingly sought to leave nothing and no one out at all.[48]

Pound was especially well positioned to appreciate the global character of London and the international flavour of its thought and art at the start of the twentieth century. Not only was he profoundly influenced by the Decadents before, during and after his arrival in London (Victor Plarr writes that Ernest Dowson was 'a kind of classical myth' for Pound, 'just as the ancients are a myth to us all'), but he became, along with Eliot, intensely preoccupied with Gautier just as he was embarking on his most Decadent writing (on the above definition), *The Cantos*.[49] Pound was, simultaneously, acutely conscious of his status as an American in the world of English letters. In the first place, he inherited what he would later term a 'language of verse' that was Romantic and Celtic in the main, and entirely unsuited to communicating with his compatriots.[50] He tried very hard to overcome the disadvantage of his own rude speech before realising that his effort to adopt the prevailing literary dialect was artistically futile. John Agard has much more recently summed up his experience as a marginal writer: 'Muggin de Queen's English / Is the story of my life', he writes.[51] A comparable process of 'muggin' official language is apparent in Pound's earliest verse and in his most admired verse alike – he even explains in one of his radio broadcasts that he has in the course of his life 'given most of [his] time to muggin' up kulchur'.[52] His approach does not simply involve the passive assimilation of 'the language of verse', but a constant wrestling with traditional and current, official and marginal Englishes.[53] If Pound began by sheepishly adopting English spellings over American ones, grotesquely imitating foreign languages, and replicating the idiom of his Pre-Raphaelite predecessors, he quickly learned the value of inter-linguistic exchange as a means of broadening the scope of English verse and refining its purchase on experience. Inevitably, this sometimes led to confused and confusing literary concoctions, but his status as a literary margin-alien immediately and inherently opened up new possibilities of expression by emphasising the sound of language and by exploiting its material aspects; it posed the question of style in a thoroughly relativistic way, emphasising the emergence of civilised and civilising sense from the incomprehensibility of barbarian speech (or, it may be, vice versa).

Initially, Pound's own dialect posed acute impediments to his literary aspirations; he approached the canon by which his achievement would be measured as an outsider. He felt himself uneasy with American English, as his relationship with his immediate literary forebears attests. His Viconian premise seems to be that an author begins without the necessary means of expression at his disposal. Lacking language, the poet must always 'make it new'. In more recent times, this has become one of the dominant critical paradigms of literary criticism. Gilles Deleuze, for example, contends that literary style amounts to discovering 'the foreign language within language', normalising a predicament that the modernists took to be exceptional.[54] He suggests, moreover, that this conception is quintessentially American, and that American literature is 'the minor literature par excellence, in so far as America claims to federate the most diverse minorities'.[55] Deleuze has in mind the multiplicitous aspects of Walt Whitman's poetry here, a feature that is still more discernable in the work of Ezra Pound, but he is essentially reading American literature in French, Decadent terms.

At a time when critics are increasingly drawn to non-canonical, regional literatures and explicating their quirks and oddities as if they were mere curiosities, independent of rigorous formal and aesthetic process, hermetically and hermeneutically sealed in their respective cultural grottos and troves, we would do well to remember Pound's fascination with regional literature, and the federating function (to pick up Deleuze's term) of Decadent and modernist literature. Some critics have argued that post-colonial literatures present not simply new experiences, but new categories of aesthetic experience. Evelyn Ch'ien, for example, observes that

> with increasing frequency in Literature, readers are encountering barely intelligible and sometimes unrecognizable English created through the blending of one or more languages with English. Currently these literatures are classified as ethnic or minority literatures, and their vernaculars are objects of cultural rather than literary study. This book [*Weird English*] aims to show that weird English constitutes the new language of literature and that it brings new literary theory into being.[56]

Ch'ien's demand for aesthetic consideration of 'ethnic or minority literatures' is an urgent one. Without this kind of attention, post-colonial literatures risk being perceived as anomalous and artless. The first step towards a more equitable reception, however, involves the recognition that literature, and especially poetry, is more often 'weird' than Ch'ien supposes. Ethnic and minority writers very often proceed in strictest accordance with the aesthetic practice of canonical authors, as outlined by the canon's most venerated theorists. Such authors have, it is true, very often different means at their disposal, but the process of charging standard forms with 'the extra dimensions of a foreign language', thereby 'weirding' English, is a mechanism that even Aristotle recommends.[57] Ezra Pound pioneered this kind of literature in the twentieth century, as Chi'en acknowledges, and there is no shortage of literary jargoners in the years intervening between Aristotle and Pound.

The solace of linguistic and cultural independence is surely real and necessary when faced with the exploits of monolithic empire. But in the process of evoking exotic places in 'weird' and marginal tongues, literature ranges far beyond the locales and linguistic communities that it depicts: the desire, the necessity of what Wallace Stevens terms the 'maker's rage to order words [. . .] / Words of the fragrant portals, dimly-starred, / And of ourselves and of our origins' mandates that art will always struggle to shape life, and that no experience is so inchoate as to be intemperable to its informing touch.[58] Ch'ien's point that 'today, varieties of English are codes for communities – the less orthodox and more subversive, the stronger the impact' appears to me to be an important one.[59] But the mere fact of this encoding, this transformation of language into literature, needs itself to be considered. It suggests something more fundamental about the way meaning is constituted and about the ways language and literature always work: literature is a process of *asserting* meaning and imposing sense on sound, often with a great deal of effort and, to succumb to the modernist cliché, a great deal of violence to official forms of communication. Baudelaire already recognises this as a central tenet of Romanticism, insisting that 'before being admitted into the sphere of art every object should undergo a metamorphosis that should fit it for that subtle realm, by idealizing it and removing it from trivial truth'.[60] It remains crucial to recognise this revival of what Chi'en terms 'the aesthetic experiential potential of English' in the later twentieth century, and to acknowledge that there is not a single 'way of reproducing meaning' (if indeed literature is primarily concerned with 'reproduction' and not production, if 'meaning' is even to be preferred in a narrow and explicit, paraphrasable sense). Accordingly, it is imperative that the non-discursive elements in literature, those 'dimensions unconnected to the transference of meaning', be incorporated into literary study.[61] As Nietzsche points out: 'one does not only wish to be understood when one writes; one wishes just as surely not to be understood'.[62] Literature, especially poetry, is about more than simply 'transferring' ideas.

Notes

1. Qtd in Heaney, 'Burns's Art Speech', p. 216. This statement may be indebted to Pound's proclamation that 'an artist's statement is made in and by his work. His work is his biography, and the better the artist the more this applies. "There is my autobiography" said Jean Cocteau one day when

we were expressing mutual annoyance with the series of importunates who return again and again to requesting it' (*Gaudier Brzeska*, p. 141).

2. It is typically assumed that birds and birdsong are especially Romantic themes in poetry. A casual survey of modern poetry reveals how erroneous this assumption is. Yeats's bird symbolism is perhaps the most thoroughly documented, although it has usually been considered in a Romantic light. T. S. Eliot makes birds do and say some very odd things in his most famous poetry ('Sweeney Among the Nightingales', for example). One can scarcely turn a page in Robert Frost's first volume without encountering a bird or a birdsong. Wallace Stevens is haunted by Shakespeare's 'bare ruined choirs' in his last poetry. Thomas Hardy, D. H. Lawrence, Gerard Hopkins all have important bird-poems. I do not mean to suggest that these poets use the image in the same way – some are more modern or more romantic than others – but it is vital to appreciate the real extent of bird symbolism in this poetry.

3. Aviram, *Telling Rhythm*, p. 109.
4. 'Jargon', *Oxford English Dictionary*.
5. Ibid.
6. Albright, *Quantum Poetics*; Tiffany, *Radio Corpse*.
7. Coleridge, *Coleridge's Poetry and Prose*, pp. 81–3; ll. 358–66.
8. This may of course have been Chaucer, and the word also occurs in *The Merchant's Tale* ('He was al coltish ful of ragerye / And ful of Iargon as a flekked pye' [ll. 603–4]).
9. Pound, *Guide to Kulchur*, p. 148; p. 150.
10. For most of the twentieth century, these scenes have been credited to George Wilkins and have often been cut in production as a result; Pound was probably aware of this scholarly debate, and attracted to these scenes because of the additional obscurity and notoriety, coupled with the studied antiquarianism of the presentation of Gower.
11. Gower, *Confessio Amantis*, vol. 3, p. 160; ll. 5690–700.
12. Ovid, *Metamorphosis*, p. 200.
13. Coleridge's 1798 version of 'The Ancyent Marinere' gives 'Lavrock' for 'sky-lark' in l. 348.
14. Gower, *Confessio Amantis*, vol. 3, p. 125; ll. 4098–104.
15. There may well be a faint echo of these lines in 'The Tree', a poem that Pound always placed first in his oeuvre; it, too, contains a metamorphosis (Daphne's transformation into the laurel tree):

> 'Twas not until the gods had been
> Kindly entreated and been brought within
> Unto the hearth of their heart's home
> That they might do this *wonder thing*.
> Naethless I have been a tree amid the wood
> And *many* new things understood
> That was rank folly to my head before. (Pound, *Poems and Translations*, p. 14; ll. 6–14; emphasis added)

16. Cf. 'The brasin durra iargis on the marble hirst' (*Æneis* I, vii, 57, in *Columbia Granger's World of Poetry*); 'At last with horrible soundis trist

/ Thai wareit portis, iargand on the hirst' (*Æneis* VI, ix, 88, in *Columbia Granger's World of Poetry*).

17. John Locke's response to this dilemma is instructive: he was clearly fascinated by the word 'jargon', and introduced into English preposterous variant forms like 'jargogle', which nicely encapsulates the oddness and arbitrariness of much scientific jargon (I will not have occasion to use this word, nor can I conceive of an occasion when its use would be warranted on Locke's own principles, which is, no doubt, the point). In *An Essay Concerning Human Understanding* (1690), Locke negotiates a position somewhere between disallowing jargon and admitting it into the bosom of philosophy. His argument rests on a quibble that exploits precisely the discrepancy between the original and modern senses of the term. Locke was perfectly aware that both precision and consistency are required of language if it is to avoid muddling its object of inquiry. No word, however particular, arcane or specialised, is objectionable to Locke if it surrenders its concept directly and unambiguously, and if it is treated in a consistent manner. As he explains in his correspondence with Edward Stillingfleet, the Bishop of Worcester: 'Your Lordship adds, "but now it seems, nothing is intelligible but what suits with the new way of ideas." My Lord, *the new ways of ideas*, and the old way of speaking *intelligibly* was always and ever will be the same. And if I may take the liberty to declare my sense of it, herein it consists: 1. That a man use no words, but such as he makes the signs of certain determined objects of his mind in thinking, which can make known to another. 2. Next, that he use the same word steadily, for the sign of the same immediate object of the mind in thinking. 3. That he join those words together in propositions, according to the grammatical rules of that language he speaks in. 4. That he unite those sentences in a coherent discourse. Thus and thus only I humbly conceive, anyone may preserve himself from the confines and suspicion of jargon, whether he pleases to call those immediate objects of his mind, which his words do or should stand for, ideas or no' (Locke, *Essay Concerning Human Understanding*, p. 646). Jargon is best avoided: (1) by finding the most univocal and unambiguous sign for the object of inquiry; (2) by using this sign consistently; and (3) in accordance with the generally accepted principles of grammar and syntax. Evidently, Locke was more concerned that the philosopher should avoid twittering away like a bird than that his language should become too recondite or abstruse. Nevertheless, his comments reveal that the popular meaning of the word 'jargon' had shifted from the prior sense that he invokes here to the sense we are now familiar with.

18. Swift, 'On Poetry: A RHAPSODY', *Major Works*, p. 541; ll. 233–54.

19. 'Rhapsody', *Oxford English Dictionary*.

20. Johnson, 'Preface' to *Dictionary*, §86.

21. In the twentieth century, this dual concern would become the leitmotif of Pound's critical endeavour, because of his desire to consolidate and rectify language, on the one hand, and to vitalise and multiply the means of expression, on the other. Conceiving of literary style as a kind of jargon thus involved a profoundly relativistic approach to aesthetics, and encouraged comparisons of current literary style with past literary styles, especially unfavourable comparisons.

22. Graves, *White Goddess*, p. 101.
23. Yeats, *A Vision*, p. 23.
24. Yeats, *Poems*, p. 380; l. 25.
25. Ellmann, *James Joyce*, p. 171.
26. Joyce, *Finnegans Wake*, p. 383.
27. Cornell, *Trial of Ezra Pound*, p. 2.
28. Pound and Spoo, *Ezra and Dorothy Pound*, p. 177.
29. Ellmann, *James Joyce*, pp. 524–5.
30. Matthew, *Oxford History of Britain*, p. 573. I have chosen the *Oxford History* to emphasise the uncontroversial nature of the argument about technology in the early twentieth century.
31. 'Science', *Oxford English Dictionary*.
32. Matthew, *Oxford History of Britain*, p. 567.
33. Wordsworth, *Major Works*, p. 607.
34. Pound, *Ezra Pound Speaking*, p. 91.
35. Nietzsche, *Gay Science*, p. 343.
36. Qtd in Diepeveen, *Difficulties of Modernism*, p. 112.
37. Leavis, qtd in Diepeveen, *Difficulties of Modernism*, pp. 99–100. Language has appeared as a code for specialised knowledge, especially to poets, since its inception. According to Barry Powell, 'there is sufficient evidence . . . to show that the inspiration [for alphabetic writing] was poetic – more specifically, Homeric. The Greek alphabet was invented because of the desire to record epic' ('Who Invented the Alphabet: The Semites or the Greeks?'). Whether we accept this hypothesis or not, and there is some controversy about the matter, it should be clear that early alphabetic writing must have appeared to the majority of Greeks to have been indecipherable; *much more* indecipherable than the sights and sounds of birds, the makeup of intestines and entrails, involuntary or unlooked for motions and coincidences, etc. Samuel Johnson speculates along the same lines much later: 'As language was at its beginning merely oral, all words of necessary or common use were spoken before they were written; and while they were unfixed by any visible signs, must have been spoken with great diversity, as we now observe those who cannot read to catch sounds imperfectly, and utter them negligently. When this wild and barbarous jargon was first reduced to an alphabet, every penman endeavoured to express, as he could, the sounds which he was accustomed to pronounce or to receive, and vitiated in writing such words as were already vitiated in speech. The powers of the letters, when they were applied to a new language, must have been vague and unsettled, and therefore different hands would exhibit the same sound by different combinations' ('Preface' to *Dictionary*, §7). The modernist poets, and Pound especially, in many ways return to this primordial conception of language and meaning as a 'wild and barbarous jargon', in part, no doubt, because of their scepticism about the universality, and about the stability, of the forms of language they inherited and perpetuated.
38. Qtd in Stock, *Life of Ezra Pound*, p. 136.
39. Gautier, 'The Magic Hat', *Works*, p. 39; p. 40.
40. Ibid. p. 40; p. 42.
41. Ibid. pp. 39–40.
42. Matthew, *Oxford History of Britain*, p. 559.

43. Ibid. p. 565.
44. Qtd in Carr, 'Imagism and Empire', p. 79.
45. I prefer this voicing of Pound's 'marginalian' for reasons that will become increasingly apparent (Pound, *Literary Essays*, p. 35).
46. Williams, *The Politics of Modernism*, p. 45.
47. See Appendix for more details.
48. Curiously, this unbridled experimentalism is precisely what renders *Finnegans Wake* an 'unimportant ... bourgeois diversion' for Pound (Pound, *Ezra Pound Speaking*, p. 129).
49. Plarr, *Ernest Dowson*, p. 28.
50. Pound, *Selected Prose*, p. 461. Margaret Fisher supposes that he only arrives at a suitable means of addressing his American audience in the 1930s, in his radiophonic and operatic works, and in certain cantos composed around this time: 'He defended his use of dialect as the only appropriate language with which to address the American listener, who, Pound asserted, was not receptive to "solemn" or "formal" pronouncements' (Fisher, *Ezra Pound's Radio Operas*, p. 199).
51. Agard, 'Listen Mr Oxford Don', *Mangoes and Bullets*, p. 44.
52. Pound, *Ezra Pound Speaking*, p. 7. The two poets probably utilise different and possibly opposed semantic and cultural associations here: my explanation follows Agard's likely usage.
53. Pound, *Selected Prose*, p. 461.
54. Deleuze, *Essays Critical and Clinical*, p. 113.
55. Ibid. p. 57.
56. Ch'ien, *Weird English*, pp. 3–4.
57. Ibid. pp. 6–7.
58. Stevens, 'The Idea of Order at Key West', *Collected Poetry and Prose*, p. 106.
59. Ch'ien, *Weird English*, p. 5.
60. Gautier, 'The Magic Hat', *Works*, p. 47. This is Gautier's paraphrase.
61. Ch'ien, *Weird English*, pp. 6–7.
62. Nietzsche, *Gay Science*, p. 343.

Chapter 2

'Toils Obscure, An' A' That': Romantic and Celtic Influences in 'Hilda's Book'

Many poets begin the process of learning their craft by mimicking a favourite predecessor; for Ezra Pound, this process amounted almost to the learning of a foreign language, complete with its own peculiar lexicon, grammar and morphology. Before he came to know Browning or Bertrans de Born, the poet's tongue sounded Romantic and Pre-Raphaelite in the main to the young Idahoan, with something of a rising Celtic brogue. For this reason, 'Hilda's Book' may come as a bit of a surprise for those most familiar with the Pound who, along with Yeats and Eliot, was instrumental in expelling Romantic sonority and Pre-Raphaelite affectation from poetry for the best part of the twentieth century. Pound's verse from this very early period has not often received much consideration due to its derivativeness and poor quality. It has also been hard to come by (until the publication of Richard Sieburth's *Poems and Translations*) and scholars interested in Pound's earliest poetry have sometimes found themselves guessing at its nature.[1] Since, however, Pound's most characteristic poetic accomplishments have so often had their origins in the assimilation of a foreign language or idiom – and, more importantly, a corresponding demeanour – a circumspect examination of his earliest volume seems overdue.

In 'Hilda's Book', a handmade volume collecting early work from 1905–7 produced by Pound in celebration of his undergraduate love, Hilda Doolittle ('H. D.'), we see the poetic novice at a familiar task: invigorating language with studied antiquarianism and barbarism. These effects are often calculated to appear strange to the eye, and their aural qualities are more outlandish still. In these early poems, we see Pound fumbling towards a poetry based on jargon, and the arcane and hieratic style he would later perfect. This style is founded in equal measure on deliberately obscure diction and on the most conspicuously acoustic language he can muster. It appeals, therefore, to the modern sense of the word 'jargon' that designates a specialised, erudite language, as well as the ancient sense of jargon that designates birdsong, a language that, according to the science of augury, brought divine wisdom to ordinary mortals. In both the ancient world and the modern world, jargoning has been an essential part of the poet's repertoire, and these two antipodes, ancient and modern, provide the defining impulse of much of Pound's verse, which comes thereby to be a hybrid speech arising from a multitude of languages.

Pound most memorably announces his commitment to this sort of poetry in the craggy, tight-knit idiolect of 'The Seafarer'. His controversial translation begins with a rather cryptic invocation. The speaker asks in an inimitable, tortured way, for the power of self-honesty, to evaluate and finally set down his song of himself: 'May I for my own self song's truth reckon, / Journey's jargon.'[2] Pound began the process of discovering this language much earlier than this seminal poem, however, in an attempt to orient himself towards several Romantic and post-Romantic predecessors. At the outset of his career, writes Thomas H. Jackson, 'the poetic language of the nineties was his natural speech', and indeed, his notorious anti-Romantic sensibility seems to be proportional to the irrepressible appeal of Celtic Romanticism in his first verses.[3]

'Hilda's Book' returns to one figure again and again: the aeolian harp.[4] As Hugh Witemeyer notes, Pound employed this trope extensively throughout his early volumes.[5] He undoubtedly met the figure in Coleridge's poem of the same title, from which he derives a substantial portion of the imagery in 'Hilda's Book'. The rest is supplied by Yeats's reconfiguration of the image in his 1899 volume *The Wind Among the Reeds* (the aeolian harp was a particularly germane idea to Yeats, since the winds were popularly regarded as the voice of the Sidhe in Ireland).[6] The following passage, where Coleridge describes the sort of music that the aeolian harp produces, seems to have left a particularly indelible impression on Pound, and served as the point of departure for his subsequent consideration of the nature of poetic speech:

> Such a soft floating witchery of sound
> As twilight Elfins make, when they at eve
> Voyage on gentle gales from Faery-Land,
> Where *Melodies* round honey-dropping flowers
> Footless and wild, like birds of Paradise,
> Nor pause, nor perch, hovering on untam'd wing.[7]

The sound of the aeolian harp is associated with magical spells and incantations; it has the qualities of spontaneity and natural authenticity, being 'footless and wild'; it is, in particular, associated with birdsong (and thereby with divine utterance). Coleridge makes this point again in 'The Nightingale', and these associations recur throughout Pound's first volume, as we shall see.[8] A persistent interest in obscurity and musicality, which will grow throughout subsequent volumes into Pound's more characteristic modern jargoning, emerges from this conventional Romantic symbol of poetic utterance.

Pound's first offering is exponentially more windswept than anything in Coleridge or Yeats. His beloved future-poetess is treated to the dreamy delights of 'a lapping wind', a 'wondrous' wind, a 'waning wind', a 'listless and heavy' wind, 'a little lonely wind' but, most refreshing of all, to a persistent, singing wind.[9] In several poems this wind is explicitly metaphorical in the conventional Romantic fashion: in 'The Banners' Pound invokes it as his 'wandring brother' because, presumably, it is as 'wild' as he;[10] in 'Domina' it becomes his 'murmured prayer' as a penitent, and his suitor's song; in 'Li Bel Chasteus' it is his 'undersong'; and, in 'The Wind', a full-blown emblem of the Romantic poet's art.[11] The female interlocutor of this last poem equates the wind with a special kind of speech:

> Without a little lonely wind doth crune
> And calleth me with wandered elfin rune
> That all true wind-blown children summoneth.[12]

This is assuredly not the way we are accustomed to Pound presenting himself and his work; nevertheless, the 'true wind-blown children' are evidently Ezra and Hilda, and the bond that ties them to each other, and to the wind, is poetry. Poetry is conceived as the strange and archaic lore it appears to be in Coleridge's poem, as a sequence of 'wandered elfin rune[s]'. Poetry often appears thus in Pound's apprentice work, as a mysterious, runic language. Fred Robinson quotes an aborted translation of the Anglo-Saxon 'Wanderer' made by Pound around this time that involves such an understanding:

> Seafowl bathing foist (?) forth their feathers
> brawl rime and hail falling with snow mingled
>
> So saith the plausible in mind, sat him apart at ⎰ rune
> ⎱ counsel
> ⎰ mystery [13]

These lines suggest not only that antique diction is essential to Pound's nascent understanding of poetic speech, and that it has its own mysterious wisdom, but that it already has an affinity with birdcalls in the poet's mind, perhaps as a result of his early exposure to Anglo-Saxon poetry. The word 'wandered' (besides being a conspicuous borrowing from Yeats) further emphasises the oblique and indirect nature of the special kind of language that unites the inspired children, and implies a degree of psychic removal from the more prosaic world. In these aborted lines and in 'The Wind', we already find Pound casting about for an emblem of the obscurity and musicality that inhere in poetic speech.[14]

'The Wind', like other poems in this volume, also reveals two distinctive features of much of Pound's later verse. In the first place, it playfully exhibits the more estranging forms that English has since cast off. Thomas F. Grieve provides a comprehensive summary of these oddities, noting that for most contemporary and subsequent critics, they amount to 'the most obvious fault' of Pound's early publications (and not just 'Hilda's Book'): their 'glut of poetic diction'. He writes:

> Pound's offenses against spoken idiom cover the spectrum: they range from the almost constant but relatively innocuous habit of using 'thou' and 'ye' and 'hast,' 'hath,' 'doth,' and 'eth' forms of various verbs; to the more distracting poeticisms of 'an' for 'and if' . . . or handfulls of Lo's and O's, of *mine* for *my*, *twain* for *two*, and *me* for *I* (for example, 'Me seemeth some-wise thy hair wandereth,' a line from 'Comraderie' where 'hair' offers momentary relief, the oasis in a desert of poetical jargon); to the disconcerting contractions for the sake of the meter in 'Th'alternate,' 'Evan'scent,' ''gainst,' 'o'er,' 'e'en,' ''tis,' and, without doubt the nadir, 'm'effulgent' . . . all the way to the outright archaisms of 'dight,' 'ellum,' 'sith,' 'queynt devyse,' 'Nathless,' and 'lang syne.' To this dismal catalog we should not forget to add the dismaying preponderance of Celtic Twighlightisms, that come, almost invariably, in hyphenated form: 'wind-runing,' 'night-wonder,' 'lily-cinctured,' 'dusk-clad,' 'dream-lit,' 'the wee wind,' and 'druidings.'[15]

These are no doubt offences against the spoken idiom, and rightly deserve the designation of 'poetical jargon'. After all, these mannerisms have been wrested from literary antiquity by Pound, sometimes with little sensitivity to the historical, cultural and psychological contexts in which they arise. Rather than dismissing this 'dismal' jargoning summarily, however, we would do well to ask whether or not, and under what circumstances, it might be more effective. As Michael King maintains, 'Pound never lost his taste for archaic diction, even in *The Cantos*, and it is instructive to see him stumbling here with techniques that he would later learn to handle surely.'[16] Pound remains fundamentally attached to 'poetical jargon', though he will in due course seek it elsewhere.

Grieve emphasises that early critics were repulsed by these idiosyncrasies of style and yet, paradoxically he claims, attracted by the 'saving grace' of Pound's 'distinct personality', 'adventurous spirit' and 'vigorous individuality' (quoting F. S. Flint, Edward Thomas and

W. L. Courtney respectively), as if these could be dissociated from the poet's mannered diction.[17] Grieve follows Thomas in suggesting that there is something slightly disingenuous about these criticisms, since Pound's poetic passion found outlet 'in a jargon that was different in degree but not in kind from what was understood to be the received proper language of poetry'.[18] The importance and accuracy of this early assessment should not be overlooked. Literary convention ruins much Georgian verse as surely as Pound's linguistic contrariety ruins much of his early output. Though Grieve goes on to suggest that Pound abandons this jargoning in favour of 'natural speech, the language as spoken', at the behest of a mawkish Ford Madox Ford, it seems fairer to say that he simply discovered a less worn, more urgent and precise tongue.[19] If this new lexicon is still less transparent to his contemporaries than the private, wind-blown language of 'Hilda's Book', this is because, from the time of his first notable publication, Pound remained convinced that 'good art . . . begins with an escape from dullness'.[20]

The above lines from 'The Wind' bear witness to a second consistent feature of Pound's style, exemplified by the word 'crune' (or 'croon'): a delight in unorthodox orthography that spans his whole career. I would like to focus on this idiosyncrasy in some detail, using this word as an example. Pound was clearly fascinated with the aesthetic possibilities presented by outlandish orthography from the beginning, and even the minimal deviation between English and American English was usually too much for the poet to resist. A letter to Homer Pound written in New York and dated 22 July 1903 (when Pound was just seventeen) survives and illustrates this curiosity. The letter has been widely reproduced, though for present purposes Noel Stock's discerning summary makes the important point more directly.[21] He points out that

> We find three of the characteristics which to a greater extent and more force-fully mark the correspondence of his mature years: the use of foreign language, dialect, and strong English. Thus the letter begins in German ('Lieber Vater'), and includes both a foreigner's broken English ('oderwise dings vas az dey vas'), and straightforward speech, as when he apologizes that the letter was written 'by bum gas light'. Queer spellings and a great variety of dialect voices gradually begin to creep into his letters: sometimes, it seems, for emphasis, but often for the sheer fun of it. In later years he often developed oddities of typing, with strange spacing, phrasing and line-breaks, often reinforced by an array of underlinings and marginal interpolations in ink.[22]

Later in *The Cantos* there is much talk of letters being written 'in cypher', and this is an apt description of Pound's own epistolary mode from the moment he began to conceive of himself as a literary stylist.[23] It demonstrates, moreover, the central and persistent investment in verbal personae, both in his correspondence and in his poetry: the later cantos as much as these early sonnets show that the same technique of babelising could be adapted to both.

In these lines from 'The Wind', then, the word 'crune' is arresting and opulent in itself, since it makes the rhyme orthographically stranger and more familiar at the same time. It indicates the soft murmuring nature of poetic speech ('murmur' is another ubiquitous word in this volume, and is synonymous with croon). At the same time, it also means chatter, prattle or babble, impressing a jargonish conception of poetic speech upon the reader still further.[24] The word (though not the spelling) became popular in English only after Robert Burns's use, most conspicuous in his masterpiece 'Tam O'Shanter' where the unlikely hero finds himself 'crooning o'er some auld Scots sonnet'.[25] Pound was entirely familiar with Burns's achievements as a poetic jargoner. We have just seen him lift two of Burns's three most famous words ('lang' and 'syne', though in fact Burns picked these up from Allan Ramsay); more convincingly, perhaps, he identified with Burns enough to set some whimsical verses, 'To Hulme (T. E.) and Fitzgerald (A certain)' to the tune of 'Song—For a' that and a' that—':

> Ye see this birkie ca'ed a bard,
> Wi' cryptic eyes and a' that,
> Aesthetic phrases by the yard;
> It's but E. P. for a' that.[26]

This poem turns on the enduring poverty experienced by both Burns and Pound, as well as on an important stylistic affinity. Pound refers to the abundant poeticisms in his early verse, suggesting that they are both standard and legitimate, and yet somehow enigmatic. In these satirical lines, the poet clearly identifies with Burns's linguistic as well his physical 'toils obscure'.[27] Not for the last time, Pound defends his art with the example of a poet whose language is based on regional dialect rather than urbane 'aesthetic phrases', assuming that each in its own way supplies a necessary jolt to received English. Burns's presence makes a powerful rejoinder to those who would disparage the poet's obligation to write in a language that, however barbarous, dim or opaque to the publishing industry at large, nevertheless gets the poetic job done.

The importance of dialect verse to modernism is now well known. In *The Dialect of Modernism*, Michael North demonstrates that modernism 'mimicked the strategies of dialect and aspired to become a dialect itself', and that this stylistic effort culminated in Pound's *Pisan Cantos*, which 'let onto the page, as onto the psyche of their author, more different dialects and idiolects than any other poem ever printed, approaching at times . . . invented language . . . or . . . secret speech'.[28] North is mostly concerned with American dialects in his study of Pound and rightly so, since Pound achieves more poetic success with them and since, moreover, the cultural and political aspects of his appropriations are more vexed and instructive. The origins of Pound's interest in dialect and foreign diction remain unexplored; he was, however, developing a poetic style based on exotic climes and foreign linguistic matter already during this Romantic apprenticeship.

There are many instructive examples among Pound's dialectical borrowings. His odd spellings are usually calculated both to estrange the reader and to direct the meaning and mood of his composition in particular ways, and 'crune' is a fine example of this process. But just where did he pick up this spelling, and what purpose does it serve, in local terms, in this poem? This is a difficult matter to be certain about, but the possibilities are intriguing. The first is that Pound encountered this spelling in the anonymous Middle English lyric 'Worlde's blisse, have good day!' He does not explicitly mention this poem to my knowledge, but it is almost inconceivable that he was not familiar with it from an early age; tellingly, however, 'crune' clearly means 'crown', or head, in this poem, not song: 'Fro the crune to the to / Thy body was ful of pine and wo', the anonymous poet says.[29] The second possibility, which I will pursue at some length, is that Pound was influenced by the traditional Scots usage of the term. Most of the few instances listed in *Granger's World of Poetry* are ascribed to Scots dialect poets.[30] It occurs in two poems each by Robert Ferguson, Allan Ramsay and Robert Leighton. Ferguson uses the term in a rather bawdy context that significantly deviates from the meaning in Pound's poem; in both other poets, however, the usage is compatible with Pound's.

Today, Robert Leighton (1822–69) is regarded as an obscure poet if he is regarded at all, but he was praised by Longfellow and Emerson during his lifetime, and so perhaps transmitted this odd Scotticism to American dialect poets like James Whitcomb Riley and hence to Pound, and I will consider this connection in more detail directly. For the moment, I simply want to observe that Leighton consistently associates the word with the wind, for example in 'Lady Margaret', where 'Wild Boreas, wi' an eerie crune / Is drivin' ower the hills o' Seidlie'; elsewhere (in 'Widow Salmon's Prayer, On the Approach of Rent Day') 'The eerie wind comes whistlin' through the wa's, / And wi' its frichtsome crune' disturbs the speaker's sleep because of some haunting, mysterious property.[31] Indeed, the word's onomatopoeic qualities make it the perfect acoustic vehicle for the kind of noisome blast it designates in Pound's poem.

Before Leighton, the word and spelling were used by Allan Ramsay, a more significant poet (who nonetheless remains rather obscure). Two telling instances of the word 'crune' occur in his poetry. In his verse-epistle 'Health: A Poem. *Inscrib'd to The Right Honourable the Earl of Stair*', Ramsay examines a variety of different humours before coming, around the middle of the poem, to a figure named Marlus 'who regards / The well-mean'd Verse, and generously rewards / The Poet's Care.'[32] Ramsay goes on to describe how the world appears to this obscure character:

> The whole of Nature, to a Mind thus turn'd,
> Enjoying HEALTH, with Sweetness seems adorn'd.
> To him the whistling Ploughman's artless Tune,
> The bleeting Flocks, the Oxens hollow Crune,
> The warbling Notes of the small chirping Throng,
> Delight him more than the *Italian* song.[33]

Marlus appreciates poetry, and finds it most perfectly embodied in the noises of animals in pasture, and in the quiring of small birds rather than in more conventional archetypes. The word 'crune' refers to simple and natural utterances, and it suggests a corresponding type of 'artless', and therefore authentic, poetry.

The kind of rustic simplicity of language that Ramsay evokes here, and that will become virtually synonymous with the art of Burns, the 'ploughman poet', is so effective in grounding the poet in his world that his 'cruning' takes on mysterious properties, including a capacity to effect that world. Ramsay accordingly uses the word 'crune' to show the power of this kind of language elsewhere in his verse, for example in *The Gentle Shepherd, a Scots Pastoral Comedy* where, in Act II, ii, he introduces a witch thus:

> Hear *Mausy* lives, a Witch, that for sma' Price
> Can cast her Cantraips, and give me Advice.
> She can o'ercast the Night, and cloud the Moon,
> And mak the Deils obedient to her Crune.[34]

This supernatural context suggests subsequent uses of the word in Burns and Pound. The word is motivated by the mysterious nature of Mausy's incantatory language, something that is no less essential to Pound's aesthetic statement in 'The Wind'. Oddly enough, Ramsay's usage seems to veer away from the exact visual coincidence that a conventional spelling would provide, where Pound uses the rhyme for precisely this effect. But Pound, unlike Yeats, found no problem in writing for the eye as well as for the ear, as *The Cantos* make clear on every page.

Little, if anything, has been written about any possible connection between Pound and Ramsay. It is clear that Pound studied classical and modern pastoral poetry in his adolescence, and Ramsay may well have been one of the authors he encountered during these studies.[35] Ramsay was instrumental in reviving dialect poetry in Scots after centuries of relative neglect. 'There is nothing can be heard more silly', he writes in one of his prefaces, 'than one's expressing his *Ignorance* of his *native Language*.'[36] He achieved recognition following the publication of his *Gentle Shepherd* in 1725. The volume is famous for its powerful admixture of classical English and vernacular Scots, which had more often been combined for burlesque (as it would be in Burns's 'Holy Willie's Prayer') than in serious literary productions. Ramsay's 'toils obscure' significantly occur in the context of the 1707 Act of Union. His poetic language is, in every sense, a kind of lingua franca calculated to conciliate English and Scots audiences. The situation is comparable to Anglo-American relations at the end of the Victorian era: Pound's poetry also arises out of an attempt to mediate two cultures with a shared literary inheritance and significantly divergent contemporary idioms. Both poets are compelled to write in dialects that only partially resemble the narrow range of those traditionally available in English poetry, and as a result both are indeed 'stupidly condemn[ed] . . . as barbarous'.[37] Like Pound, Ramsay was plagued by charges of oddity and parochial obscurity, but chose to affirm these features to the bemusement of his detractors and, he maintained, to the benefit of his art.

Ramsay not only practised a deliberate oddness in his orthography and in his practice as a poet, but explained the poetic value of this strategy in several important prefaces to his work. His provincial idiom, Ramsay argued, was crucial to maintaining what he took to be an authentic attitude towards his subject matter. At the same time, however, he felt it necessary to effect some compromise between his regional speech and that of his English audience. Ramsay insisted, for instance, that although his spellings were often Scots, the words themselves were English; even if this vestigial form was lacking, he maintained that the 'the Idiom or Phraseology' was nevertheless Scots.[38] This compromise ensures that Ramsay's urbane audience could follow him and that his poetry would yet remain infused with an authentic parochialism that spoke of his different way of looking at the world. This notion of a 'phonetic approximation that an urban audience could follow' is at the heart of Pound's aesthetics from his celebrated translations through the dialogue sequences of *The Cantos*. This 'phonetic approximation' is driven by the necessity to both make sense according to the highest strictures of the Queen's English and yet use a plausibly naturalistic, speakable dialect; the sort that might 'under the stress of some emotion', actually be heard.[39] Poetry involving regional dialect claims veracity through this curious admixture of obscurity and authenticity, since it is bound up immemorially with the objects it is concerned with, and not merely an abstraction sanctified by specialists. Ramsay's divergence from metropolitan literary English has the collateral effect of ensuring that the literati would encounter his verse in as purely musical a form as is possible.

The difficulty of defending a regional, and therefore to some extent insular, poetic language was acute for Ramsay. He was aware that in fully embracing his native dialect, his verse became jargonish in the modern sense: specialised and, for most of the literary audience, unnecessarily opaque. As a result, he took pains to distinguish his own efforts from those admixtures of language that were for him more dubiously derived. In the following passage from '*Bag-Pipes no Musick*: A SATYRE on *Scots* Poetry', he defends the poet's right to speak in 'rustick jargon', and yet maintains that poetry that is obscure for other reasons remains suspect:

> Sooner shall *China* yield to Earthen Ware,
> Sooner shall *Abel* teach a singing Bear,
> Than *English* Bards let *Scots* torment the'r Ear.
> Who think their rustick Jargon to explain,
> For anes is once; lang, long; and two is twain,
> Let them to *Edinburgh* foot it back,
> And add their Poetry to fill their Pack,
> While you, the Fav'rite of the tuneful Nine,
> Make *English* Deeds in *English* Numbers shine.
> Leave *Ramsay's* Clan to follow their own Ways,
> And while they mumble Thistles, wear the Bays.[40]

Ramsay's own Scots poetry surely appeared to many as the very essence of incomprehensibility, which is perhaps why, in this instance, he addresses this part of his audience in their own vernacular: neoclassical English, and heroic couplets. The use of 'jargon' in combination with the satirical elements of this poem suggests that he is dwelling on the received metropolitan opinion of Scots verse here, as does his decision to transliterate his Scots when writing in this urbane fashion; Pound, of course, does exactly the same throughout *The Cantos*.

Remarkably, Ramsay succeeded in using the most common objections to his verse in his own favour, as a way of distinguishing natural writing in dialect and writing in the suave, affected mode of neoclassical poetry. In 'The Scribblers Lash'd', he frankly opposes his own poetic obscurity to the less germane kind of obscurity that arises when poets seek out technical vocabularies:

'Tis to correct this scribbling Crew,
Who, as in former Reigns, so now
Torment the World, and load our Time
With Jargon cloath'd in wretched Rhime,
Disgrace of Numbers! Earth! I hate them!
And as they merit, so I'll treat them.[41]

In this poem, the modern sense of the word 'jargon' governs Ramsay's critique. He cautions against dainty lexical fussing, which leads to overburdened verse, 'load[ed]' or 'fill[ed]' with 'affected Delicacies and Studied Refinements'.[42] Recondite sentiment and language are seen to be incompatible with true poetry – and specifically with the musical elements of poetry as indicated by Ramsay's extolling of 'Numbers' – and no amount of ornament can make good the deficit. That he describes the offenders as scribblers rather than writers or poets makes the point about urbane jargon rather well: the problem with overly technical or specialised language is that it is conspicuous and difficult to integrate; at best it leads to ornament, at worst it effectively amounts to cipher.[43]

Ramsay was acutely conscious of the proximity of these two forms of jargoning, yet he believed that it was possible and essential to distinguish between authentic and mechanical poetry on the basis of this distinction. We see this paradox in his juxtapositional treatment of the two forms of jargon in 'Grubstreet nae Satyre':

DOUP down doilt Ghaist, and dinna fash us
With *Carpet Ground* and *nervous* Clashes;
Your *Grubstreet Jargon Dryden* wounds,
When mixt with his Poetick Sounds.
You *pace* on *Pegasus*! Take Care,
He'll *bound o'er furrow'd fields* of Air,
And fling ye headlong frae the Skies,
Never a second Time to rise.[44]

The 'Grubstreet Jargon' Ramsay singles out as particularly offensive to poetry is constituted by trite and misapplied adjectives, unlikely and conventional metaphors.[45] For Ramsay, jargon (in the modern sense) is entirely incompatible with the sonic excellences of poetry. To the makeshift poetry of metropolitan hacks needing to make ends meet he opposes his own vernacular, best exemplified in the vigorous first line above, which means something like: 'Sit down, dumb cretin, and don't bother us'. The ancient and modern meanings of jargon have become entirely dissociated, so that it is essentially possible at this point to claim that true poetry consists in natural, musical language, albeit with its own sonic obfuscations, and that poor and derivative poetry consists in cheap scientificism, the conceptual yoking of incompatible elements so as to abstract and estrange the reader from (a much more lyrical) reality.

In the same preface, Ramsay makes the tenor of this critique more explicit by detailing the distinct values of poetry grounded in a regional sensibility. He emphasises the conceptual and poetic precision ('that natural strength of thought and Simplicity of Stile') that arises from intimate daily contact with one's local surroundings ('their *Images* are native, and their *Landskips* domestick; copied from those Fields and Meadows we every Day behold').[46] This amounts to a rather well-developed (and proto-Romantic) critique of neoclassical literary values. Pound levels the same critique at Georgian poetry: the glut of poeticisms, cliché and mixed metaphors sanctioned merely by superficial observation and cheap repetition were redundant and, what is worse, detrimental to clear thinking about the modern world and to authentic poetry about it. Thus, in practical and theoretical terms, Ramsay appears to anticipate Pound's poetic and critical project. The parallel has more to recommend it: a shared interest in the classics, especially Horace; an important debt to Villon (evident in Ramsay's 'Lucky Spense', a poem narrated in part from the point of view of a brothel-keeper); and a shared near-veneration of Gavin Douglas.[47]

Critics are often troubled by a perceived crudeness in Pound's representation of foreign idioms. The tendency to view this stylistic feature in the context of his later anti-Semitism, for example, is strong and legitimate, but it must be borne in mind that Pound's desire to mimic and appropriate foreign speech is a feature of both his verse and prose from the beginning. He is, in fact, extraordinarily open-minded and inclusive in his borrowings from foreign languages, much more so than most writers, and he advises the poetic novice to acquire facility in, if not mastery of, foreign speech (and so foreign modes of thought) for the express purpose of becoming a better poet. His receptiveness to Burns and Ramsay probably began, however, in a much more parochial way, through the influence of James Whitcomb Riley. Riley had a profound and well-known admiration for Robert Burns. As his recent biographer Elizabeth Van Allen makes abundantly clear, Riley himself encouraged the view, almost ubiquitous throughout the second half of the nineteenth century, that he had achieved for Indiana (and the US Midwest more generally) what Burns had achieved for the Scottish Borders. Both poets, at any rate, transformed their native environs into an idyllic poetic landscape and made powerful claims that the diction of its inhabitants constituted an essential, poetic register.[48] Pound was of course familiar with Riley, and he would have known of his admiration for Burns; known, too, that the experiments in dialect he was then making in his correspondence and increasingly in his poetry had this celebrated precedent.[49] There is a certain irony in the fact that an American could appreciate the urgency of Scots dialect poetry at a time when literary London could not. English poets were writing in dialect at the time, and writing very well – Thomas Hardy is the best example – but it was perhaps not until Pound and his allies liberated poetry from late Victorian convention that dialect poetry would again assume its previous importance.

Pound would have been aware of Riley's poem addressed to Burns. It is a powerful tour de force though it does not significantly depart from the popular nineteenth-century caricature of the Scots national poet. It presents Burns in an overly Romantic light. The following passage illustrates the power of Riley's assimilation of Scots dialect, despite its rather staid imagery:

> Frae where the heather bluebells fling
> Their sangs o' fragrance to the Spring,
> To where the lavrock soars to sing,
>   Still lives thy strain,
> For a' the birds are twittering
>   Sangs like thine ain.
>
> And aye, by light o' sun or moon,
> By banks o' Ayr, or Bonnie Doon,
> The waters lilt nae tender tune
>   But sweeter seems
> Because they poured their limpid rune
>   Through a' thy dreams.[50]

These lines are both typical of the public estimation of Burns, and of the kind of poetic sensibility Riley believed he shared with the 'ploughman poet'. Here, too, the twittering of the birds is equated with the expression of a particular kind of poetic genius, and both amount to a runic language profoundly invested in nature. Significantly, perhaps, this presentation of Burns does not substantially deviate from Ramsay's presentation of Marlus, almost a century before Burns wrote anything at all.

James Whitcomb Riley was proud of popular comparisons between his poetry and that of Burns, but it seems to most modern critics that his admirers have been rather indulgent of this association. The more revealing Scots counterpart to Riley is Ramsay. When Riley visited Burns Country in 1891 he would have been hard pressed not to hear of the reinventor of Scots dialect poetry. Ramsay's depiction of a lost golden age of rustic poetry, too, would have suggested an affinity between the two. Twelve years prior to this visit, moreover, in 1879,

Riley drafted a poem, 'To the Wine-God Merlus', that seems to derive from Ramsay's invocation of Marlus in 'Health', examined above. Both poems depict an obscure figure whose chief delight is poetry. In Ramsay's poem, however, Marlus is an emblem of moderation and propriety when it comes to other passions: 'The cheering glass he with right friends can share / But shuns the deep debauch with cautious care';[51] the wine-god is not so restrained in Riley's poem, as the final apostrophe makes clear:

> Drink thou my ripest joys, my richest mirth,
> My maddest staves of wanton minstrelsy;
> Drink every song I've tinkered here on earth
> With any patch of music; drink! and be
> Thou drainer of my soul, and to the lees
> Drink all my lover-thrills and ecstasies;
> And with a final gulp—ho! ho!—drink me,
> And roll me o'er thy tongue eternally.[52]

This passion involves both kenosis and apotheosis for 'Jucklet', one of Riley's personae. In surrendering his self and 'soul', the poet attains divine speech and all that that implies. The tragic dimension that arises in Riley's poem, we may imagine, is in part supplied by the example of Robert Burns, who becomes transformed (in the popular imagination at least) into a sort of rustic wine-god, or Marlus-figure, himself. In any case, Riley's critics have not been able to shed much light on this figure, and have usually assumed it to be of his own invention; it seems to derive, however, from Ramsay, and to be associated with an ideal, poetic type of rustick jargon in the Scots-pastoral tradition.

Riley's pastoral leanings, his admiration and imitation of Burns, and his own reflections on the use of dialect in poetry all point to Ramsay as an importantly elided poetic influence. The Hoosier poet was extremely vocal in defence of the use of dialect in poetry. In Marcus Dickey's account of a lecture given by Riley around the time he composed his poem 'To the Wine-God Merlus', after comparing his native dialect to the 'Cantie blether o' the hielands', Riley argues that the natural authenticity of regional dialect is too often missed by his critics in their simple, stupid amusement at its novelty:

> However dialectic expression may have been abused, certain it is that in no expression is there better opportunity for the reproduction of pure nature. In artlessness of construction the dialectic poem may attain even higher excellence than the more polished specimens of English. Its great defect seems to be that, as written or printed, the real feeling it contains is overlooked by the reader in the contemplation of its oddity.[53]

The paradox of local idiom, for Riley, is that it presents a language that is both more familiar and authentic to those who use it in their daily lives, and yet, because of this uncommon power, it recedes into spectacle and obscurity for those who do not. Riley's opposition of his own poetry (and the hoosierisms it incorporates) to 'more polished specimens', suggests that he too is concerned with a scientific understanding of language. He goes on to explain that because of a general reluctance to probe the subtleties of regional expression, 'dialectic' poetry is often poorly received by critics and weakly imitated by opportunistic journalists. 'With our fickle knowledge of all its deeper worth and purity', he remarks, 'it is little wonder that its mission is so often debased to serve the ends of the rhyming punsters and poetical thugs of our "Comic Weeklies"'.[54] Michael North, paraphrasing Paul Laurence Dunbar, reminds us that dialect verse fared similarly in the United States in the early part of the twentieth century: it became 'a trap because readers would pay attention to nothing else'.[55] Convinced, as Ezra Pound was, that poetry might be diversely charged by regional and by specialised linguistic forms, his early poems did not escape this trap. Early critics were perhaps guilty of overlooking the 'real feeling' of his early poems in 'contemplation' of their 'oddity'.[56] Pound persisted in his early volumes, however, and moved gradually towards another lyric voice from the past, that of the troubadours. This defence of 'poetic jargon' does not originate with Pound or Dunbar, James Whitcomb Riley or even with Burns, but with Allan Ramsay and his contemporaries, as we have seen. In Ramsay, too, there is a similar and understandable distrust of cheap imitation of dialect by writers of magazine verse, and other 'Grubstreet hacks'. This makes both authors uncomfortable because it threatens to exploit the superficial similarity of authentic 'rustick jargon' on the one hand, and inveterate urban jargon, on the other hand.

His emphasis on obscure forms of language – which, by the very fact of their frustration of ordinary prose meaning become more sensible in poetic contexts – leads Pound from the aeolian harp toward a new symbol of his art. In several of his 'stale creampuffs' (as Pound referred to the early poems that subsequently embarrassed him), his druidy woodlands are populated by other, more natural, songsters. In the Petrarchan sonnet entitled 'The Lees', for example, the wind mingles with the song of birds, provoking a comparison between the poet's art and theirs:

Low soundeth a murmurous minstrelsy
A mingled evensong beneath the breeze

Each creeping, leaping chorister hath ease
To sing, to whirr his heart out, joyously;
Wherefor take thou my laboured litany
Halting, slow pulsed it is, being the lees
Of song wine that the master bards of old
Have left for me to drink thy glory in.[57]

This particular stale creampuff has the merit of forcibly illustrating
a number of interesting and persisting features of Pound's style. The
curious spellings continue: when an English and American alternative lie
open for the poet, as in the word 'laboured', Pound tends to opt for the
English alternative. Though always chameleonic, this is more than a case
of the cosmopolitan poet assuming local convention. The poeticisms
persist: not only does 'White-flower-o-the-Jasamin' conflate the conventional (and more botanical) *jasmine* with 'the ordinary "Jessamine"
of English literature', but the aspiring poet couches the new term in an
elaborate compound phrase more reminiscent of the hoopoe's solo in
Aristophanes' *Birds* than the Celtic Twilight.[58]

Pound was fond of repeating Ford Madox Ford's advice to would-
be writers, to get a 'DICtionary / and learn the meaning of words', but
it seems that he held this principle dear even before he embarked on
his conquest of London.[59] His leaning towards recondite learning and
trouba-lore underpin the structure of this poem on a much more basic
level. It demonstrates a firm and well-judged commitment to poetic
diction as 'the language of exploration' by probing the manifold senses
of the poem's title: the earliest sense of 'lees', meaning a shelter or
bower, is combined with the later sense, popularised in the late medieval period, meaning the dregs of a drink. These two senses of the word
seem, moreover, to be different philologically – the former derives from
Romance languages (notably, Provençal) and the latter is Gaulish or
Celtic (though Pound's impulse was possibly supplied by Chaucer). The
poem is a skilful exercise in both diachronic and synchronic barbarism;
his language approximates the 'Elfin runes' he aspires to in 'The Wind'.[60]

This poem also deserves attention because it demonstrates Pound's
assimilation and concentration of a number of the early influences
examined above. The immediate source of its most conspicuous poeticism is probably Coleridge's 'Eolian Harp': 'our cot o'ergrown / With
white-flower'd Jasmin, and the broad-leav'd Myrtle, / (Meet emblems
they of Innocence and Love!)'[61] This poem also suggests that Pound was
familiar with James Whitcomb Riley's poem 'To the Wine-God Merlus'
and the imagery therein. That poem, let us recall, concludes with a
prayer for intercession:

> Drink! and be
> Thou drainer of my soul, and to the lees
> Drink all my lover-thrills and ecstasies;
> And with a final gulp—ho! ho!—drink me,
> And roll me o'er thy tongue eternally.[62]

In describing his effort to write poetry in the modern world and to come to terms with the erotic feelings that are co-original with this art, Pound comes back to this image of consumption and consummation offered by Jucklet's wine-god. 'The lees / Of the song-wine' that is left to Pound (and Hilda) to drink are the sweeter for having also inspired the 'master bards of old', whom we can still detect in the smattering of allusions in the poem, though this is of little consolation to the speaker and his beloved, who feel that little genuine poetry is left to them.

If a poetic reorientation seems requisite to the speaker of this poem, his description of the birds (which also appears to owe a debt to 'To the Wine-God Merlus') seems calculated to escape in some measure the hackneyed image of the Romantic songbird. Pound is particularly contemptuous of too-easy recourse to bird images as a way of articulating the poet's own state of being, as his remarkable (and later) 'Song in the Manner of Housman' whimsically suggests:

> The bird sits on the hawthorn tree
> But he dies also, presently.
> Some lads get hung, and some get shot.
> Woeful is this human lot.[63]

This poem skilfully scorns the automatic currency that the image of the bird enjoyed in Housman and Pound's day, and parodies the formulaic manner in which it has been incorporated ready-made into much post-Romantic poetry (and, it should be pointed out, unconsciously picks up Allan Ramsay's objection to the urbane 'scribbling crew' of his day, whose verse was 'load[ed]' or 'fill[ed]' with 'affected Delicacies and Studied Refinements'). In 'Vorticism' (1914), Pound explains his gripe with decorative poeticisms: 'all poetic language is the language of exploration. Since the beginning of bad writing, writers have used images as ornaments.'[64] His double objection in this poem to Housman and poorly deployed bird images anticipates this point by a number of years. Thomas Grieve fails to afford enough weight to this distinction in his discussion of Pound's move towards Fordian realism: poeticisms, according to Pound, may be either obsolete or viable, and viable in so far as they are neither ornamental nor conventional. Pound's trouba-lore is much more obviously explorative, much less ornamental, than his more conventional archaisms, and it was probably for this reason that he preferred this mode of writing.

'Each creeping, leaping chorister' does not present a figure of pathos, an emblem of freedom or its opposite, but of frenetic and effusive religious stricture.[65] The word 'chorister' came to have strong avian associations in the sixteenth century, though its principal meaning denotes one of a band of singers, especially in a religious choir. The religious aspects of the image are not ancillary to Pound's poem either. Beginning in the second line with the description of the 'hallowed' bower, they help the attentive reader understand the odd activity of these 'creeping, leaping' birds. The first word here is surprising: one does not typically think of the terrestrial movement of birds as being particularly lithesome or stealthy. Yet the word precisely conveys their very close proximity to the ground, and at the same time evokes the special religious sense of the word (prominent in the Adoration of the Cross, the Roman Catholic service for Good Friday), where devotees are said to *creep to the cross*, suggesting a prone position and an ideal of humble ponderousness.[66] The movement of the poet's verse, his 'laboured litany / halting, slow pulsed it is', perhaps adds to this image of processional religious worship, though the context marks it as pagan rather than Christian in nature (unless the 'song wine' also evokes the Eucharist).[67] This language suggests that Pound is consciously seeking an aesthetic impulse from his subject matter: it powerfully imitates the chirruping of the birds themselves. 'Each creeping leaping chorister hath ease' is a fine example of how poets since Aristophanes have, as Leonard Lutwack suggests, sought to approximate birdsong by supplying 'phonetic equivalents of the sounds made by the bird'.[68] Supplying an auditory equivalent for the phenomenon being described invests this poetry with something of the recondite musicality of augury, where birdcalls convey the secrets of the gods to humanity. Though the image might confuse at first, Pound's usage is consistent with the precise nature and historical development of the language he employs; the special religious sense governs the meaning of the poem subtly and surely, in a vital rather than ornamental fashion. The language and the strange diction conspire to release these songbirds from the spell of Romantic and post-Romantic introspection, much as they do in the closing lines of Eliot's 'Sweeney Among the Nightingales', and result in a new but tentative poetic register.

Though the poem is not a magnificent achievement, and has been overlooked, it is an excellent metaphorical tour de force that uses language to span a cultural and historical abyss and, as such, is a wonderful early specimen of Pound's pioneering juxtapositional and mythopoeic strategies. We also observe in this poem how 'linguistic imitation and racial masquerade are so important to transatlantic modernism', as North has discovered in a different context; that is to say, 'because they allow the writer to play at self-fashioning'.[69] The poem already anticipates Pound's later jargon in a number of ways; in its resistance to the mellifluous lilt of post-Romantic poetic phrasing; in privileging heterogeneous sounds and voices rather than a single, modulated musical phrase, the beginnings of what Michael King calls 'the polyglot paganism of Pound's later work'; in its mystery and in its obscurity; in its polysemy.[70]

Notes

1. T. S. Eliot encouraged this line of speculation with his introduction to Pound's *Selected Poems*. Cf. N. Christoph de Nagy's fine book, *The Poetry of Ezra Pound: The Pre-Imagist Stage*: it is to de Nagy's credit that his surmises have generally been found to be true (for example, p. 24; p. 75).
2. Pound, *Poems and Translations*, p. 236; ll. 1–2.
3. Jackson, *Early Poetry*, p. 176. We must agree with de Nagy in rejecting John Berryman's dismissal of 'the illusion of Pound's Romanticism' at this primordial stage (*Pre-Imagist Stage*, p. 14).
4. An aeolian harp, whose name derives from Aeolus, the god of the winds, is an ancient stringed instrument sounded by the wind; it was favoured by the Romantics as a symbol of the kind of natural music they aspired to as poets.
5. Witemeyer, *Poetry of Ezra Pound*, pp. 53–5.
6. De Nagy prefers to trace this 'call of the wind, calling man away from the earth . . . the vaguely symbolic wind . . . in a vaguely symbolic landscape' to Fiona MacLeod, but it is hard to see how the symbol does not 'occur . . . with . . . frequency' in the author of 'The Unappeasable Host', or 'He Reproves the Curlew', for example (*Pre-Imagist Stage*, p. 94; Yeats, *Poems*, pp. 75–6; p. 79).
7. Coleridge, 'The Aeolian Harp', *Poetry and Prose*, p. 18; ll. 21–6.
8. Ibid. p. 102–5; see for example ll. 81–2.
9. Pound, *Poems and Translations*, p. 5; p. 6; p. 6; p. 9; p. 16.
10. Professor Doolittle, Hilda's father, prevented his marriage to Hilda in 1908, reasoning that he was 'nothing but a nomad' (Pound, *Poems and Translations*, p. 1209).
11. Pound, *Poems and Translations*, p. 10; p. 7; p. 13; p. 16.
12. Ibid. p. 16; ll. 6–8.
13. Robinson, 'The Might of the North', p. 205.
14. This imagery is a key element in what Witemeyer calls Pound's 'spiritual romanticism'. He summarises as follows: 'Its main elements are (1) disembodied spirits seeking incarnation in an earthly form or union with the divine essence; (2) a magical wind conveying sometimes death but more often a transcendental inspiration; (3) dawn, and especially the false dawn, the strange illusory harbinger of day, real and unreal; and (4) dreams,

symbolizing rare psychic states of contemplation and insight. In addition, fire is an ubiquitous symbol of inspired spirituality, and the literary tradition of the past is a vague but potent influence in the form of runes, legends, druidings, and old songs' (Witemeyer, *Poetry of Ezra Pound*, p. 51).

15. Grieve, *Early Poetry*, p. 38.
16. King, 'Go, Little Book', p. 352.
17. Grieve, *Early Poetry*, p. 38.
18. Ibid. p. 39.
19. Pound, *Literary Essays*, p. 362.
20. Pound, *Spirit of Romance*, p. 8.
21. For example, in Carpenter, *A Serious Character*, p. 44.
22. Stock, *Life of Ezra Pound*, p. 16.
23. Cf. Canto XXXI, LXIX, LXX, for example.
24. 'Croon', *Oxford English Dictionary*.
25. Burns, *Poems and Songs*, p. 445; l. 84.
26. Pound, *Poems and Translations*, p. 175; ll. 17–20. Barry S. Edwards also discovers Burns's influence in 'Ballad of the Goodly Fere' ('The Subtler Music', pp. 32–3).
27. Burns, *Poems and Songs*, p. 602.
28. North, *Dialect of Modernism*, p. v; p. 98.
29. 'Crune', *Columbia Granger's World of Poetry*.
30. This regional usage of the term may well prove to be a development of earlier usage in lyrics like 'Worlde's blisse, have good day!' The only other example cited in *Granger's* – six instances of the term in Robert Southey's ballad, 'Brough Bells' – seems to derive from the regional usage.
31. 'Crune', *Columbia Granger's World of Poetry*.
32. Ramsay, *Works of Allan Ramsay*, vol. 2, p. 11.
33. Ibid. p. 12.
34. Ibid. p. 229.
35. Cf. Stock, *Life of Ezra Pound*, p. 14. Two surveys of Pound's library in Rapallo have been conducted and the results published in *Paideuma* (Tim Redman, 'Pound's Library: A Preliminary Catalog' and Dannah Edwards, 'Addendum to the preliminary Catalog of Ezra Pound's Library'). There is no mention of Pound being in possession of Ramsay's poems at this later time, although the method of both studies is to include only books inscribed by Pound.
36. Ramsay, 'Preface' to *The Ever Green*, *Works of Allan Ramsay*, vol. 4, p. 237.
37. Ibid. p. 237.
38. Ibid. p. 20. As his editors Kinghorn and Law note: 'Ramsay did not coin vocabulary. He converted a number of Scots words and expressions into a phonetic approximation that an urban audience could follow; but he was not consistent in his reproductions of a given word in phonetic convention (e.g. bain/bane, curtchea/kurchie; unco/unko/uncko). His orthography in a very general fashion accommodated itself to English usage (e.g. laigh for laich; sleigh for sleich) but in other cases introduced peculiarly Scottish conventions (pouer, shaw, snaw)' (Kinghorn and Law, *Poems by Allan Ramsay and Robert Fergusson*, p. xvi).
39. Pound, *Selected Letters*, p. 39.

40. Ramsay, *Works of Allan Ramsay*, vol. 3, p. 32.

41. Ibid. vol. 1, p. 84.

42. Ibid. vol. 4, p. 236.

43. Ramsay probably alludes to Alexander Pope's 'First Epistle of the Second Book of Horace Imitated' here, where Pope contends that 'those who cannot write and those who can, / All rhyme, and scrawl, and scribble, to a man' (*Poems of Alexander Pope*, vol. 3, p. 642; ll. 187–8).

44. Ramsay, *Works of Allan Ramsay*, vol. 3, p. 33.

45. 'Grub Street' appears in Johnson's *Dictionary*, where it is described as 'originally the name of a street near Moorfields in London, much inhabited by writers of small histories, dictionaries, and temporary poems; whence any mean production is called grubstreet'. It is, itself, a sort of literary code-word for inferior literary productions (p. 227).

46. Ramsay, *Works of Allan Ramsay*, vol. 4, p. 236.

47. See Chapter 7 for a discussion of Bishop Douglas's influence on Pound.

48. Van Allen, *James Whitcomb Riley*, pp. 239–40.

49. Pound included a poem by Riley in his anthology *Confucius to Cummings* (1964).

50. Riley, *Complete Poetical Works*, pp. 160–1.

51. Ramsay, *Works of Allan Ramsay*, vol. 2, p. 11.

52. Riley, *Complete Poetical Works*, p. 152.

53. Dickey, *Maturity of James Whitcomb Riley*, p. 84.

54. Ibid. p. 83.

55. North, *Dialect of Modernism*, p. 23.

56. Dickey, *Maturity of James Whitcomb Riley*, p. 83.

57. Pound, *Poems and Translations*, p. 8; ll. 3–10.

58. Ibid. p. 13; 'Jasmine', *Oxford English Dictionary*.

59. Pound, *The Cantos*, p. 739.

60. Pound also uses the word 'whirr' in accordance with this careful deployment of etymological detail (almost Greek in intensity). It originally means: 'to throw or cast with violence and noise', a meaning that was reinforced in English by onomatopoeia. In the word 'murmur', remarked above, Pound revives a medieval meaning of the word that specified 'the sound of a light breeze' (c. 1555; *Oxford English Dictionary*).

61. Coleridge, *Poetry and Prose*, p. 17.

62. Riley, *Complete Poetical Works*, p. 152.

63. Pound, *Poems and Translations*, p. 160.

64. Pound, *Gaudier Brzeska*, p. 88.

65. Pound, *Poems and Translations*, p. 8.

66. 'Creep', *Oxford English Dictionary*.

67. Pound, *Poems and Translations*, p. 8.

68. Lutwack, *Birds in Literature*, p. 8. The other feature that Leonard Lutwack points to in Aristophanes, describing 'the song in words arranged in rhythmic patterns that imitate the musical pattern of the song itself', is evoked somewhat by the return to the onomatopoeic internal rhyme sound at the end of the line – more concerted feats of rhythmical arrangement being unavailable to the writer of this 'laboured litany' (Pound will subsequently pronounce the sonnet an obsolete form in English and reject iambic rhythm as an even worse vice). Pound will later champion the Absolute or internal

poetic form in English – a concept that is epitomised by Aristophanes in Greek and by the hoopoe's solo in *Birds* especially (Pindar, who also wrote in heterogeneous metre, was 'the prize wind-bag of all ages' for Pound [*Letters*, p. 87]).

69. North, *Dialect of Modernism*, p. 11.
70. King, 'Go, Little Book', p. 356.

Chapter 3

'Opacity is NOT an American Quality'

What Pound discovered in Burns, and to a lesser extent in Allan Ramsay and James Whitcomb Riley, was a rustick jargon that claimed poetic veracity by being soundly articled to some distinctive local culture. He did not cultivate this jargon for Romantic or naturalistic reasons, but as a means of allowing language to come into full possession of its representational and acoustic properties. The semantic torsion produced by this jargoning is therefore not at all undesirable; neither is it just a feature of some poetry for Pound but the intrinsic signature of all genuine poetry. It produced the kind of trepidation that he hoped to excite in his own verse and accounts for much that he admired in others' work. When, some years later, he was publicly accused of anti-Americanism and (what was surely harder for him to take) of being a detrimental influence on young American poets, Pound stressed that modern poetry was essentially both foreign and opaque: 'The thing that saves your work is opacity, and don't forget it', he says bluntly to his friend and accuser, W. C. Williams, adding: 'Opacity is NOT an American quality.'[1] What Pound discovered, in different degrees, in Coleridge, Burns, Ramsay, Riley, and what he also found to admire in W. C. Williams, was in each case a 'foreign fastness'; an opacity that he felt he could make his own.[2]

The modern sense of this word is liable to mislead us here if we are not careful; the sense indicating 'obscurity of meaning; resistance to interpretation; impenetrability' is largely a twentieth-century phenomenon.[3] It may even arise as means of designating some elemental quality in the literature of this age. Pound was not simply being abstruse, however; opacity is not the same thing as circumlocution, ornament or obscurantism. On the contrary, the term is a precisely physical one ('scientific' in the sense discovered in Chapter 1): it describes a 'quality or condition of not transmitting light; lack of transparency or translucency; inability to be seen through'. Crucially, opacity implies a material obstruction to the transmission of light; it comes from the Latin *opācus*, meaning 'partly through'.[4] If any single word can satisfactorily convey what Pound's lyrical art always involves, this is the word.

This terminology involves a departure, then, from the obscurity examined in the last chapter. Pound's assimilation of Celtic and Romantic diction is obscure because it occludes his meaning with foreign matter. This interposition results in a strange remoteness, which is in fact the etymon of 'obscurity' (he uses the word thus, for example in 'Clara', the second poem in 'Mœrs Contemporaines'). Much of Pound's poetry is indeed obscure: its meaning is not directly available to sense, but is semantically eclipsed, as it were. As we shall see, however, it increasingly appeared to Pound that the estranging qualities of poetry were more often due to the medium of language itself than to the arbitrary interposition of poeticisms. The essential quality of poetic language is after all transmission rather than occlusion, even if this transmission involves reflection and refraction of the sense. By insisting on its own, dim materiality, poetic language retains the capacity to tincture and transform its subject, and thereby to obtain it most surely. Often, this very materiality slows the act of comprehension just long enough to permit flashes of insight to accompany the sedentary accretion of prose sense.

Pound always maintained that a certain amount of materiality inhered in poetic speech. This is evident above all in his translation of 'The Seafarer', where the speaker's wanderlust is ever bent on some distant, unattainable security. The most obvious aspect of this concern with security is thematic, but the poet-speaker also seeks a referential security in his language. The poem, and the translation, are both attempts to 'seek out a foreign fastness', suggesting that the referential rectitude that the speaker requires is bound up with the strange opacity of his speech.[5] He invokes the material density and pithiness he requires of poetic language, which at once situates language more securely within the salty milieu the poet wishes to evoke and allows the formal, traditional and associative qualities of the language to interpose their weird sense. This understanding of language can be traced to Plato's *Phaedrus*, which Pound read when he was eighteen and recalled when he was writing *The Spirit of Romance*. Leon Surette notes that Pound inscribed a copy of Dante's *Paradiso* with a passage from the *Phaedrus*, and it is clear that he associated the glimmering world of Cavalcanti and Dante's *Paradiso* with the linguistic materiality he encounters here.[6] Pound's Cavalcanti essay, for instance, evokes

> the radiant world where one thought cuts through another with a clean edge, a world of moving energies, *'mezzo oscuro rade,' 'risplende in sè perpetuale effecto,'* magnetisms that take form, that are seen, or that border on the

visible, the matter of Dante's *paradiso*, the glass under water, the form that seems a form seen in a mirror.[7]

He notices a residual sturdiness about the world of Dante and Guido that refuses to yield its meaning transparently or totally.

The poet's overwhelming task is archetypically set forth in Cavalcanti's 'Donna Mi Prega', a poem that exerted a fascination over Pound for decades. It eventually appears in resplendent English in Canto XXXVI, but Pound's earlier attempt to capture its inquisitive but aloof take on mystifying experience helps explain the incongruity of language and metaphysical experience to the apprentice poet. Cavalcanti's defiant lover insists:

> save they know't aright from nature's source
> I have no will to prove Love's course
> > or say
> Where he takes rest; who maketh him to be;
> Or what his active *virtu* is, or what his force;
> Nay, nor his very essence or his mode;
> What his placation; why he is in verb,
> Or if a man have might
> > To show him visible to men's sight.[8]

Language, even poetic language, is an imperfect medium for the lover's lofty thought, which does not wholly survive its transubstantiation into unsuited and unsuitable words. Cavalcanti's meaning, to paraphrase John Berryman, is not entirely soluble in language, which can, at best, offer sporadic and partial insight to those who are already persuaded of its sensibility.[9] If 'opacity is NOT an American quality', then, it is probably to be associated with this European lyrical tradition. This emphasis is not surprising, since the canonical text that Pound prized above all others begins in the middle of a '*selva oscura*'.

Despite overwhelming inherent difficulties and the poet's understandable reluctance, the essential materiality and intractability of verse alone allows poetry to act as a suitable medium for the most trenchant terrestrial insights and the loftiest transcendental wisdom; this is what Pound discovered in Dante and Cavalcanti. He traced their enigmatic lyrical precision in two more modern influences: François Villon and Algernon Charles Swinburne.[10] Pound views each of these poets as being capable of seeing and presenting their several worlds with extraordinary clarity, and he considers their distinct jargoning to be the decisive signature of this genius. The question of poetic style is inextricably linked with these poets' fascination with light and with lyric vision, and Pound learned from them a distinctly more lucent and visionary approach to his subject matter.

Swinburne is arguably the cardinal influence in terms of Pound's vatic jargon. When he arrived in England he had the opportunity to meet the 'king of the cats', as Yeats famously referred to his Victorian predecessor, but demurred, and ended up regretting it (as he tells us in Canto LXXXII).[11] Swinburne died in 1909. Pound's endorsement of the elder poet's hieratic qualities is pronounced. In 'Salve O Pontifex – for Swinburne; an hemi chaunt' for instance, he celebrates his 'entangled music that men may not / Over readily understand'.[12] The title of the poem alone provides a number of important clues to Pound's fledgling art, and N. Christoph de Nagy expounds its lore in an invaluable footnote to his study of the Pre-Imagist poetry. He establishes Pound's identification of Swinburne with Aristophanes, and with the Greek prosody that he enjoyed so much success in adapting. 'Few English poets had the intimate knowledge of Greek poetry Swinburne possessed, none used so many Greek themes and metres', observes de Nagy, and Pound would appear to have been especially drawn to the conspicuous example of Swinburne's fine translation of Aristophanes' chorus in *Birds* (discussed at length in the Appendix) which undertakes a virtuoso rendering of almost every poetic metre known to the Attic stage.[13] The title of Pound's poem goes some way, also, in explaining the repeated invocation of *Iacchus*: an identification with the god Dionysus is only part of the story in de Nagy's analysis, the more revealing detail being Iacchus's association with Prosephone and Demeter; hence 'the invocation . . . is ultimately linked with the Mystery of Eleusis' that so enthralled Pound.[14]

'Salve O Pontifex' emphasises the Dionysian basis of Swinburne's esoteric art and advances the understanding of poetic speech in 'Hilda's Book' in one crucial respect. It insists that the function of poetry is a religious one: to reveal what secrets the dark words of god possess, and to aid in their supplication. This sacred function is the *raison d'être* of the opacity that poetic language presents. At the heart of this understanding is the notion that poetic language should not be too transparent lest its mysterious power lose efficacy; understanding is permitted, but is reserved for that special caste of mortal who alone can experience its insights and ecstasies. This kind of poetry founds a community of knowledge based on what Thomas Grieve has termed 'the isolated sublimity of the poet and his compensatory companionship with like-minded spirits in priesthood of Gnostic awareness', which, he demonstrates, is a leitmotif in Pound's early verse.[15] Since meaning is fully manifest only within this exclusive, linguistically guaranteed coterie, Pound implicitly claims that certain privileges and rights accrue to the adept. Poetic vision is, of course, one of these privileges. Accordingly, Swinburne's eyes are said to 'look out unto the infinitude / Of the blue waves of heaven' and to be capable of surveying human destiny like the Fates.[16] In another passage, Swinburne is said to enable hidden things to materialise; peculiar things like 'hamadryads that hold council concealed / In streams and tree-shadowing / Forests on hill slopes'.[17] A world of immanent myth is thus discovered, thanks to Swinburne's priestcraft, beyond the ordinary world of experience.

These hieratic qualities are singled out elsewhere in Pound's early verse, for example in 'Swinburne: A Critique'. Tellingly, this poem does not follow Pound's customary practice of assimilating foreign – English – spellings when available, and is probably therefore among the earliest of his extant verse compositions. Here is this piece of juvenilia in its entirety:

> Blazes of Color intermingled,
> Wondrous pattern leading nowhere,
> Music without a name,
> Knights that ride in a dream,
> Blind as all men are blind,
> Why should the music show
>   Whither they go?
> I am Swinburne, ruler in mystery.
>   None know the ending,
>   blazes a-blending   in splendor
> Of glory none know the meaning on,
> I am he that paints the rainbow and the sunset
> And the end of all dreams,
>   Wherefor would ye know?
>   Honor the glow
> Of the colors   care not wherefor   they gleam
>   All things but seem.[18]

The prevailing mood is of 'mystery' in the ordinary sense – of that which is not 'over readily' understood – as well as in the sense of a 'secret rite of an ancient religion or occult society to which only the initiated are admitted' in which Swinburne instructs the younger generation.[19] Pound calls attention to Swinburne's prosodic experimentation, which palpably expanded the repertoire of metre and form available to English writers, and a capacity to stymie his readership and delight them at the same time: his 'wondrous pattern leading nowhere'.[20]

As readers of the early verse have long realised, Pound's appreciation of Swinburne is consistent with a general reception that placed 'emphasis upon the surface musical qualities of language'; of his 'verbal music [which] has always been considered to be the peculiar way in which the words as bearers of meaning are fused with – and subordinated to – their sound quality'.[21] Pound's is scarcely an original way of addressing Swinburne or describing his poetic manner, therefore, and these ideas and images – especially the lucent and visionary qualities that make even phantasmagoric things apparent – derive directly and manifestly from Swinburne's most famous poems. Charles Baudelaire epitomised this capacity for insight to Swinburne in turn, and was in turn presented in these terms in 'Ave Atque Vale'. The poem begins thus:

> Thou sawest, in thine old singing season, brother,
>   Secrets and sorrows unbeheld of us:
>   Fierce loves, and lovely leaf-buds poisonous,
> Bare to thy subtler eye, but for none other
>   Blowing by night in some unbreathed-in clime;
>   The hidden harvest of luxurious time,
> Sin without shape, and pleasure without speech;
>   And where strange dreams in a tumultuous sleep
>   Make the shut eye of stricken spirits weep;
> And with each face thou sawest the shadow on each,
>   Seeing as men sow men reap.[22]

Here is that visionary 'subtler eye' sought by Pound as well as by Swinburne, that surveys both time and space; open or closed, it is trained on something beyond terrestrial matters. Pound departs notice-ably from the Apollonian chiaroscuro we find in Swinburne's own descriptions of light and vision, and presents a more colourful, a wilder and more phantasmagorical type of poetic vision. The ending of Pound's tribute also adds a Neoplatonic dimension to this depiction. Such ideas are ubiquitous in Pound's early verse in poems like 'The Flame', where 'Nature herself's turned metaphysical', or 'Masks', where the poet finds he must 'Ponder in silence o'er earth's queynt devyse'.[23]

To fully appreciate Swinburne's importance to Pound's develop-ment, however, it is necessary to examine his role in introducing Pound to another Frenchman: François Villon. For Pound, Swinburne's own achievements and those of Villon are often inseparable. He quips that 'Swinburne's Villon is not Villon very exactly, though it is perhaps the best Swinburne we have.'[24] This begins to sound more like a compliment in the context of Pound's own labours as a translator. We can begin to appreciate Swinburne's intermediary function and Pound's sense of Villon's urgency by considering Swinburne's tribute to the 'Prince of All Ballad-Makers' in his 'Ballad of François Villon'. It is perhaps even more typical of *Poems and Ballads* than 'Ave Atque Vale', particularly because of the presentation of Villon as one of countless birds strewn throughout the volume. Here is the first stanza:

Bird of the bitter bright grey golden morn
   Scarce risen upon the dusk of dolorous years,
First of us all and sweetest singer born
   Whose far shrill note the world of new men hears
   Cleave the cold shuddering shade as twilight clears;
When song new-born put off the old world's attire
And felt its tune on her changed lips expire,
   Writ foremost on the role of them that came
Fresh girt for service of the latter lyre,
   Villon, our sad bad glad mad brother's name![25]

Villon's achievement is marked in vatic terms; the 'far shrill note' of his jargon is endowed with the capacity to 'Cleave the cold shuddering shade as twilight clears'. As this phrase suggests, his poetry is new and strange in the context of the 'old world' in which it appears. His 'latter lyre' resounds like something from the Attic stage.[26]

Villon's original embodiment of the sure vision he will come to share in brotherhood with Baudelaire and Swinburne, 'the stubborn persistency of one whose gaze cannot be deflected from the actual fact before him', on the one hand, and a language capable of delineating this vision, on the other, results in his depiction as a gallows-bird.[27] With unflinching omniscience these poets look into the sordid soul of their respective ages and prove art's capacity to astonish and transmogrify in the most unlikely circumstances. Villon's jargon is a triumphant fusion of the perceptual and the representational, the visual sensation and the aural articulation – explaining Swinburne's preposterous repeton. This shrill caw of lamentation, absurd as it must perhaps seem to a twenty-first-century readership, anticipates Pound's modernising experiments in his translation of 'The Seafarer'. Bird cries, such as we find here, are traditionally reckoned to appeal to the senses, and Villon's are no exception: Swinburne champions his pre-eminence as the original and 'sweetest' of all modern poets. The paradox here helps to explain what makes Villon paradigmatically modern. How can his verse be both shrill *and* sweet? His subjects are vulgar and his language often raucous and lewd; but he discerns and declares the truth with great honesty, courage and impeccable technique: 'In Villon filth is filth, crime is crime', Pound writes, 'neither crime nor filth is gilded. They are not considered as strange delights and forbidden luxuries, accessible only to adventurous spirits.'[28] Villon presents the sordid vagaries of his world directly and immediately to his audience, without pretence or exoticism; he exposes filth and crime for what they are. Such candour, for Pound, is an aesthetic as much as a moral quality.[29]

Robert Louis Stevenson had already famously presented Villon in these terms in *Familiar Studies of Men and Books*: 'this gallows-bird was the one great writer of his age and country, and initiated modern literature for France', he argued, citing in particular his 'callous pertinent way of looking upon the sordid and ugly sides of life' as the revolutionary modern quality in his verse.[30] Stevenson extols Villon's acumen and audacity in equal measure. Pound was familiar with Stevenson's essay from an early age; in Humphrey Carpenter's appraisal, Pound's early villonauds 'really have more of Stevenson about them than of fifteenth-century France'.[31] The quality that recommends Villon is his pertinence in the face of repugnant physical circumstance. Many of Swinburne's French contemporaries were actively engaged with similar themes, and Swinburne met and corresponded with the most eminent of them (especially Mallarmé).[32] For Pound, who was attempting to found a truly modern style in English by looking at his world steadily and without flinching, Villon provided a formal example and hinted at an idiom that would be central to this effort.

There is another crucial element in Villon's influence on Pound, however, and it was also very much part of the Victorian lore surrounding the poet. Stevenson, in the same essay, describes Villon's style as 'something between the slap-dash inconsequence of Byron's *Don Juan* and the racy humorous gravity and brief noble touches that distinguish the vernacular poems of Burns', and he notes a special affinity with the latter, both having

> a certain rugged compression, a brutal vivacity of epithet, a homely vigour, a delight in local personalities, and an interest in many sides of life, that are often despised or passed over by more effete and cultured poets. Both also, in their strong, easy, colloquial way, tend to become difficult or obscure; the obscurity in the case of Villon passing at times into the absolute darkness of cant language. *They are perhaps the only two great masters of expression who keep sending their readers to the glossary.* (Emphasis added)[33]

Stevenson does all he can to exonerate these poets from the charge of obscurantism by presenting their undoubted difficulties in natural and informal terms; he notices their 'rugged compression', 'brutal vivacity', 'homely vigour' and their 'strong, easy, colloquial way' of becoming 'difficult or obscure'. This, for Stevenson and for Villon's first readers, was the key point. The word 'cant' means, emphatically in this instance, 'the secret language or jargon used by gypsies, thieves, professional beggars, etc.' or, by extension, 'any jargon used for the purpose of secrecy'.[34] It directs our attention to Villon's legendary mendicancy and his alleged association with the Coquillards, a group of truants and blackguards, card-cheats and homicides active in Paris in the sixteenth century.

Obscurity, it may be inferred, was cultivated by the poet as a necessary precaution against discovery by the law. Villon's first editor, Clément Marot, emphasises very much the same points just two generations after Villon was writing:

> As for the artistry of the bequests that Villon made in his testaments, to understand it truly one would have had to live in the Paris of his day and to have known the places, events, and men he speaks about.[35]

The 'absolute darkness' Stevenson associates with Villon's language is ascribable in part to historical remoteness, but the fact that it was encountered as early as 1533 suggests that it was also due to the lyric style of the poems themselves. Marot suggests as much by focusing not on the meaning of the poems, but on their 'artistry'; for him, difficulty is a function of poetic craft: opacity, as well as obscurity, concerns him here.

These qualities are most evident in Villon's *Ballades en Jargon*, a series of (more or less) eleven ballads written in the jargon of the Coquillards, six of which appear in the first published edition of his poetry in 1489. These poems pose a considerable problem for editors and translators. Although nominally written in Middle French, they defy understanding because of their reliance on Coquillard slang. If this lingo was ever comprehensible to those outside the fraternity, it has long since ceased to be. To the Victorians, this indecipherability appeared to be a very deliberate attempt by Villon to avoid discovery or any clear statement of culpability. He continually urges his 'Companions, Robbers, Thieves, and all' to be watchful and cautious, to 'seize those who spy upon [their] band; / Make them afraid their tongues to loose', and advises them to 'take care . . . dreamers, what ye say'.[36] As the word 'dreamers' gently urges, there is continual commerce between the criminal's and the artist's business in these poems; Villon cautions his fellow 'tricksters versed in all [their] trade', for instance, to 'play not [their] game without great care'. That criminals too should learn and take solace from verse, and that poets may benefit from furtive tricks, is among Villon's most idiosyncratic insights.

Some of Villon's tricks in these poems are worth dwelling on since they anticipate several of the techniques Pound will make synonymous with modernism. Pound even came to think of poetic techniques as 'tricks', no doubt under the influence of Villon.[37] Most obviously, Villon delights in puns and linguistic gamesmanship throughout his verse – part of what Pound will later term 'logopoeia'. One famous example, the second poem from the *Ballades en Jargon*, begins thus:

To brothers of the Cockle-shell –
At fair Ruel not long ago,
I sung to you a warning lay;
I spoke to you in whispers low,
And counseled that ye'd best away.[38]

According to David Fein, 'Rueil is a town near Paris, but *aller à Rueil* is slang for "to attack" or "to murder".'[39] The dissimulation allows a complex under-song to emerge here, which is then taken to be characteristic of the poet's language (explaining why Villon describes his verse as 'whispers low'). Pound's language, even before this point, is often polysemous and on occasion, for example in 'Na Audiart', he exploits this polysemy for bawdy, Villonesque ends.[40]

At such moments in the *Ballades*, it is clear that effective communication is sought with a relatively select audience of initiates. Wayne Booth provides a useful explanation of this 'trick':

> Whenever an author conveys to his reader an unspoken point, he creates a sense of collusion against all those, whether in the story or out of it, who do not get the point. Irony is always thus in part a device for excluding as well as for including, and those who are included, those who happen to have the necessary information to grasp the irony, cannot but derive at least part of their pleasure from a sense that the others are excluded.[41]

Latent references prevent a poem's eroticism, say, becoming so obvious as to titillate the popular imagination or rouse the suspicion of the authorities, and at the same time secure the firm attention of the poet's intimates, who are familiar with the characters and the tenor of the jokes. This last point is important because it demonstrates that opacity need not have a negative impact in literary reception; this was as well known to the priests of high modernism as it was to the College of Augurs. As N. Christoph de Nagy remarks, Pound inherited this notion of artistic community from the Decadents, and in his earliest poetic trials he 'does not speak in his own name alone, using the first person singular, but for a collective, using the first person plural, without, however, giving direct indications who the members of the collectivity are'.[42] To those permitted access, at least, these strategies ensure that the poems are more meaningful and not less so, though they may appear that way to the uninitiated. The hermeticism of Yeats, Pound, Joyce and Eliot more characteristically utilises myth and literary precedent to effect its dissimulation, but the principle, and the estranging effect on all but the initiated in the audience, is much the same.

Another strategy that contributes significantly to the difficulty of Villon's poetry, again with a conspicuous modern parallel, is the ubiquitous references to contemporary personages, often personal acquaintances, that the annals of history have otherwise ignored. Stevenson noticed this trick, and Pound was evidently quite taken by it. He populates 'A Villonaud: Ballad of the Gibbet' with characters from Villon's own poetry, including the poet himself, and replicates the feat more astoundingly in his first opera, *Le Testament*.[43] Villon supplied a clear precedent for poetry that deals with real people – with characters, that is to say, who have more or less discrete existences apart from any literary or historical gossiping about them. *The Cantos*, too, are full of historical and literary figures who often appear in a stark Villonesque light that disentangles them from the myths in which culture has implicated them. Many of these countless cameos have already become peripheral to the poem in much the same way as Villon's fellows have become peripheral to his *Testament*, so that Allen Tate can write with some justice that 'the secret of [Pound's] form is this: conversation. *The Cantos* are talk, talk, talk; not talk by anyone in particular to anyone else in particular; they are just rambling talk'.[44]

Tate's description – 'just rambling talk' – is equally apt for much of the spoken English language, in distinction to the sung French verse, of Pound's *Le Testament* of 1931: Margaret Fisher explains that the opera is written in an 'amalgam of American and British dialects' contrived precisely to eliminate anything that might individuate (and, by extension, incriminate) the dramatis persona.[45] This is dramatically expedient, since it facilitates a climax that refuses to divulge if Villon is among the dead or, if he is, how he came to be so; it also reveals Pound's abiding commitment to an opaque lyrical form even when extensive narrative matters are involved.[46] This strategy enables the prose banter of the opera to obtain a more striking counterpoint to its sung verse, since they are both, in essence, different asymptotes of Villon's original lyrical jargoning.

The disorientating amalgamation of linguistic forms that appears in Pound's first radio production only realises the aesthetic possibilities that are already latent and incipient in conventional Victorian presentations of Villon. The word Stevenson employed in his famous portrait, 'cant', derives from the Latin *cantus*, meaning singing, or musical sound. For Stevenson as well as Pound, the opacity of Villon's verse is directly related to its aural and musical qualities. Villon's influence on Pound is just as emphatically towards more musical verse as towards more hermetic diction, more direct and more rugged idiom. Indeed, in his important 'Cavalcanti' essay, Pound coins a term that draws upon this crucial double significance. The 'cantabile values' of a poem are the formal features that register when the poem is spoken, chanted or sung.[47] They include the particular qualities of a given poetic line (Pound discusses the relative virtues of Italian hendecasyllables and English blank verse, for instance), strophe and stanza arrangement, and also include rhyme, both internal and external to a strophe (with the canzone as example), etc. Cavalcanti's poetry – and especially his canzoni – cannot be fairly appraised without due attention to 'its lyricism, in the strictest sense'; to those formal features that accommodate the spoken utterance to its musical accompaniment.[48] Pound's example is pronounced and extreme; of the canzone strophe he notes that '52 out of every 154 syllables are bound into pattern'; whatever the meaning of the strophe and poem is, the acoustic edifice is essential to its way of meaning.[49]

Accordingly, the two villonauds in *Personae* display Pound's growing technical mastery by utilising *coblas unissonantis* (using the exact same rhymes in the exact same positions of each stanza) and avail themselves of two and three rhyme sounds respectively ('Villonaud for this Yule' also manages the Spenserian or Yeatsian coincidence between period and stanza much admired by Pound). In order to demonstrate the musical distinction of Pound's verse, T. S. Eliot, in his study *Ezra Pound: His Metric and Poetry*, quotes the whole first stanza of 'Canzon: Of Incense', from *Canzoni* (1911), noting that 'within the iambic limits, there are no two lines in the whole poem that have an identical rhythm'.[50] Such metrical virtuosity inspires these verses with an air of intense concentration so well suited to the poem's theme as to be a necessary, even essential, part of the meaning conveyed. The study of Villon's form was doubtlessly part of Pound's attempt to achieve in these villonauds 'an expression akin to, if not of, the spirit *breathed* in Villon's own poeting'.[51] The italicised word is important here. The pneumatic quality, equated with the psychological essence of the poem, arises through the skilful manipulation of form and rhythm. By emulating the sonic and rhythmical qualities of the original, Pound hoped to inspire his poem with the same emotional qualities too. This is, let us recall, the author who maintained that 'the perception of the intellect is given in the word, that of emotion in the cadence'.[52]

Crucially, the 'cantabile values' of a poem register the opaque elements that are intrinsically and inexorably musical, and therefore poetic in the sense that Pound champions (both the verse and the prose of *Le Testament*, for instance, function in this cantabile way). The idiosyncrasy of the Poundism should not lead us to suppose that this is an unconventional idea. As I remarked in the Introduction, Amittai F. Aviram demonstrates that this understanding of poetry has a long tradition and crucial implications for literary criticism.[53] The putative distinction between the 'communicative content' of language and its 'physical, nonmeaning substance', to use Aviram's language, is precisely what

Pound wished to avoid; his exertion converges, rather, in the sensuous unity of sound and sense. As we have seen, his verse is characterised by tendencies towards opacity and even non-discursivity; in this above all he reveals himself to be a devoted student of Swinburne. These elements, in his understanding, accentuate the lyrical or 'cantabile' features of his poetry: its sound and rhythm. Pound's critical interest in Villon and Cavalcanti, like most of his criticism, is also marked by a reluctance to dwell on the 'communicative content' of their language, and a strong effort, in the face of contemporary critical opinion, 'to preserve a sense of [its] distinctness [as] poetry'.[54]

Pound's lifelong absorption in the 'cantabile' values of Guido's canzone is the ground of his rebuttal of the prevalent critical opinion that Cavalcanti's poems were, purportedly like Villon's, written in cipher. Leon Surette provides a comprehensive discussion of Pound's ten-year involvement in this controversy in '"Dantescan Light": Ezra Pound and Eccentric Dante Scholars'. His account examines the theory that, as Pound himself put it, 'Guido and his correspondents [chiefly Dante] are a gang (secret) of Nonconformists, aching to reform mother church, plotting and corresponding in hyper-heretical cipher.'[55] As Surette's title implies, this idea is not given much credence now, and was afforded only slightly more indulgence at the time. Its chief exponents were Luigi Valli (with whom Pound is most concerned) and Gabriele Rossetti, whose dogged pursuit of this theory adversely affected his career as a critic (Ugo Foscolo and Giovanni Pascoli were also advocates of this theory). According to Surette, there were two distinct positions among advocates of the 'Love Code', as Pound calls it in *Spirit of Romance*: 'Rossetti's arguments overlap with that of Foscolo, Pascoli, and Valli himself in so far as all three believed Dante to be writing in code, cipher, or jargon. But Rossetti, unlike the others, identified Dante's secret as a pagan survival.'[56] The 'others' thought of Dante as a 'member of a secret society dedicated to the reform of Church and papacy corrupted by the temporal powers'.[57]

According to Surette, the controversy has two main problems as far as Pound was concerned. First:

> Valli's claim that Cavalcanti and Dante can be decoded easily was undoubtedly what most offended Pound. After all, by 1929 he had spent nearly twenty years teasing out the profound and mystical meaning of Cavalcanti's poetry, and even longer contemplating passages of Dante.[58]

Second: 'Valli's central claim that, once decoded, the poetry ceased to be vague, stylized, monotonous, cold' offended Pound, no doubt because it makes poetic difficulties, which he considered inherent, seem ancillary and disposable.[59] This second objection expresses the essentially Romantic preference for symbol over allegory, and Surette is right to foreground Pound's wariness about poetic transparency. While Pound was sympathetic to the notion that Cavalcanti's poems, and especially 'Donna Mi Prega', contained irreducible difficulties, he believed that these difficulties were not the result of deliberate obscurantism for its own sake, esotericism or allegory, but essentially lexical and lyrical. He concedes that 'there is no reason to ignore his [Valli's] intuition that there is often a hidden or indirect meaning in these poems. The most materialistic critic concedes that there are incomprehensible allusions.'[60] He further explains in *Guide to Kulchur*:

> Valli's wanderings in search of a secret language (for Dante, Guido, and the rest of them) are, at mildest estimate, unconvincing. 'Something' behind it? Certainly 'something' behind or beyond it. Which the Police called 'Manichaean' knowing nothing either of Manes or of anything else.[61]

The question is not whether there exists in Guido's poems some essential opacity, but what the nature of that opacity is.

The very qualities that make an utterance poetic, Pound argues, whether Cavalcanti's, Villon's or his own, render it, by definition, opaque precisely in so far as it differs from prose. Pound observes: (1) that 'there are places where attempted application of his [Valli's] code would turn a good poem into a mere piece of priggishness and vain theory, in no way accounting for its manifest lyric impulse, or for the emotional force of its cadence',[62] suggesting that much of the perceived difficulty results from the poems' lyrical features; and (2) that the language may heighten these difficulties by technical precision and acoustic elaboration rather than cryptic obscurantism. He maintains 'there is still perfectly solid ground for arguing that the language of Guido is secret only as the language of any technical science is secret for those who have not the necessary preparation'.[63] The comparison of poetry to technical science is a suggestive one: Pound's point is that criticism that treats poetry simply as a vehicle for meaning thereby transforms that poetry into something it is not – this is true, apparently, even without recourse to elaborate theorising about ciphers and secret codes. Poetry cannot be paraphrased, or reduced to its 'communicative content'. This same understanding of poetry governs Pound's estimation of both Villon and Cavalcanti. Rather than a necessity to evade discovery, behind which might lurk any number of delicious horrors or a pleasing nicety, the jargonish aspect of their verse is part of the generic inheritance of every poet who would write accurately and intimately about their world and yet remain a poet.

Margaret Fisher has quite recently offered a startling reaffirmation of his position: Pound was indeed tempted to write in cipher on at least one occasion – in his opera on *Cavalcanti*, no less – but he apparently scrambled his clandestine meaning, if there is one, in a musical rather than semiotic code. We learn that Pound 'tried to decode [Cavalcanti's] poems thinking the cipher is in the words whereas the cipher is really in the music' (Pound's words): he transplants this furtive musical burden to the climax of his opera where, in Fisher's analysis, the listener is invited to decipher the sound that Rico attempts, and fails, to learn by heart.[64] Guido's gravest concern is consequently bewildered, and lost to posterity. Fisher's attempt to reconstitute his message by solmisation ('or sol-fa singing . . . a system of Latin syllables to help singers reach their pitches') demonstrates at the very least just how sensible Pound thought music or rhythm could be, and offers a tantalising asymptote to his more customary jargoning.[65]

The idea that the aural and lexical aspects of language must be considered in their coincidence is the datum of Pound's art, and we find him worrying the consequences of this approach at a basically dictionarial level too. His choice of words is vital to the successful conjuration of the spirit of Romance. As he says in the essay on 'Cavalcanti', begun around 1910: 'What we need now is not so much a commentator as a lexicon. It is the precise sense of certain terms as understood at that particular epoch that one would like to have set before one.'[66] The difficulties of technical language are outweighed by its capacity to signify exactly. For Pound, medieval language had the further benefit, because 'the Medieval mind had little but words to deal with, [of being] more careful in its definitions and verbiage' than the language of the early twentieth century.[67] He tries to exemplify this habit of semantic precision in his translations from Cavalcanti. 'Canzone: Of Angels' stands out among these translations as the most thoroughly developed lexically, drawing on minute mineralogical discrepancies to evoke the ineffable with the utmost acumen:

> That azure feldspar hight the microcline,
> Or, on its wing, the Menelus weareth
> Such subtlety of shimmering as beareth
> This marvel onward through the crystalline,
> A splendid calyx that about her gloweth,
> Smiting the sunlight on whose ray she goeth.[68]

Mineralogical jargon, combined with Pound's antiquing of English verb forms, evokes something of the alchemical metaphysic of Cavalcanti's verse; this trick gives the poet 'voices at last to voice [his] heart's long mood' even if, as in the first line here, it will inevitably stymie those without the 'necessary preparation' to comprehend him (presumably most of his readership).[69] Hugh Witemeyer demonstrates that mineralogy is integral to Pound's symbolic use of light in the poems of 1911; 'precious stones and rare metals' often provide a conventional index of his muse's brilliance.[70] The materiality and luminosity of the mineral, its capacity to tincture the light, to refract and reflect it, make it an apt emblem for poetic language as I have been describing it here.

Failure of the discursive intellect is a ubiquitous feature in Cavalcanti's visionary poems; indeed, it is often precisely what establishes that his vision is genuine, as we have seen already. Sonnet VII summarises the connection between visionary experience and the failure of intellection nicely. In Pound's translation, the suitor asks:

Who is she coming, drawing all men's gaze,
Who makes the air one trembling clarity
Till none can speak but each sighs piteously?[71]

The poet's lyric capacity, however, makes good the deficit. Hugh Witemeyer summarises the trope succinctly: 'the lady radiates an ambience of light as she approaches, and the rational mind is powerless to comprehend her glories'.[72] For both Cavalcanti and Pound, language is charged with expressing this dialectic. For those unfamiliar with the lexicon and unwilling to investigate it, 'Canzone: Of Angels' makes difficult sense, is bland and colourless; for those who are prepared to consort and become familiar with it, it becomes refulgent.

Language itself, then, is tasked with enacting revelation for the reader, allowing those who are prepared to follow the poet faithfully to share in his vision, obscuring it for those who are not. As Giorgio Agamben reminds us, the basic material and semiotic condition of language simultaneously involves 'unconcealment and concealment, alētheia and lēthē': the very fact of its manifesting some thing in discourse transforms that very thing into a sign.[73] Language always has a flashing, revelatory quality to it. By clinging resolutely to the opaque, Pound's diction tends to sieve his audience, functioning as a kind of lyrical gatekeeper or litmus test. His experience and insight demand rarefied and highly wrought expression, and an audience capable of (very nearly) the same shades of discrimination as the poet. In his Cavalcanti translations as well as in his own writing of this period, Pound establishes a firm connection between technical language and the vision it is capable of sustaining. In 'The Flame', for example, he affirms the following:

There *is* the subtler music, the clear light
Where time burns back about th' eternal embers.

We are not shut from all the thousand heavens:
Lo, there are many gods whom we have seen,
Folk of unearthly fashion, places splendid,
Bulwarks of beryl and of chrysoprase.[74]

This is at once the same conjunction of musical and optical imagery we discovered in Pound's treatment of Villon and Swinburne, and a very Poundian reflection on the capacity of the artist to rouse the dormant gods.

There are sound and essentially Romantic objections to this kind of poetry, of course, as Wordsworth indicated in his 'Preface' to *Lyrical Ballads*.[75] Cavalcanti evidently considered that he lived in a time when 'the remotest discoveries' of the scientist, to use Wordsworth's phrase, were fair game for the poet; Pound did too. For his generation, the innermost workings of science were probably no more apparent than in Wordsworth's day, but the language that contained these secrets was incalculably more current. Equally important as lexical precision, however, is Pound's avoidance of Romantic mannerisms in his verse by treating a wider variety of subjects. As he remarks in *Gaudier Brzeska*,

> It is to be noted that one is not forbidden any element, any key because it is geological rather than vegetable, or because it belongs to the realm of magnetic currents or to the binding properties of steel girders and not to the floppings of grass or the contours of the parochial churchyard.[76]

This passage implies that modern poetry would be discovered in places that the Romantic poet neglected to look, and Pound would make this an explicit theme in 'I Gather the Limbs of Osiris': 'Science is unpoetic only to minds jaundiced with sentiment and romanticism', he proclaims: 'the great masters of the past boasted all they could of it and found it magical'.[77]

Science, then, was no longer to be the adversary of art. So much did he feel this was the case that Pound, like Eliot, when he needed to find a way of explaining poetry as clearly as possible to the largest number of people, almost invariably turned to scientific metaphors. Instances are far too numerous to mention here, although one remark, from the *ABC of Reading*, is irresistible. Pound insists that

> a limited amount of communication in re special subjects, passes via mathematical formulae, via the plastic arts, via diagrams, via purely musical forms, but no one proposes substituting these for the common speech, nor does anyone suggest that it would be either possible or advisable.[78]

If a subject is amenable to poetic treatment it is, by definition, special in this sense for Pound; this is particularly true of the Tuscan and

Provençal translations made around this time. Again, though, poetry is considered to be closer to esoteric and abstract, even non-rationalisable, non-denotative discourse than to ordinary English prose or actual speech. Pound sees nothing obviously wrongheaded or unfortunate about this identification.

Pound knew, however, that the requisite quotient of precision could (and perhaps should) be supplied by non-technical means. Rather than utilise an exclusive, learned and private language, or a passively inherited set of poeticisms, he increasingly foraged for historically and culturally remote language. The capacity to signify unambiguously becomes a function of this very historical and cultural remoteness. Thomas Jackson offers an excellent distinction in this regard. Cavalcanti, Villon, Swinburne and other writers of hieratic bent taught Pound a critical lesson: 'He comes to depend less upon the outré imagery, more and more upon rhythm and upon a much more adroit appeal to strange diction and word order', he says.[79] Pound's early preference for the glamorous word (rather than the right word) made way for a more nimble and discriminating art. He moves away, as I have been arguing, from simple obscurity for its own sake toward embracing the ontological opacity of language in meticulously significant ways. The one crucial advantage of this kind of jargoning is that the language remains concrete and urgent for all its opacity – it is not an abstract vocabulary that struggles to pertain to the lives of those who wield it, but is on the contrary a living vocabulary tailored to meet the expressive demands of the dramatic and socio-historical situations his speakers find themselves in.[80]

Consequently, Pound continues to emphasise the particular importance of poetic barbarism – of foreign language adoptions, that is – in both his poetry and his critical prose. As he remarks later in 'How to Read' (1928): 'Different languages – I mean the actual vocabularies, the idioms – have worked out certain mechanisms of communication and registration.'[81] In the two villonauds from *Personae* we see Pound exploring a different semantic terrain than in most of his early poems for just this purpose. Words and phrases like 'noel', 'everychone', 'gueredon', 'skoal', 'wining', 'foison' and 'mere' are markedly different from the Anglo-Saxon and Celtic vocabulary of 'Hilda's Book'. This vocabulary lends these poems a thoroughgoing outlandishness that is capable of evoking, if not medieval France exactly, then something of its music and habits of association. This complex of unique experience (whether real or ideal) and just the right language and form to obtain and faithfully articulate it becomes the stated poetic objective with the advent of Imagism.

In some of his earliest published criticism, Pound is quite explicit about the role of this foreign diction in his verse. In his essay 'The Serious Artist' (1913), for instance, this textual strategy is already firmly associated with conceptual and emotional precision:

> In the writers of the duo-cento and early tre-cento we find a precise psychology, embedded in a now almost unintelligible jargon, but there nevertheless. If we cannot get back to these things; if the serious artist cannot attain this precision in verse, then he must either take to prose or give up his claim to being a serious artist.[82]

Poetry, in opposition to prose, is characterised by its jargonish aspects. In order to hit the correct psychological note it is necessary to adopt some of the jargon that arises historically and culturally to express that psychology. Again, Pound clearly realises that this will inevitably present difficulties, but the gain in precision and texture is reckoned to be worth losing a few casual readers for.

What Pound hopes to reproduce for a contemporary audience is therefore neither the original word nor the original referent simply, but the original relationship between a remote language and the world view it comprehends. We may appreciate just how this works by considering an example from 'Villonaud for this Yule':

> Then when the grey wolves everychone
> Drink of the winds their chill small-beer
> And lap o' the snows food's gueredon
> Then makyth my heart his yule-tide cheer.[83]

The image is quite straightforward in itself. Pound sets the scene for his lament by depicting a pack of wolves banqueting on the scant provisions of bleak winter: wind and snow. Words like 'everychone' (presumably a contraction for *every which one*) and 'gueredon' (*guerdon*) do not refer to anything that might be readily experienced in Georgian England – they force the reader to take account of their cultural and literary milieu. Pound's outlandish spellings, 'everychone', 'gueredon', 'Disdeign', etc., like Allan Ramsay's, further these logopoeic aims. Typically, the words are perfectly intelligible phonetically; their strangeness is a property of their appearance on the page and their relation to the other sounds in the line or lines in which they appear. The disparity is enough to force the reader to hesitate momentarily or to strain (audibly or silently) the voicing of the word, to *make it new* quite literally, from the aural stuff.

In this most famous mantra, the emphasis has routinely fallen on the last word. If Pound's own poetry is anything to go by, the first two words are at least as crucial, perhaps more so. The poet, as makar, must return to the anvil and reforge a language whose cutting edge has been worn and eroded by centuries of unthinking usage expressly for his or her present purpose. Some of this effort is even foisted on the reader. For Pound, this operation usually involves utilising a word in particular etymological and contextual ways, and in a particularly involved sonic and prosodic fashion. In the case of 'gueredon', for instance, Pound proffers a more precise term than 'reward' or 'recompense', invoking a hierarchical yet equitable world of fealty in which the wolves are nevertheless denied the just reward of their seasonal labours from their guardian. Their condition is emblematic of the speaker's. Having lost the source of his sustenance he cries: 'Where are the joys my heart had won?' The strange sounds of these words as much as their denotational obscurity – the Latinate rhyme, the shrill medial sound of 'everychone' that so uniquely evokes the skirl of the wolves' communion with the wind (as well as the quality in Villon remarked above), the assonance in the final line – all these effects contribute significantly to the liveliness and precision of the image, which is constituted on the basis of what Aristotle terms $\gamma\lambda\omega\tau\tau\alpha$, 'expressions unknown in the language of common life'.[84] As Pound would say in a different context, he hoped to 'charm . . . by being not too unfamiliar'.[85]

Since this composition, too, is written 'in a jargon that was different in degree but not in kind from what was understood to be the received proper language of poetry', to return to Edward Thomas's initial appraisal of Pound's technique, these strategies are doubly appropriate as a means of escaping prosaic expression and hackneyed poeticism.[86] The rare denotational precision and the musical properties of the language, in combination with outright barbarisms like 'morte saison', and penetrating parochialisms like 'Drink of the winds their chill small-beer', ensure that the image is exact and that the emotional milieu of the original is, as far as possible, re-established. For Pound, this kind of opaque and yet trenchant poetics – which, because of its opacity, is lucent and revelatory in the strongest sense – vindicates his pretensions as a 'serious artist'. Ford Madox Hueffer was, famously, far from convinced.

Notes

1. Qtd in Wilhelm, *American Roots*, p. 119.
2. Writing to Harriet Monroe with Williams in mind, he underlined the necessity for the aspiring American poet to encounter foreign traditions: 'You know perfectly well that American painting is recognizable because

painters from the very beginning have kept in touch with Europe and dared to study abroad. Are you going to call people foreigners the minute they care enough about their art to travel in order to perfect it?' (Pound, *Letters*, p. 37). Similar statements abound; the following, to the Editor of the *Boston Transcript*, for example: 'I think it unwise that you should encourage that type of critic who limits the word "American" to such work as happens to flatter the parochial vanity. It is not even Chauvinism. It is stupid' (ibid. p. 63).

3. 'Opacity', *Oxford English Dictionary*.
4. Ibid.
5. Pound, *Poems and Translations*, p. 237.
6. Surette, 'Dantescan Light', p. 328.
7. Pound, *Literary Essays*, p. 154.
8. Ibid. p. 155.
9. Berryman, *Collected Poems*, p. 70.
10. As N. Christoph de Nagy points out, however, both authors were already passé by the 1890s, and his interest in them was simply 'another proof that the young Pound, at this early stage, was "behind the times"' (*Pre-Imagist Stage*, p. 69).
11. Pound, *The Cantos*, p. 543. Yeats's comment is widely discussed. Cf. R. F. Forster, *W. B. Yeats: A Life, vol. 1*, p. 616, n. 69.
12. Pound, *Poems and Translations*, p. 52; ll. 58–9.
13. De Nagy, *Pre-Imagist Stage*, p. 159, n. 174. Swinburne contextualised his effort by noting that Aristophanes' 'marvelous metrical invention of the anapæstic heptameter was almost exactly reproducible' and by proceeding to reproduce it, very nearly 'foot by foot and pause for pause, in English' (Swinburne, *Selected Poems*, p. 262).
14. Ibid. pp. 159–60.
15. Grieve, *Early Poetry*, p. 44. Cf. de Nagy, *Pre-Imagist Stage*, pp. 52–3.
16. Pound, *Poems and Translations*, pp. 50–1; ll. 16–17.
17. Ibid. p. 51; ll. 36–8.
18. The poem is provided by Louis L. Martz in his essay 'Pound's Early Poems', p. 58.
19. 'Mystery', *Oxford English Dictionary*.
20. This is kinder than, but substantially similar to, Eliot's famous remark that 'ways of saying nothing are not interesting. Swinburne's form is uninteresting, because he is literally saying next to nothing' (qtd in de Nagy, *Pre-Imagist Stage*, p. 72).
21. Jackson, *Early Poetry*, p. 126; de Nagy, *Pre-Imagist Stage*, p. 76. The latter's account of Swinburne's art (pp. 68–80) is illuminating in the context of Pound's prosody and technique in the stricter sense.
22. Swinburne, *Poems and Ballads*, p. 73.
23. Pound, *Poems and Translations*, p. 45; l. 14.
24. Pound, *Literary Essays*, p. 36.
25. Swinburne, *Poems and Ballads*, p. 126; ll. 1–10.
26. Villon's depiction in this stanza, lines 3–4 especially, closely parallels the depiction of Prokne in Aristophanes' *Birds* – a part comprised solely of the melody of the aulete rather than verse. See Appendix.
27. Pound, *Spirit of Romance*, p. 168.

28. Ibid. p. 173.

29. He offers an extended discussion of this topic in 'The Serious Artist' that begins: 'This brings us to the immortality of bad art. Bad art is inaccurate art. It is art that makes false reports . . . ' (Pound, *Literary Essays*, p. 43).

30. Stevenson, *Familiar Studies*, p. 222; p. 223.

31. Pound, *Letters*, p. 93.

32. McGann, *Swinburne*, p. 57.

33. Stevenson, *Familiar Studies*, p. 221; p. 222.

34. 'Cant', *Oxford English Dictionary*.

35. Qtd in Fein, *François Villon and His Reader*, p. 23.

36. Villon, *Jargon*, p. 16.

37. Cf. 'It is a great thing, reading a man to know, not "His Tricks are not as yet my Tricks, but I can easily make them mine" but "His message is my message. We will see that men hear it"' (Pound, 'On What I Feel About Walt Whitman', *Selected Prose*, pp. 145–58). He also begins the first of his 'Three Cantos of a Poem of Some Length' of 1917 in this way: 'Hang it all, there can be but one Sordello! / But say I want to, say I take your whole bag of tricks / Let in your quirks and tweeks, and say the thing's an art-form . . .' (Pound, *Poems and Translations*, p. 318).

38. Villon, *Jargon*, p. 17.

39. Fein, *François Villon Revisited*, p. 127.

40. Witemeyer's reading of the poem demonstrates Pound's Villonesque skill in this regard (Witemeyer, *Poetry of Ezra Pound*, pp. 75–8).

41. Booth, *Rhetoric of Fiction*, p. 304.

42. De Nagy, *Pre-Imagist Stage*, p. 38. De Nagy concludes that 'one is justified in assuming that the "we" – if it can be reduced to a simple formula at all – stands for "artists" or, by extension, "lovers of beauty," as opposed to "Philistines" who appear in some poems as indifferent to the arts, in others as merely enjoying them without offering any help to their creators and in some as seeing in the products of art merely a source of profit' (ibid. p. 39).

43. Fisher, *Ezra Pound's Radio Operas*, p. 32. Fisher provides the following 'Synopsis of Action' for Pound's first opera: 'the outlawed Villon moves back into Paris despite an outstanding warrant for his arrest in that city. His closest friends gradually assemble around him – Ythier, a former girl-friend named Rose, the old prostitute Heaulmière, her protégés Gantière, Blanche, and Guillemette. Joined by Villon's mother, the group urges Villon to flee for his life, but to no avail. Villon pens his last will and testament. By evening the gathering crowd has grown quite large and quite drunk. Their singing and dancing attract the attention of the police. Villon is arrested. A final tableau depicts six lads hung by the neck' (ibid. p. 34).

44. Tate, 'Ezra Pound', p. 351.

45. Fisher, *Ezra Pound's Radio Operas*, p. 97.

46. Cf. 'Pound's choice to write a hybrid vernacular was apparently an informed and artistic one. He had used colloquial speech to more precisely identify individual characters in *The Cantos* by their psychology as well as their nationality and race . . . Here it would be used to remove such indicators. The blurring of dialects would have created a very broad stereotype,

preventing the listener from misinterpreting characters as specific persons' (ibid. p. 97).

47. Pound, *Literary Essays*, p. 167.
48. Ibid. p. 163.
49. Ibid. p. 168.
50. Qtd in Sullivan, *Ezra Pound*, p. 70.
51. Pound, *Selected Letters*, p. 3.
52. Pound, *Poems and Translations*, p. 193.
53. See p. 11.
54. Aviram, *Telling Rhythm*, p. 109.
55. Pound, *Literary Essays*, pp. 178–9.
56. Surette, 'Dantescan Light', p. 333.
57. Ibid. p. 332.
58. Ibid. p. 334.
59. Ibid. p. 334.
60. Qtd in Anderson, *Pound's Cavalcanti*, pp. 8–9.
61. Pound, *Guide to Kulchur*, p. 295.
62. Pound, *Literary Essays*, p. 181.
63. Ibid. p. 182. This argument derives from Samuel Johnson: 'These complaints of difficulty will, by those that have never considered words beyond their popular use, be thought only the jargon of a man willing to magnify his labours, and procure veneration to his studies by involution and obscurity. But every art is obscure to those that have not learned it: this uncertainty of terms, and commixture of ideas, is well known to those who have joined philosophy with grammar; and if I have not expressed them very clearly, it must be remembered that I am speaking of that which words are insufficient to explain' ('Preface' to *Dictionary*, §55).
64. Fisher, *Ezra Pound's Radio Operas*, pp. 183–4.
65. Ibid. p. 188.
66. Pound, *Literary Essays*, p. 162.
67. Ibid. p. 22.
68. Pound, *Poems and Translations*, p. 139; ll. 34–9.
69. Ibid. p. 139; l. 60.
70. Witemeyer, *Poetry of Ezra Pound*, pp. 92–3.
71. Pound, *Poems and Translations*, p. 199.
72. Witemeyer, *Poetry of Ezra Pound*, p. 89.
73. Agamben, 'Tradition of the Immemorial', p. 105.
74. Pound, *Poems and Translations*, p. 169; ll. 23–8.
75. See pp. 24–5.
76. Pound, *Gaudier Brzeska*, p. 125.
77. Pound, *Selected Prose*, p. 28.
78. Pound, *ABC of Reading*, p. 33.
79. Jackson, *Early Poetry*, p. 144.
80. This understanding of poetic language is as long lived as it is serviceable. To take a somewhat extrinsic example, John Barton advises Shakespearean actors to envisage a situation in which language is psychologically or emotionally *required* by the dramatic situation and characterisation and not a prefabricated given that they need to memorise and trot out (Barton, *Playing Shakespeare*, p. 18; p. 50).

81. Pound, *Literary Essays*, p. 36.
82. Ibid. p. 54.
83. Pound, *Poems and Translations*, p. 28; ll. 3–6.
84. Aristotle, *Poetics*, p. 1479; §22.
85. Pound, *Poems and Translations*, p. 1124.
86. Grieve, *Early Poetry*, p. 39.

Chapter 4

'Caliban Casts Out Ariel':
Ezra Pound's Victorian Barbarian

From my foule Studie will I hoyst a Wretch
A leane and hungry Meager Canniball
Whose [j]awes swell to his eyes with chawing malice
And him Ile make a Poet

Anon. Mucedorus, c. 1598[1]

A Lume Spento (1908), *A Quinzaine for This Yule* (1908) and the initial *Personae* (1909) plainly suggest that, for Ezra Pound, one of the most characteristic Victorian achievements in poetry was the discovery of a certain kind of literary barbarian. In these volumes, he rejects many of the conventionally poetic qualities of his earliest verse: the Celtic diction, the crepuscular, Romantic and *fin de siècle* imagery of 'Hilda's Book' make way for a more natural and robust idiom, and his subject matter becomes noticeably less precious and literary. Bold, stubborn and abstruse, this new poetry anticipates his more recognisable and influential modern style. In these early volumes we can see how Pound's stylistic innovations emerge from a critical engagement with Victorian ideas about the Barbarian, and with authors who championed an associated kind of literary primitivism. Revisiting this period in his development a decade later in 'Hugh Selwyn Mauberley', Pound discovers the perfect symbol for this earlier self: Shakespeare's Caliban. For the Victorians, Caliban was the quintessential foreigner, and typically an American; both Pound and Caliban hailed from the same 'half-savage country'.[2] The poem focuses upon Pound's struggle to reconcile his initial enthusiasm for the role of the literary barbarian with the barbarities of World War I, and Caliban appears in a profoundly ambiguous context. He is symbolically aligned with the tea parties and mass-produced musical instruments of the first stanza; with the Christ of modern religion rather than the Dionysus of ancient religion; and with the 'tawdry cheapness' of the modern world.[3] His earlier volumes present an uncritical and uncluttered view of the matter, and we can appreciate how his experience as a linguistic margin-alien in literary London leads him to embrace the role of poetic interloper in thematic and formal terms in his verse, providing a decisive foundation for his mature, modern style.

The rugged and seemingly unrefined voices of Robert Browning and Walt Whitman supply the immediate impetus for Pound's new direction, and Browning's poem 'Caliban upon Setebos: or Natural Theology on the Island' (with which Pound was certainly familiar from an early age) offers contemporary readers a convenient place to begin to trace how a Victorian discourse of barbarianism impacted the twentieth century. The poem is a dramatic monologue and an extraordinary one, since Caliban 'talks to his own self, howe'er he please': it asks to be read or heard as a soliloquy. The subject is to be Setebos (Caliban's God) and it is an irksome subject to Caliban – 'to talk about Him, vexes – ' but he delights in it regardless, exclaiming: 'ha, / Could he but know! and time to vex is now.' Caliban's task is irreverent and urgent, and he gets on with it, 'letting the rank tongue blossom into speech'.[4] Everything about this type of communication appeals to Pound and he aspires to it often in his early verse. Caliban's notion of self-satisfying self-communion, and his blunt indifference to the effect this speech arouses in his audience, is particularly evident in several of Pound's own early dramatic monologues, as we shall see. His earliest letters show him already 'letting the rank tongue blossom into speech', although it is not until his debutant London volumes that he seeks out a literary audience for his meaner experiments in diction, and their significance as a systematic literary strategy can be appreciated.[5]

Browning's famous lines conceive of sound and speech as a kind of spectrum or gradient, the 'rank tongue' at one end and the 'blossom' of speech at the other. This idea is central to Pound's poetic effort from his Cavalcanti translations to his most polyglot cantos, where language and poetry are seen in their nascence and emergence from mere sound.[6] This concern with the acoustic datum of linguistic and poetic communication is intrinsic to notions of barbarism from the outset of Western literature.[7] The ethical or moral gradient that these lines imply is equally ancient and important, but is made ambiguous by Browning here, in part because of the fundamental uncertainty surrounding the term 'rank' (as indeed of 'barbarism' itself) in the late nineteenth and early twentieth centuries.[8] This ambiguous discourse provides the backdrop for Pound's poetic entrance.

The prose writers of the age also worried about the dichotomy between English civilisation and the perceived barbarity of cultures over which England claimed jurisdiction. Already in 1869, Matthew Arnold could describe the culture of the barbarian ('an exterior culture mainly consist[ing] principally in outward gifts and graces, in looks, mannerisms, accomplishments, prowess') in essentially the same terms he uses for the accomplishments of the English aristocracy.[9] More important for Ezra Pound, however, was Arnold's resolute insistence that barbarism embodies 'that staunch individualism, as the modern phrase is, and that passion for doing as one likes, for the assertion of personal liberty'.[10] Powerful and passionate action, the exhibition of personality and freedom – here barbarism is recognisable by its positive traits and civilisation demeaned for its 'outward gifts and graces'. William Morris is even more sceptical. He privately confesses

> no more faith than a grain of mustard seed in the future history of 'civilization,' which I *know* now is doomed to destruction, and probably before very long: what a joy it is to think of! and how often it consoles me to think of barbarism once more flooding the world, and real feelings and passions, however rudimentary, taking the place of our wretched hypocrisies.[11]

The persistent problem is the inauthentic, artificial, false nature of contemporary culture. In Morris's analysis the ancient dichotomy remains, but the traditional values of civilisation and barbarity are reversed: he esteems 'real feelings and passions' over the 'wretched hypocrisies' of colonial self-satisfaction and post-Romantic idealism.

This criticism is perhaps now most familiar to readers of Oscar Wilde, however. He extolled the *fin de siècle* only in so far as it compensated for an otherwise bland and pedestrian civilisation: 'all that is known by that term I particularly admire and love', he claimed: 'it is the fine flower of our civilization: the only thing that keeps the world from the commonplace, the coarse, the barbarous'.[12] Victorian 'civilization', that is to say 'the commonplace, the coarse, the barbarous', was only redeemed by its absurd and sickly outgrowths, the implosive decadence of its final throes. The characteristic argument about barbarism during the *fin de siècle* was therefore not only geographical and colonial, but also fundamentally historical, many writers feeling, with Wilde and the Decadents, that English culture had somehow decayed. For many writers, this feeling was what gave the Decadent movement its name and what coherence it possessed in the first place.[13]

These remarks demonstrate that the dubious relationship between England and the colonies, between civilisation and its ancient foil, involved an intrinsically literary dilemma for the authors of the age. The criticism and commentary of Victorian England hints at the utility of barbarism from a strategic, intellectual point of view, but stops short of embracing its artistic possibilities in literature: Pound would have to look to other sources to realise this. First, perhaps, among those to recognise the aesthetic potential of a kind of stylistic primitivism in a modern context, is Giambattista Vico. In his *New Science* he argues that Pound's most beloved troubadour, Arnaut Daniel, roundly embraces barbarism in his verse:

> With the recourse of barbarism in Europe, new languages were born. The first language of the Spaniards was that called '*el romance*,' and consequently that of heroic poetry, for the *romanceros* were the heroic poets of the returned barbarian times. In France the first writer in vulgar French was Arnaut Daniel Pacca, the first of all the Provençal poets, who flourished in the eleventh century.[14]

Pound learned much from En Arnaut: that poetry quite often achieves much of its lyric potency by adopting strange and foreign words, thereby heightening its non-discursive and acoustic qualities; to 'file and preen, / and cut words clean', as Arnaut has it, honing his technique until he discovered the terse 'modern' style of his mature verse.[15]

At this stage of his career, however, the question of literary barbarism seemed urgent to Pound largely because of George Santayana's treatment of the topic in 'The Poetry of Barbarism'. Santayana's essay is systematic and situates discussion of the literary barbarian in a specifically American context. The essay turns upon what its author sees as the false pre-eminence of Anglo-American modernity and its cultural accomplishments. He argues that poetry had become separated from the highest ideals of Classicism and Christianity; that its language had become sundry and provincial, muddied like the languages of Babel. Paradoxically, 'the comparatively barbarous ages had a poetry of the ideal; they had a vision of beauty, order and perfection', Santayana contends; 'this age of material elaboration has no sense for those things. Its fancy is retrospective, whimsical, and flickering; its moral strength is a blind and miscellaneous vehemence. Its poetry, in a word, is the poetry of barbarism.'[16] Like William Morris, Santayana undermines the complacency that seemed to come with the many advances of the nineteenth century by transposing the terms of the dichotomy on which it was based.

Santayana's essay was enormously influential, especially on two young American poets about to make a name for themselves abroad and give literary modernism a decisive shove. In an obvious and general way, 'The Poetry of Barbarism' anticipates the dialectical understanding of history championed by Pound and Eliot by some years.[17] In former ages, Santayana suggests, they thought of all reality as in a sense contemporary, and in considering the maxims of a philosopher or the style of a poet, they were not primarily concerned with settling his date and describing his environment. The standard by which they judged was eternal.[18]

This resonates with Eliot's advocacy of what he termed a 'historical sense' that 'involves a perception, not just of the pastness of the past, but of its presence . . . a sense of the timeless as well as of the temporal, and of the timeless and the temporal together'.[19] The coincidence is not surprising since Eliot studied 'Art and Science and their historical development' with Santayana in 1909.[20] These methodological statements are also consistent with Pound's demand, in *The Spirit of Romance*, for a 'literary scholarship, which will weigh Theocritus and Yeats with one balance, and which will judge dull dead men as inexorably as dull writers of today, and will, with equity, give praise to beauty before referring to an almanac'.[21] Here, the language is clearly indebted to Eliot's former instructor. The continuing importance of this idea in twentieth-century criticism can best be gauged, however, by the durability of E. M. Forster's notion of the canon being simultaneously composed by its authors 'in a room, a circular room, a sort of British Museum reading-room'.[22]

One implication of Santayana's demand that the critic consider literature in 'eternal' or absolute terms is therefore a concomitant intolerance for parochial and faddish forms of criticism and creative writing. This was the leitmotif of Pound's reviews and criticism in the Teens and early Twenties: that provincialism, and the provincial attitude of literary editors in particular, 'rewards not the best work . . . but the best local product'; paradoxically, he associated this almost entirely with elite, metropolitan culture.[23] His modernism begins, in a sense, as a reaction to the provincial and irrelevant attitudinising of the Georgian literary establishment, with the double aim of shocking contemporary tastes and calling attention to the deliberate and facile exclusivity of the institutions that support them. Michael North demonstrates the vitality of this international gesture, observing at the same time its pronounced American dimensions. American modernists, including Pound,

> assume the traditional American pose, that of vital, new, raw, egalitarian, common men against the gray cultural authorities established in Europe, and they also remodeled it so that it can become a component of literary modernism with its general revolt against old literary conventions.[24]

North sees the aspect of the barbarian as an acutely American problem, stemming from the literary needs of a generation whose 'language branded them as cultural interlopers'.[25] His analysis shows how this style and attitude originate in Eliot and Pound's private experiments with African-American dialect, but it has a traditional and public basis as well, as the context above demonstrates. The barbarian attitude itself is riddled with paradoxes, as T. S. Eliot insists when he comments: 'the artist is more *primitive*, as well as more civilized, than his contemporaries'.[26] The emphasis here is Eliot's, but this corroborates North's thesis neatly by calling attention to the paradox of the modernist author's need to be seen as elite and vulgar at the same time.

This critical legacy aside, Santayana's essay develops a crucial reading of modern poetry in general, and of Whitman and Browning in particular. He claims that the modern style exemplified by these writers is fundamentally sensual rather than rational, suggestive rather than discursive:

> The poetry of barbarism is not without its charm. It can play with sense and passion the more readily and freely in that it does not aspire to subordinate them to a clear thought or a tenable attitude of the will. It can impart the transitive emotions which it expresses; it can find many partial harmonies of mood and fancy; it can by virtue of its red-hot irrationality, utter wilder cries, surrender itself and us to more absolute passion, and heap up a more indiscriminate wealth of images than belongs to poets of seasoned experience or of heavenly inspiration.[27]

Whereas Santayana ultimately sees these as inferior and desultory charms, Pound embraces them, at least for the time being, and hopes they will help him write authentically and enduringly about the world he inhabits. Santayana's dichotomy is, after all, quite germane to Pound's ideas about Yeats, Burns, et al. as discussed in Chapter 2 – ideas that are plainly consonant with Matthew Arnold's more famous account of Celtic literature – and the development of Pound's more barbaric style must therefore have seemed to him and his readers to be a quite natural progression. As an account of Pound's poetic efforts between 'Hilda's Book' (1905–7) and *Ripostes* (1912), indeed, Santayana's description can hardly be equalled.[28]

The aspects of literary barbarism that Pound inherited from the nineteenth century, then, may be summarised in the following way: first, the obvious point needs to be made: barbarisms are of course borrowings from a foreign tongue. This makes meaning obscure and accents the lyrical dimension of the given utterance, as has been well known since the Greeks.[29] Pound's persona of the perennial margin-alien, his status as a 'poetic interloper' in London, his rhetorical and critical emphasis upon 'individualism' and 'personal liberty' – or, as North says, his 'vital, new, raw, egalitarian, common' qualities – are calculated and traditional poetic strategies.[30] Second, we must also note (following Strabo) the primal or animalistic dimension of such a language: it supposedly belongs to some proto-human stage of development, and the sense of *belonging to the primate* in 'primitive' helps us to appreciate the 'half-savage' nature of Pound's poetry. From these two basic premises follow many of Pound's critical foibles, especially his antagonistic and shrill attitude towards more traditional Brits. As an American, one does not blindly follow a foreign tradition but prefers 'doing as one likes'. Paradoxically perhaps, Browning is briefer and clearer on this matter. His Caliban, remember, 'talks to his own self, howe'er he please' and seems not to consider his audience (his God, that is) except to annoy. This will remind many readers of the controversy-courting, combative stance of modernism in general, which is also 'bold, stubborn [and especially] abstruse'. Browning's word 'vex' is crucial here. The early twentieth century was, for the modernists, 'the time to vex': that is, to interfere with the quaint prevailing peace and quiet; to cause agitation, commotion, controversy, grief; and even to court mental and spiritual agitation in their audience with their 'miscellaneous vehemence'.[31] In terms of subject and treatment, Pound and his contemporaries would flaunt the classical 'ideal' of simple beauty, become 'elaborate', ruminating 'play[fully]' and 'whimsical[ly]' upon 'coarse', 'material' and 'modern' subjects, while retaining a decadent interest in superficiality and style per se, in 'outward gifts and graces', in looks, mannerisms and exterior accomplishments.

There are countless examples of these tendencies in Pound's early volumes. 'Anima Sola' is a fairly representative poem of this period: an unrestrained *ars poetica* that nonetheless provides a useful précis of Pound's emerging aesthetic. Thomas Jackson offers a memorable description of the poem as a 'druidic snake dance' whose 'effect could be gained with much less incense', but it is an instructive example all the same.[32] The poem is a dramatic monologue written from the point of view of what Pound had earlier conceived of as a 'wind-blown' child-poet, now grown-up, estranged and exiled from any society capable of sustaining his artistic needs.[33] The wind symbolism of this poem derives in part from his pneumatic experiments in 'Hilda's Book', a fact underscored by the prefatory remark ascribed to Empedocles: the discovery of air is often credited among the ancient philosopher's accomplishments. The persona also mitigates the strident and explicitly barbaric tone somewhat, as Empedocles is usually represented as arrogantly believing that study had made him a god.

The title of the poem – meaning 'solitary soul' – evokes Caliban's situation in Browning's poem, and suggest a speaker who also 'talks to his own self, howe'er he please'. As the poem begins, the speaker consequentially insists upon his own cantankerousness:

> My music is weird and untamed
> Barbarous, wild, extreme,
> I fly on the note that ye hear not
> On the chord that ye can not dream.
> And lo, your out-worn harmonies are behind me
>   As ashes and mouldy bread.[34]

With this 'weird and untamed' music Pound strikes a Dionysian note and lays claim to an art that will be heterogeneous and spontaneous. The speaker is a self-styled barbarian and he does not expect to receive intelligent or sympathetic response from contemporary auditors, being a Swinburnian prophet of the savage past; he recognises that this kind of barbaric art will be misunderstood and debased by those whose ears are attuned to more harmonious (and, in this view, less urgent) forms, and delights in having his meaning all to himself.

Significantly, these lines allude to the last section of 'Song of Myself', where Walt Whitman meets the objection of barbarianism indignantly:

> The spotted hawk swoops by and accuses me, he complains of my gab and
>   my loitering
> I too am not a bit tamed, I too am untranslatable,
> I sound my barbaric yawp over the roofs of the world.[35]

Whitman imagines himself as a bird surveying the world, with a language that is correspondingly harsh, querulous and 'barbaric'. The allusion is signalled in terms of the discourse of barbarism outlined above: the bestial qualities, emphasised in the word 'untamed', the hint of accusation from one's established (in this instance, avian) peers, and the impossibility that they themselves might appreciate either the 'harmon[y]' or the meaning of the 'yawp' since it is fundamentally 'untranslatable'. George Santayana singles out these lines in 'The Poetry of Barbarism', noting how 'the "barbaric yawp" is sent "over the roofs of the world" in full consciousness of its inarticulate character'; indeed, the word 'yawp' was chiefly used of bird cries prior to Whitman.[36] For Santayana, this inarticulacy constitutes a serious flaw, but it is at least a representatively modern flaw; for Pound, Whitman's 'yawp' was a necessary but not a sufficient adjunct to the spirit of modern (and American) poetry. His early endorsement of literary barbarism, so pronounced and supercilious in 'Anima Sola', will soon become tempered by a deference to craft that appears at first to be deliberately scorned. In 1912, for example, he writes to Harriet Monroe that 'The "Yawp" is respected from Denmark to Bengal, but we can't stop with the "Yawp." We have no longer any excuse for not taking up the complete art.'[37] The genius of modern American poetry is this feral urge to expression but, for Pound, only the beginning of a fully-fledged art: it simply clears the throat for fuller lyric expression (the other meaning of Whitman's 'hawk').[38] His barbarism, thus aligned with Whitman's, is seen as partial and ambivalent, but he will return to this simple lyrical formula often enough – in the keen cries and screams of the seabirds in 'The Seafarer', for instance.

The words 'weird' and 'untamed' recur in 'Anima Sola', and they accent Pound's primitivism nicely. The ordinary modern sense of 'weird' – meaning strange, unusual or fantastic – becomes prominent only in the Romantic period (and is a favourite of Shelley), where it is frequently applied to strange sounds. In the barbaric and pagan context of the poem the dominant sense is literary, indicating the power to control fate or destiny, after the Weird Sisters made famous by Shakespeare (three more thoroughgoing and thaumaturgical barbarians one could scarcely encounter). In this poem, both the poet and his poems are so described; the poet himself 'pendant sit[s] in the vale of fate', which is especially suggestive of the Empedoclean mood in which the poem originates.[39] Pound emphasises the mysterious, runic nature of poetry here: he seeks an uncommonly potent, even visionary language and he will not be deterred by mere abstruseness. These associations are repeated and elaborated throughout:

> My music is your disharmony
>   Intangible, most mad,
> For the clang of a thousand cymbals
> Where the sphinx smiles o'er the sand,
>   And viol strings that out-sing kings
> Are the least of my command.
> Exquisite, alone, untrammeled
> I kiss the nameless sign
> And the laws of my inmost being
>   Chant to the nameless shrine.[40]

The passage gives access, first, to a remote and mythy landscape (more than reminiscent of that presided over by Shelley's Ozymandias), and then to deeper communion with a 'nameless sign'. The image is an appropriately strange and opaque one, not yet modern, but it evokes the neophyte muttering his offices clearly enough: poetic language is inherently weird and will remain so even to the poet who wields it, his meaning coming only partly through. The poet claims that ecstasy arises out of his loneliness and the incantatory power of his dithyramb. The language is by now familiar; patterned, even. The aural qualities of his 'yawp' – its 'mad', 'clang[ing]' 'disharmony' – are obnoxious to many in his audience though musical to the speaker, and are, moreover, privileged above the 'nameless' discursive qualities obscurely signalled in the last few lines. The paradox is heightened by the curious use of the word 'intangible' here, which is clearly chosen to echo 'clang', making it of course very tangible *in* the poem. 'Clang' itself is highly onomatopoeic, and its earliest usages, like those of 'yawp', refer to the echoic ring of certain birdcalls (often in imitation of the Greek), making it a natural way of describing utterances that are both strictly non-discursive and yet emotive and suggestive of meaning. Significantly, the word establishes yet another important inter-text in Pound's 'runic rhyme': Poe's 'The Bells', which 'can only shriek, shriek, / Out of tune, / In a clamorous appealing.'[41]

By emphasising liberty and individualism, this passage also illustrates another key aspect of Pound's engagement with Victorian ideas about barbarism and the swerve away from conventional poeticism that it occasioned, and invites a complementary reading of the poem. The phrase 'solitary soul' is often associated with the suffering of the devoutly religious, and especially with the Carmelite pursuit of an isolated, contemplative life. Carmelites are a silent order, whose members are, however, permitted to worship in chant and song, making them a suitable analogue for the lyric poet who would scorn society and conversation for more sublime communions.[42] The poet may have been familiar with the order from his childhood since his parents were actively religious, and Dutch Carmelites founded houses at two Pennsylvania locations – in Pittsburgh and Somerset counties – in 1870.[43] Although the brash tone makes this passage seem entirely removed from the religious context that the title invokes, the debate enacted in the poem involves a basically Carmelite antinomy. The limitation placed on Carmelite participation in vocal devotion is precisely what increases the intensity of that expression when it does occur. A strange kind of communication results, which is characterised by long stretches of ascetic, silent self-absorption, and sudden, profuse outbursts of song. This is the same dynamic that Pound avers for his art in this poem. Through isolation and contemplation, Pound claims access to profounder knowledge: 'Exquisite, alone, untrammeled', his speaker says, 'I kiss the nameless sign / And the laws of my inmost being.'[44] At the same time, he stresses the vestigial musical qualities of his art. He can effortlessly command 'the clang of a thousand cymbals / And viol strings that out-sing kings' – these remain, however, potential and 'unresolved' in the poem. 'Your outworn harmonies are behind me', says the speaker; his discordant notes cannot be appreciated by those trained in the old ways.[45] The irony of this identification is, of course, that while Pound's periodical outbursts both derive from his lack of able (if not willing) interlocutors and result in a similar invocation of 'nameless' signs and truths, they are infinitely more noisome and abrasive than Carmelite 'harmonies'.

Pound's early poems abound in similar aesthetic pronouncements. In 'Aegupton' he vouches that his mouth is ready to 'chaunt the pure singing', though he wonders 'who hath the mouth to receive it'.[46] His endorsement of an abstruse poetic jargon is still more pronounced in 'Salve O Pontifex', considered in the previous chapter, where he celebrates that 'Entangled music that men may not / Over readily understand'.[47] Swinburne's prosody is so complex that his meaning tends to dissolve in his music, baffling the untrained popular audience more perfectly in this way than by his professed decadence or frequent, startling impieties. He continues in this vein in 'Sandalphon', where he bids his audience 'marvel and wonder' as he gives 'to prayer new language';[48] and in 'An Idyl for Glaucus', where the literary ideal is 'strange words', the meaning of which the speaker 'did not know / One half the substance'.[49] Everywhere, speech that is esteemed as poetic smacks of these same confounding properties.

Everywhere we see Pound render his lyricism more potent and coherent by charging it with arcane meaning. This will prove to be one of his most characteristic poetic strategies – logopoeia – which 'employs words not only for their direct meaning', but also 'takes count in a special way of habits of usage, of the context we *expect* to find with the word, its usual concomitants, of its known acceptances, and of ironic play'.[50] In 'Anima Sola' Pound selects remote literary and historical ideas and arranges them for his audience so that their similarities may emerge. He places his own personal experience in Crawfordsville, Indiana, one of profound social and artistic alienation, within a more prestigious context by considering these other famously contemplative souls, and with surprising subtlety, given the vituperative tone of the poem. With this technique, Pound effectively ventriloquises the words of yet another literary figure, that of the glutton Caccio, who, subdued and reduced to a spectre by the heavy rain in Dante's *Inferno*, laments: 'E io *anima* trista non son *sola*'; that is to say: 'And I, sad soul, am not the only one' (emphasis added).[51] As N. Christoph de Nagy explains, literary allusions like this one are often keys to discovering the 'personal attitude' of Pound's early poems:

> quotation and allusion sometimes serve to support Pound's personal attitude or personal view by showing their similitude to those other poets; sometimes

quotation and allusion serve to contrast the present state of the artist with a more favourable position he enjoyed in the past. Even in 'In Durance', one of the few strongly subjective poems Pound ever wrote, he looks into the past in search of artists who were faced with the same difficulties as he is, and, by quotations, brings their experience to bear upon his.[52]

By seeking to embody obscure historical figures and adopt neglected literary postures, and by allowing forgotten voices to claim the reader's attention in the iridescent way Browning had done, Pound became a sort of foreign correspondent for literary London long before he assumed that position in an official capacity for *The Little Review* or *Poetry* magazine. He derives a technique – what Eliot will later call 'the mythical method' – from what is perhaps initially just the solace of literature.[53]

Like Santayana, Pound initially finds the perfect embodiment of this barbaric aesthetic not in Whitman's, but in Robert Browning's verse. His most ingenious tribute to his Victorian predecessor, 'Mesmerism', firmly establishes a Browningesque mood by severely curtailing the poem discursively and by eliminating ratiocination almost entirely. It begins in the following way:

> Aye you're a man that! ye old mesmerizer
> Tyin' your meanin' in seventy swadelin's,
> One must of needs be a hang'd early riser
> To catch you at worm turning. Holy Odd's bodykins![54]

While much of *A Lume Spento* has been censured for exhibiting a 'glut of poetic diction', featuring conspicuously precious words and endings, disconcerting elisions and 'Celtic Twilightisms', this poem stands out as a rare example of a faithful, comic evocation of what passes for naturalism in Browning, despite being written largely in dactyls.[55] We can only suppose that Pound thought this was the sort of thing that might actually be said 'under the stress of some emotion' – by Browning at least – but is it any clearer or more transparent than his more slighted verse?[56] However one answers the question, we have here a significant early example of his barbarian speech; colloquial, blunt and tormented.

Arguably, the degree and quality of the lyrical opacity is warranted by the subject matter of 'Mesmerism'. The second line, for example, provides a pithy description of Browning's vertiginous poetic style: his refusal to beautify or to set his audience at rhythmical ease. The discursive core of Browning's poetry – his meanin' – is described as being carefully concealed by numerous layers of bandaging; the process of contriving such a style is described as a sort of winsome deceit. Meaning is present, but it is occluded by something else in Browning's style.

Although his obscurantism is usually reckoned among Browning's difficulties or faults, Pound singles it out as a unique and endearing quality. In ll. 3 and 4 he implies that with a certain amount of resilience and cunning the difficulty disappears, suggesting that the prospect of coming to unravel the stylistic exterior is the essential part of the poet's appeal. These verses are also full of mutilated expletives, such as 'Hang'd' and 'Holy Odd's bodykins'; most significantly of all, however, meaning itself must be distorted if it is to appear in this poem. All of these contribute tangibly to the tone of voice and to the dramatic situation, but contribute nothing, or virtually nothing, to the discourse in a direct, denotative way. The archaeological effort to unravel the mummy's threads and to make sense of the phatic ciphers results in a kind of poetry that withholds as much meanin' as it manifests. The humour is in the style as much as the substance of the speech, which is fitting since Browning is said to transcend the fads of his day by virtue of his stylistic idiosyncrasies – his 'individualism' – arriving at truth by clear-sighted perversity. This gap, between the indecorous exterior style and the putative interior truth, is perhaps what makes Browning seem so authentic to the modernists, Pound especially, and although we should be wary of false antitheses, Browning offers an important reminder or re-emphasis here, nudging the late nineteenth century away from style that comes only at the cost of substance.

Pound, at any rate, hoped to avoid the fads of *his* day in more or less this manner, as he announces frankly in the unpublished poem 'Have I Not':

> When I have something real to say
>   I blurt it out bald as Browning
> no tom foolery, no tinsel
> no pre-Raphaelite zitherns and citoles
> to make ecstatic holes in the pants of my meaning.[57]

Citoles and zitherns, lyre-like instruments related to the aeolian harp, had much inspired Pound in 'Hilda's Book'.[58] The latter term appears to have been coined by Pound as a linguistic compromise between zither and cittern (it does not appear in the *Oxford English Dictionary*), and is probably intended to remind the reader of the antiquarian pretensions of the poetry he is lampooning, as though reminding one's audience that one is working from the Greek were more important than any substantial part of the poem. Pound is mocking the preciousness of his own earlier verse here, opposing what he now regards as its sham Pre-Raphaelite glamour with a more individualistic and direct voice borrowed, of course, from Browning.

This poem differs stylistically from the ghost-enamoured crepuscular effusions of his own earlier verse and that of most of his early contemporaries, and his reliance on Browning for this impetus is critical as he makes clear with the pneumatic imagery in this poem. Not only does Pound relate Browning to his central early figure for poetic speech, the wind ('sound in your wind past all signs o' corruption'), but he provides a hardly equalled description of the discordant note that Browning often strikes in his verse: 'You wheeze', says Pound, 'as a head-cold long-tonsilled Calliope'.[59] His reliance on pneumatic and percussive effects demonstrates the corporal and animalistic dimension of his poetry of barbarism. The locus of Browning's wheezing is the tortured, gustatory rhythm and colloquial idiom of 'Soliloquy of a Spanish Cloister', for example, which Pound mimics here. The wilfully perverse spellings exhibited by this poem, coupled with the egregious contractions, are of the same ilk as Browning's 'Gr-r-r – you swine!' and at points virtually banish the sense to oblivion (Pound uses a similar effect at the beginning of 'Sestina: Altaforte'). What, for example, are we to make of 'man-kin'ards'? The holes in the pants of his meanin' are vast indeed.[60]

Browning's influence on Pound during this period is evident in less localised ways as well, and the young modernist evidently found his predecessor's eccentric approach to prosody especially enabling. The image of 'seventy swadelin's' may offer an insight into this matter: according to the Oxford English Dictionary, swaddling clothes (which I take it he means) consist of 'narrow lengths of bandage wrapped round a new-born infant's limbs to prevent free movement' (emphasis added). Pound may well be referring to the hieratic qualities of Browning's writing mentioned above – Tacitus, for instance, notes that secret messages were often sent into a besieged city on manuscripts that appeared to be bandages.[61] Possibly, however, Pound has another aspect of Browning's art in mind. The fact that he prescribes 'seventy' items here, or that Browning's meaning may be couched in any large number of short, narrow strands, seems to suggest that his versification is somewhat suspect, stunted and haltering as in Pound's parody, above. Oscar Wilde notoriously sanctioned Browning for not writing verse at all, but prose (albeit lineated and measured). This criticism rests on Browning's presumed inability or unwillingness to count to ten, his perceived imperviousness to harmony and predilection for short, staccato phrases ('versicles') rather than sweeping normative measures. Pound champions precisely this approach to prosody throughout his career, not just when he imitates Browning.[62] He claims, for example, to have learned around 1907 (while an instructor at Wabash College, Indiana) that Dante composed using a large but finite number of cadenced units, and had little interest in counting syllables or any notion of metrical feet, the invention of which Pound attributes to the vogue for the sonnet, 'which marks the beginning of the divorce of words and music'.[63] Whatever success can be claimed for *The Cantos*, they clearly attempt to develop such a *particular* English prosody.

Browning, then, embodies two opposed poetic tendencies for Pound: a kind of cultural hermeticism coupled with a desire to keep the reader at a distance with strategically placed non-discursive elements. He further licensed the use of idiosyncratic language and spelling – and Pound very quickly learned to utilise the inherent torsions of such devices to cultivate a series of personae and infuse his poetry with strangeness, reducing it in part to music and feeling rather than emphatic sense. As he says at the close of this poem, there is 'no need to pack cents / Into your versicles' – of course he means 'sense' as much as 'cents' here. The point, I think subtly and so aptly made, is that poets who would write to make a buck have to convey something pragmatically and unambiguously, to command the attention of a popular audience or serve a patron; those who would write for the Art's sake are free to couch their meaning in the 'verse-barrel', to make their point in formal terms, and to delight in word play and resounding sonic arrangement. Pound makes this point in another unpublished Browningesque poem in the Beinecke Library: 'Because this trick or that shall sell / at this or that per word, the jester gets / some Judas thirty for each noun and verb / that is a feater tickler to the feet.'[64] Pound's poetry will not seek to fill out the line in a mechanical way, but to develop a composite understanding of poetic form, something Pound thought that Browning, like Dante, had a better sense of than he is given credit for. If his initial offence was 'against spoken idiom', he redeems himself from here on – yet the poetry remains oddly charged with recondite fact and now, even worse, splendid gibberish.

Although Pound's stylistic primitivism often seems instinctive and merely reactive, 'Mesmerism' demonstrates that it is, to a large extent, a formal and technical poetic matter. His use of elision is instrumental here and a feature of his best poetry to the end. For his detractors, Pound's use of elision is artificial, sanctioned either by metrical convenience or blind habit; any innovative modernist ought to be wary of the practice. If his early contemporaries were sceptical of the abysmal wrenches Pound so often required of his reader, this is not because they were unfamiliar with the technique, but because they were uneasy with Pound's brash appropriation of conventions that were regarded as suitable for the stage but not for lyric or epic poetry. His elisions were insufficiently Miltonic. Robert Bridges had recently published a comprehensive study of *Milton's Prosody* that underscored the crucial role of elision in *Paradise Lost* and presented a taxonomy of supposed rules governing its application. Pound used these Miltonic elisions, but he also departed from them quite emphatically or ignored them.

It would be a mistake to see Pound's persistent use of elision as a decadent mannerism. Like Browning, he uses elision dramatically, to vitalise and particularise his verse. Although Browning often wrote in iambic pentameter, his influence contributed to its desuetude due to the exorbitant leaps and bounds that the line exhibited in his hands, and it is probably in this capacity, rather than as a staid convention sanctified by unthinking veneration or mere habit, that elision first occurred to Pound as a viable poetic technique.[65] Sometimes elision renders his poetry like the ordinary speech of his contemporaries, but more often his object is a more remote language. In 'The Ballad of the Goodly Fere', for example, he often drops the ending of a word (*quo'* for quoth, *ha'* for have, etc.) to create a plausible locutor for his ballad, who, in this instance, comes to resemble the speaker of one of Robert Burns's poems. Pound produces a realistic speech in the same way that Browning had done; his use of elision, too, undermines the coherence of the line and supplies an element of spontaneity that is wanting in much Georgian verse.

Poetic elision often serves as the signature of Pound's poetics of barbarism, the locus of its individualistic and uncouth qualities. This point is underscored when we consider a second influence on Pound's practice here: Shakespeare's. Pound never concentrated on Shakespeare when he became an influential critic because he believed that Shakespeare had no need of further apologists.[66] These early poems were written before he adopted this official stance, however, and suggest that he was as prone to this great influence as many a writer. Elision is a distinctive feature of Shakespeare's later plays, and especially of *The Tempest*, the play that provides Pound with an archetypal poetic role: that of the eloquent barbarian. The preponderance of *'st* elisions throughout *Ripostes* (1912) – 'mak'st', 'brav'st', 'thou'st', 'know'st', 'knew'st', 'call'st', 'dar'dst' and 'mad'st', for instance – evidently originate in this play, where they often serve to indicate the distinct speech of the islanders, Caliban especially. The briefest excerpt of Caliban's speech anticipates many of the elisions in *Ripostes*, as for example when he proclaims:

> This island's mine by Sycorax my mother,
> Which thou tak'st from me. When thou cam'st first
> Thou strok'dst me and made much of me; wouldst give me
> Water with berries in't.[67]

(The *in't* elision is also highly favoured by Pound in his early volumes.) Halting, slow and severe at its most lyrical, Caliban's language is primal and percussive rather than limpid and grandiloquent. As Vico realised (following Strabo, it would seem), language made up in this manner, with many diphthongs and where the consonants do not easily combine, is received as being more barbarous than fuller, more rounded forms.[68] This aspect of poetic craft has long been known to Pound's critics; Hugh Kenner, for example, observed some time ago that Pound learned this lesson well – not just from Browning and Shakespeare but also from Arnaut Daniel and Rihaku – and it became one of the signatures of his mature style. According to Kenner, Pound 'expects us to take pleasure in the separation, not the blending, of syllables, and in sound relieving, not prolonging, sound'. The language of his modernist verse 'seems to welcome separations. Its words clip, bounding the clear distinct syllables modern French has slurred . . . to make English words new meant to make them more separately audible'.[69] Pound's modern attitude and stylistic aims were clear, then, almost upon his arrival in London when he began to disturb the sonorities of Georgian poetry in this way, as if to proclaim, haltingly, with Caliban: 'The red plague rid you / For learning me your language!'[70]

The signal attitude and the first gropings after the famous style are here already. Many other early works demonstrate how Pound's interest in literary barbarianism, and his cultivation of a barbarian jargon, is fundamentally related to his most characteristic poetic concerns, but few so clearly as the 1908 poem, 'Masks'.[71] Here it is in full:

These tales of old disguisings, are they not
Strange myths of souls that found themselves among
Unwonted folk that spake an hostile tongue,
Some soul from all the rest who'd not forgot
The star-span acres of a former lot
Where boundless mid the clouds his course he swung,
Or carnate with his elder brothers[72] sung
Ere ballad-makers lisped of Camelot?

Old singers half-forgetful of their tunes,
Old painters color-blind come back once more,
Old poets skill-less in the wind-heart runes,
Old wizards lacking in their wonder-lore:

All they that with strange sadness in their eyes
Ponder in silence o'er earth's queynt devyse?[73]

These lines rehearse the same themes of Pound's staunch individualism and sense of personal liberty, his emphasis on a self-consciously stylistic presentation (largely suggested by the title and initial lines), his ambivalent attitude towards received tradition, the necessary encumbrances of artistic exile, etc. Nonetheless, something interesting begins to happen in this poem: the diction is not quite the same as what Pound's early readership would have expected; one might even call it relatively plain and natural – that is until we meet, in the last line, an absurdly contorted phrase given not to the wizened artifice of the wizard-poets Pound describes, but to the world itself. *This* is the point of Pound's objectionable poetic diction: he does not intend it to abstract us from reality but to situate us more securely within it; not in the prosaic world, to be sure, but in the imaginative world where things are ever surprising and delightful. The phrase itself is drawn from *The Tempest*:

> *Thunder and lightning.*
> *Enter Ariel like a harpy, claps his wings upon the table, and with a quaint device the banquet vanishes.*[74]

In Pound's poem, the artifice of theatrical production is attributed to the world at large; the weird poet's language is not nearly as convoluted or thaumaturgical as the 'insubstantial pageant' that he surveys, and so whatever length he may go to capture some of the strange magic of indubitable reality is warranted, necessary.

The cognitive effort, we are reminded, originates in linguistic discord, where the poet's native language flounders to communicate in 'an hostile tongue'.[75] Pound often expressed this urge to be (as he put it in 'Plunge', from *Ripostes*) 'Out and alone, among some / Alien people'.[76] Thus we see that his lifelong interest in personae begins as a sonic phenomenon, as an attempt to form a composite inter-language out of the diversely hued dialects and idioms he discovered everywhere around him, precisely as Dante had done. As R. P. Blackmur reminds us, a 'persona, etymologically, was something through which sounds were heard, and [only] thus a mask'.[77] Pound's personae allow him to liberate the sounds and sweet airs that modern civilisation has muted, and that will eventually constitute the native language of *The Cantos*, his own *vulgari eloquentia*.

Notes

1. This play is often cited as providing 'the frantic original of [Shakespeare's] Caliban' (qtd in Berryman, *Berryman's Shakespeare*, pp. 166–7).
2. Pound, *Poems and Translations*, p. 549. According to Leslie A. Fielder, 'the myth of the new and the West, which constitutes one-half of the main archetypal content of *The Tempest*, is quite simply the myth of America and

the Indian'; 'there seems little doubt . . . that America was on Shakespeare's mind' (*The Stranger in Shakespeare*, p. 208; p. 230). Fielder even asserts that Caliban creates 'the first American poem' with his drunken song at III, 2, 174–82 (ibid. p. 236).

3. Pound, *Poems and Translations*, p. 550.
4. Browning, *Works*, vol. IV, p. 492.
5. See pp. 40–1.
6. In his translation of Cavalcanti's eighth sonnet Pound writes: 'There's a deep voice heard whose sound in part / Turned into speech' (Pound, *Poems and Translations*, p. 200). For a discussion of the influence of this Tuscan idea on Pound see Chapter 6.
7. Strabo considers spoken language to be the original basis of the antithesis and conjectures that 'the word barbarian was first uttered onomatopoei-cally in reference to people who enunciated words only with difficulty and talked harshly and raucously, like our words "battarizein," "traulizein," and "psellizein" [stutter, lisp, speak falteringly].' He argues that even Homer employed the distinction (contradicting Thucydides on the matter). He also insists that the Greeks 'misused the word as a general ethnic term, thus making a logical distinction between the Greeks and all other races' (Strabo, *Geography*, 14.2.28).
8. The *Oxford Dictionary of English Etymology* notes that 'the primitive sense and later developments are uncertain', and points out a range of positive ('proud . . . rebellious . . . stout . . . strong . . . swift . . . violent . . . vigorous . . . luxuriant') as well as negative ('gross . . . coarse . . . offensively strong smell[ing] . . . ') meanings. This confusion parallels the complex-ity of the term 'barbarism' historically, particularly in the second half of the nineteenth century. The *Oxford English Dictionary* emphasises and enlarges this ambiguity, stating that 'the development of the word in Eng. is, however, far from clear, as the OE. uses are not quite the primitive ones'. In the context of Browning's usage it is also worth noting that 'the root-idea appears to be that of growing or shooting up . . . [being] restricted to height or length without corresponding breadth', suggesting that speech is a strange, unnatural kind of 'blossoming' for Caliban ('Rank', *Oxford Dictionary of English Etymology*; *Oxford English Dictionary*).
9. Arnold, *Culture and Anarchy*, p. 78.
10. Ibid. p. 77.
11. Morris, *Collected Letters*, vol. 2, p. 436; qtd in Karl Beckson, *London in the 1890's*, pp. xiii–xiv.
12. Beckson, *London in the 1890's*, p. xv.
13. Théophile Gautier writes already in his 'notice' to *Les Fleurs du Mal* in 1868: 'The style of decadence . . . is nothing else than art arrived at that extreme point of maturity produced by those old civilizations which are growing old with their oblique suns – a style that is ingenious, learned, full of shades of meaning and research, always pushing further the limits of lan-guage, borrowing from all the technical vocabularies, taking colours from all palettes, notes from all keyboards, forcing itself to express in thought that which is most ineffable, and in form the vaguest and most fleeting contours; listening, that it may translate them, to the subtle confidences of the neuropath, to the avowals of ageing and depraved passion, and to the

singular hallucinations of the fixed idea verging on madness. The style of decadence is the last effort of the Word, called upon to express everything, and pushed to the utmost extremity. We may remind ourselves, in connection with it, of the language of the later Roman Empire, already mottled with the greenness of decomposition, and, as it were, gamy (*faisandée*), and of the complicated refinements of the Byzantine school, the last form of Greek art fallen into deliquescence. Such is the inevitable and fatal idiom of peoples and civilizations where factitious life has replaced the natural life, and developed in man unknown wants' (qtd in R. K. R. Thornton, *The Decadent Dilemma*, p. 19).

14. Vico, *New Science*, p. 144.
15. Pound, *Poems and Translations*, p. 481.
16. Santayana, *Interpretations*, p. 104.
17. In the final analysis, Pound rejects a merely dialectical approach to historical criticism – but not yet. See pp. 171–2.
18. Santayana, *Interpretations*, p. 106.
19. Eliot, *Sacred Wood*, p. 28.
20. Eliot, *Letters*, p. xx.
21. Pound, *Spirit of Romance*, p. 8. De Nagy also traces this critical maxim to Provence, and observes that its earliest appearance in Pound's writing occurs in 'The Flame' (*Pre-Imagist Stage*, p. 41).
22. E. M. Forster, *Aspects of the Novel*, p. 9.
23. Qtd in Stock, *Life of Ezra Pound*, p. 225. In 'How to Read', Pound illustrates the point that 'the Britons have never shed barbarism' with an anecdote about the medieval Scottish Court: 'When Mary Queen of Scots went to Edinburgh she bewailed going out among savages, but she herself went from a sixteenth-century court that held but a barbarous, or rather driveling and idiotic and superficial travesty of the Italian culture as it had been before the debacle of 1527. The men who tried to civilize these shaggy and uncouth marginalians by bringing them news of civilization have left a certain number of translations that are better reading today than are the works of the ignorant islanders who were too proud to translate' (Pound, *Literary Essays*, p. 35). He has in mind Gavin Douglas, a poet noted (at least to Pound's readers) for his 'living tongue' (Pound, *Selected Prose*, p. 462).
24. North, *Dialectic of Modernism*, p. 82.
25. Ibid. p. 80.
26. Qtd in ibid. p. 80.
27. Santayana, *Poetry and Religion*, p. 107.
28. The shared emphasis on images is misleading, however. For Pound, images in poetry are neither indiscriminate nor opulent; Santayana would seem to have in mind the prosy expansiveness of Whitman rather than the intense concentration and contraction of *les Imagistes*.
29. For Aristotle, 'diction becomes distinguished and non-prosaic by the uses of unfamiliar terms, i.e. strange words, metaphors, lengthened forms, and everything that deviates from the ordinary modes of speech. – But a whole statement in such terms will either be a riddle or a barbarism, a riddle, if made up of metaphors, a barbarism, if made up of strange words' (Aristotle, *Poetics*, p. 1478; §22). Aristotle is quick to point out that he

does not simply mean reasonably unfamiliar words whose meanings are not precisely known by laymen, but γλωττα, 'expressions unknown in the language of common life' (ibid. p. 1479; §22). Such unknown words have an acoustic rather than denotational primacy for auditors: they are heard and are not – or not immediately and effortlessly – understood. The advantage of verse that incorporates such obscure material is precisely that it lends a literary quality: 'These, the strange word, the metaphor, the ornamental equivalent, &c., will save the language from seeming mean and prosaic, while the ordinary words in it will secure the requisite clearness' (ibid. p. 1478; §22).

30. North, *Dialectic of Modernism*, p. 82.
31. This is Santayana here, and he seems to have in mind a modern perversion of Longinus's famous definition of sublime art.
32. Jackson, *Early Poetry*, p. 137.
33. Pound, *Poems and Translations*, p. 16.
34. Ibid. p. 33.
35. Whitman, *Poetry and Prose*, p. 87; p. 247.
36. Santayana, *Poetry and Religion*, p. 108.
37. Pound, *Selected Letters*, p. 11.
38. He offers a neat soritic explanation of how to proceed from the 'yeowl and the bark . . . at last to the poem' in 'The Serious Artist' (Pound, *Literary Essays*, p. 51).
39. Pound, *Poems and Translations*, p. 33; l. 18. Pound seems to allude to 'la fortunata valle' of *Inferno XXXI* rather than Shakespeare, however.
40. Pound, *Poems and Translations*, p. 34.
41. Poe, *Spirits of the Dead*, pp. 92–3; l. 10; ll. 42–4.
42. De Nagy's formulation of Pound's conception of the author's hieratic communion with a select audience of initiates, mentioned in Chapter 3, is useful here also: 'The "We"—the poets—represent the active, progressive principle, who sacrifice their personal happiness in order to increase the sum of beauty on earth' (de Nagy, *Pre-Imagist Stage*, p. 39).
43. 'Carmelite', *New Catholic Encyclopedia*.
44. Pound, *Poems and Translations*, p. 34.
45. Ibid. p. 34.
46. Ibid. p. 47.
47. Ibid. p. 50.
48. Ibid. p. 76.
49. Ibid. p. 86.
50. Pound, *Literary Essays*, p. 11.
51. Dante, *Inferno, Canto VI*, p. 29. This is Longfellow's translation.
52. De Nagy, *Pre-Imagist Stage*, p. 27; p. 28.
53. For Eliot, the Mythical Method refers specifically to James Joyce's 'way of controlling, of ordering, of giving a shape and a significance to the immense panorama of futility and anarchy which is contemporary history' by 'manipulating a continuous parallel between contemporaneity and antiquity' (Eliot, 'Ulysses, Order, and Myth', pp. 480–3). In Pound, perhaps, the parallel is less continuous than in Joyce, but it is virtually ubiquitous and often several textual layers deep, as in this rich example.
54. Pound, *Poems and Translations*, p. 31.

55. Grieve, *Early Poetry*, p. 38.
56. Pound, *Selected Letters*, p. 39.
57. Qtd in Gibson, *Epic Reinvented*, p. 70.
58. A prose note on 'The Tradition' elaborates upon this criticism in the same terms: 'My purpose in all this is to suggest to the casual reader that the Middle Ages did not exist in the tapestry alone, nor in the fourteenth-century romances, but that there was a life like our own, no mere sequence of citherns and citoles, nor a continuous stalking about in sendal and diaper. Men were pressed for money. There was unspeakable boredom in the castles' (Pound, *Literary Essays*, p. 101).
59. Pound, *Poems and Translations*, p. 31.
60. The sense seems to be that Browning's verse is anthropocentric or humane in some primal fashion, that it *leads towards mankind*, as it were ('leanin' man-kin'ards'). There may also be a suggestion that his characters are diminutive, puny, suffering beings. The word 'mankin' can be used in both senses, and tends, in Browning's 'Caliban Upon Setebos', towards the latter. The barbarian poet is such a diminutive figure, reduced but nonetheless capable of vivid and incisive human observation. 'Pants', presumably, offers a pneumatic pun.
61. D'Agapeyeff, *Codes and Ciphers*, p. 16.
62. On this understanding, the title of the poem, 'Mesmerism', has perhaps as much to do with Yeats's famous theory of poetic rhythm, where he emphasises the hypnotic qualities of rhythm, as with Browning's poem of that name. Cf. 'The purpose of Rhythm, it has always seemed to me, is to prolong the moment of contemplation, the moment when we are both asleep and awake, which is the one moment of creation, by hushing us with an alluring monotony, while it holds us waking by variety, to keep us in that state of perhaps real trance, in which the mind liberated from the pressure of the will is unfolded in symbols. If certain sensitive persons listen persistently to the ticking of a watch, or gaze persistently on the monotonous flashing of a light, they fall into hypnotic trance; and rhythm is but the ticking of a watch made softer, that one must needs listen, and various, that one may not be swept beyond memory or grow weary of listening; while the patterns of the artist are but the monotonous flash woven to the eye in subtler attachment' (Yeats, *Essays and Introductions*, p. 159). Pound explodes Yeats's hypnotic moment in this poem.
63. Cf. 'Dante's hendecasyllables were composed in combinations of rhythm units of various shapes and sizes and . . . these pieces were put together in lines so as to make, roughly, eleven syllables in all. I say "roughly" because of the liberties allowed in elision' (Pound, 'Cavalcanti', *Literary Essays*, pp. 169–70). Cf. D. S. Carne-Ross, 'New Metres for Old' for a discussion of the bearing of Greek prosody on Pound (qtd in Sullivan, *Ezra Pound*, p. 347).
64. Qtd in Gibson, *Epic Reinvented*, p. 61.
65. Cf. Stark, 'Keep[ing] Up the Fire'.
66. His occasional references are, however, quite telling. In the Ur-Canto that begins by invoking Robert Browning, for example, Pound refers admiringly to *Pericles*.
67. Shakespeare, *The Tempest*, I, ii, 331–4.

68. Cf. 'French preserves, as Greek did, many diphthongs, which are natural to *a barbarous tongue still stiff and inept at combining consonants with vowels*' (Vico, *New Science*, p. 66; emphasis added).
69. Kenner, *Pound Era*, p. 86; p. 85.
70. Shakespeare, *The Tempest*, I, ii, 362–3.
71. W. B. Yeats's poem 'The Mask' dates from August 1910 according to Daniel Albright, but the doctrine that informs it had been formulating in Yeats's mind for some time beforehand, certainly in 1908 as the initial entries in his journal make clear (Yeats, *Poems*, p. 144; *Memoirs*, p. 138). Pound did not meet Yeats until 1909.
72. A nod to Swinburne's reincarnation of Villon, surely.
73. Pound, *Poems and Translations*, p. 45.
74. These directions occur in Act III, iii. Whether they are Shakespeare's own, or the scrivener Ralph Crane's, is a matter of some critical controversy. On the matter of stage directions in *The Tempest* Leslie A. Fielder offers an invaluable insight: 'The word "strange" appears everywhere in *The Tempest*, not only in the speeches of the shipwrecked Neapolitans but in the stage directions as well: "strange drowsiness", "strange beast", "*strange music*", "*strange Shapes*", "strange stare", "strange story" – all culminating in Alonso's description of Caliban: "This is a strange thing as e'er I looked on"' (Fielder, *The Stranger in Shakespeare*, p. 239).
75. Cf. 'the sources of all poetic locution are two: the poverty of language and need to explain and be understood' (Vico, *New Science*, p. 22).
76. Pound, *Poems and Translations*, p. 242.
77. Qtd in Sullivan, *Ezra Pound*, p. 145.

Chapter 5

'The Seafarer' and a 'Living Tongue'

With the publication of *Ripostes* in 1912, Pound embarked on what is often regarded as the most compelling and revolutionary period of his career. He effects a change in his idiom, slowly and, I believe, temporarily, veering away from his reliance on a whole spectrum of poeticisms. The immediate impulse for this dramatic about-turn was Ford Madox Hueffer's famous reception of the poet in July 1911. Pound recalled the incident in his 1939 obituary for the poet and novelist. Ford Maddox Ford, as Hueffer was known by this point,

> felt the errors of contemporary style to the point of rolling (physically, and if you look at it as mere superficial snob, ridiculously) on the floor of his temporary quarters in Giessen when my third volume displayed me trapped, fly-papered, gummed and strapped down in a jejune provincial effort to learn, *mehercule*, the stilted language that passed for 'good English' in the arthritic milieu that held control of the respected British critical circles . . . that roll saved me at least two years, perhaps more. It sent me back to my own proper effort, namely, toward using the living tongue.[1]

This passage deserves particular attention because of the significance that has been ascribed to it, by both Pound and his critics. The first thing to note is that, in retrospect, Pound found his earlier style to be erroneous, to have gone somehow astray. We have noted his preening of *Personae*, striking out its 'stale creampuffs', already. The apparently mitigating fact is that the author of these early volumes could not freely choose his language; it was somehow almost compulsory. This is an odd claim given what we have discovered so far: whatever else his early poems demonstrate, they show Pound searching somewhat diligently for *le mot juste*, discerning uncommon meanings, and discriminating carefully between connotations, etymologies and sounds. True, the search was not always a fruitful one; in many instances the language he settles upon remains too extrinsic to the experience it is supposed to arise out of and articulate, but the trajectory is clear: Pound refuses to settle for received 'good English' and is casting about in literary tradition, foreign idiom and forgotten history for alternatives.

Nevertheless, in 1939 Pound recognised what his critics had long suspected: that, for all his dedication to rare beauty, he was heavily indentured to the literary jargon of the *fin de siècle*. His counter-thrust, in *Ripostes*, is directed squarely at this literary mode. The terms he uses to deprecate his apprentice work are as precise as ever. Georgian poetry remains 'provincial' – limited and petty – in some measure because of its erudition and its stylised qualities.[2] The terms 'stilted' and 'jejune' emphasise the vapidity that inheres in his too lofty speech, its lack of substance. This description helps us to understand why Pound ultimately attached so much significance to Hueffer's reaction: it epitomised the kind of embodied, humane communication that his early verse often failed to produce. Hueffer's hilarious roll was primate-ive, material and articulate: the *res* and not merely the *verba*.

One final point about this obituary: we need to observe the chronology that Pound invokes here. Ford Madox Hueffer's rolling laugh does not launch the poet directly into the modernist poems of *Lustra* that began to appear five years later. Some of these poems, to be sure, were written shortly afterwards, appearing in late 1912, for example in the November number of *Poetry* and the December issue of *Smart Set*.[3] On the whole, the poems he composed and published in the year or so following Hueffer's antics show some of these transparent, modern qualities, but also stubbornly persist in his familiar jargon-ish ways. Onerous difficulty and extreme simplicity are juxtaposed, often rudely, in the poet's art of this decade. Rather than transforming Pound into a modernist or a Realist, it seems fairer to stick to the poet's own assessment of this transformative event: it simply led him to what he calls his 'own proper effort, namely, toward using the living tongue'.[4]

Stopping to consider more exactly what Pound means by 'the living tongue', we may well begin by distinguishing it from the 'dead language, dialects of books, dialects of Lionel Johnson, etc.' that Hueffer often cautioned against.[5] Some kind of animism, equivalent perhaps to Hueffer's great roll, is required if language is to become vital and poetic. At the same time, however, we find that 'the living tongue' is clearly not the same thing as naturalistic, everyday speech, as some critics have supposed. In 'I Gather the Limbs of Osiris', which began appearing in instalments from 30 November 1911, four months after Hueffer's dive, Pound offers the following qualification:

> We must have simplicity and directness of utterance, which is different from the simplicity and directness of daily speech, which is more 'curial', more dignified. This difference, this dignity, cannot be conferred by florid adjectives or elaborate hyperbole; it must be conveyed by art, and by the art of verse structure, by something which exalts the reader, making him feel that he is in contact with something arranged more finely than the commonplace.[6]

This definition of poetry is, to my mind, the most enduring that Pound devised. It serves equally well for his early efforts, for the direct simplicity of *Cathay*, for the concentrated Imagist poems of *Lustra*, the chiselled quatrains of *Mauberley* and the ranging organic bulk of *The Cantos*. I will return to this definition on several occasions in what follows, therefore, especially to the formalist notion that poetry may be thought of in 'curial' terms. Crucially, the poet does not abandon the aesthetics of jargon he had been pursuing up until now, but tweaks it. Meet arrangement and order supplant mere technique, and are judged according to their capacity to demarcate life in all its intensity. 'Daily speech' does not suffice for poetry because it is often insufficiently alert to the intensities of life – often, in fact, spoken language is merely phatic, inconsequential and effectively dead language. The poet's task is, on this understanding, essentially a formal resuscitation, with all the pneumatic and sonic implications this implies; 'by art, and by the art of verse structure', Pound hoped to breathe new life into the husks of ordinary language.

Pound's celebrated, and notorious, translation of the Anglo-Saxon poem 'The Seafarer' illustrates this crucial point. It is widely acknowledged to be central (rather than peripheral or prefatory) to Pound's poetic achievement; Georg M. Gugelberger, for example, describes it, along with Canto I, as representing 'Pound's poetics in a nutshell'.[7] Pound himself encouraged this view, describing it in a note to *Umbra* (1920) as 'a major persona'. At the same time, this poem stands as the culmination and vindication of Pound's early experiments with poetic jargon. The poem is, without contradiction, written in 'the living tongue' and yet also constituted by a dense and foreboding jargon. It keenly illustrates just how fundamental jargon can be to the most authentically human acts of communication. The speaker of this Old English lyric finds himself cut off from all the things that give meaning to his existence, and his lamentations find expression in a forlorn language that embodies this situation. Pound successfully finds a means of expressing the speaker's isolation, his removal from the familiar currents of life, and his estrangement from habitual and phatic discourse by subjecting the language his contemporaries knew – both everyday language and poetic language – to some quite extraordinary acts of violence. Pound did not so much abandon jargon, therefore, as learn to discriminate more finely between circumstances capable of legitimately producing it.

'The Seafarer' is included in both *Ripostes* (1912) and *Cathay* (1915). Its inclusion in the latter volume ought to challenge the assumption of critics who would see this as Pound's liminal volume, wherein he finally sloughs off his prior affectations and becomes modern. In *A Guide to Ezra Pound's* Selected Poems, an introductory companion to Pound's verse oriented towards the new student, Christine Froula offers a typical response, remarking that Pound's 'strange language, to a new reader, might itself seem to need translation'.[8] This is true to some extent of much of Pound's poetry, as I have been suggesting. This candid remark demonstrates just how mind-boggling his jargoning can be. The new reader who experiences the desire to tame and familiarise such a foreign, poetic utterance realises (as more advanced readers sometimes forget) that poetry is qualitatively different from ordinary speech. Crucially, however, Pound would always and emphatically side with the student rather than the expert on this point. The beginning of 'The Seafarer' is as opaque as anything Pound composed:

> May I for my own self song's truth reckon,
> Journey's jargon, how I in harsh days
> Hardship endured oft.
> Bitter breast-cares have I abided,
> Known on my keel many a care's hold,
> And dire sea-surge, and there I oft spent
> Narrow nightwatch nigh the ship's head
> While she tossed close to the cliffs.[9]

Hugh Kenner describes this beginning as exhibiting 'consonantal structures like rocks', which force us to hear each 'craggy monosyllable . . . one at a time'.[10] The difficulty arises from the syntactical confusion in the first line and from the taut sound patterning, which throttles expression, spectacularly de-lyricising the poem in the conventional sense. Pound's translation thus begins by foregrounding the existential and communicative impasse reached by the speaker, something he will try throughout the poem to overcome.

What appears in most translations as a simple statement of the author's purport to deal faithfully with the events of his life, here becomes a rather cryptic invocation asking for the power of self-honesty, to evaluate and finally set down the speaker's song of himself. As the next lines suggest, the difficulty posed by his solipsism makes it necessary that the Seafarer discover just the right kind of language to articulate this experience. Medievalists have not been oblivious to this detail, though they have tended not to credit Pound with adding this important nuance to our understanding of the original. In 'Genre(s) in the Making: *The Seafarer*', for example, John Miles Foley explains that

> for the Seafarer himself, the tale is individually told, grounded in and
>   quickened by subjective experience:
>   Mæg ic be me sylfum   soðgied wrecan,
> or, as Burton Raffel translates:
>   This tale is true and mine.[11]

John C. Pope attributes the discovery of the intensity of the theme of solitude to Pound, citing the relevant special sense of the Anglo-Saxon word *sylf* used in the original: the speaker's unique experience and form of expression do not simply distinguish him from others, but cause him to be quite alone and without fellows.[12] Pound decides, probably correctly, that the sort of language required of the Seafarer is bound to amount to a kind of 'jargon', in the first place because of the singular nature of his experience, and second, because, in the remoteness of his extreme wretchedness, the speaker finds the cries of the seabirds more urgent, and more authentic, than their human counterpart. Composing his 'self song' presents the speaker with a dilemma (making invocation necessary), the solution of which is the discovery of a unique 'journey's jargon'. Pound presents the best lyric poetry as a conjunction of personal experience and the private language that results from it.[13] Henceforth for Pound, poetry will always involve articulation in this double sense. Poetic language cannot be produced by habitual associations, nor is it sanctified by grammarian or expert; it is a means of orientation in the living world, homespun, whittled from life itself. The tortured jargon that Pound settles upon here is legitimised by the special significance of the word 'wrecan' in the original: it literally means 'to "drive out" words'.[14] When (in the passage from 'I Gather the Limbs of Osiris' already cited) Pound calls for 'simplicity and directness of utterance, which is different from the simplicity and directness of daily speech', he is making an analogous point: to utter means in the first instance to *issue forth* goods or wares for sale; the common idea, perhaps, is the making public of something that is privately held or owned.[15]

As Chapter 1 demonstrates, Pound was certainly aware of the ambivalence of the term jargon, and he exploits its full range of meaning in this poem.[16] Having utilised the concept throughout his apprentice work, he announces his commitment to the concept as a poetic principle in this poem. The opening of Pound's 'Seafarer' makes use of the range of meanings of 'jargon' in order to make the untenable situation of the speaker abundantly clear (despite the fact that the original lines do not necessarily license this poetic embellishment): Pound makes the poem a vehicle of his own, by now well-established, aesthetic. The word offers a neat poetic contraction of the thematic concerns of the speaker, and performs an important structural role, too, anticipating the symbolic bird-cries that will shortly resound in the Seafarer's imagination. In the following lines from the original, the hemistich 'siþas secgan' corresponds to what Pound gives as 'journey's jargon':

> Mæg ic be me sylfum   soðgied wrecan,
> siþas secgan,   hu ic geswincdagum
> earfoðhwile   oft þrowade . . .

Pound captures the initial alliterative sound as well as the internal rhyme between the second hemistich of the first line and the first hemistich of the second: 'wrecan' / 'secgan' becomes 'reckon' / 'jargon'. This internal rhyme is, strictly speaking, not required prosodically, but the Seafarer-poet (like Pound) typically indulges in such virtuosic, cantabile gamesmanship. To produce a translation with this lyric condensation and the power to convey both the sense and the sound of the original is vindication enough for Pound's continuing 'offenses against the spoken idiom'.[17]

At the most basic level, the idiom Pound creates for this translation responds to the acoustic properties of Old English as well as the thematic concerns of the poem. Pound reconfigures English into a remote but intensely personal language tethered to the arduous experiences of medieval seafaring. If the language is occasionally affected or stiff, this should be understood to result from the duress under which the language comes into being. Certainly, the original poem would have appeared in the same light to its original audience. Following the lead of Milman Parry's Homeric studies, scholars have been intrigued by the density and distribution of conventional poeticisms in 'The Seafarer'. Jackson J. Campbell, for example, provides a valuable empirical study of formulaic phrases and cola in the poem, and distinguishes three basic types of poeticism, each of which belies the oral nature of the poem's authorship or subsequent composition. The dominant poeticisms consist of: formulae that 'appear in more than one poem' (he identifies fifty-six); 'poetic words which do not appear in Old English prose' (he identifies thirty-five); and *hapex legomena*, or unique instances of a word's usage, which he divides into (a) compounds 'formed in a particularly poetic way, or favoured by poets and not prose writers' and (b) 'sole survivors, common at one time, preserved in poetry as archaisms' (he identifies twenty-one instances in total).[18] According to Campbell's analysis, then, the idiom of the original 'Seafarer' is considerably removed from the language of its audience, and indeed constitutes a kind of arcane lore that derives its immediacy and potency from this strangeness, which forces the hearer or reader to grapple with its powerful acoustic and rhythmical qualities. It thus amounts to a kind of poetic jargon. More recent critics largely concur with Campbell's conclusions. Foley contends that

> the phraseological texture of *The Seafarer* is not simply the smooth surface which we have come to expect (and therefore to demand) as the basis of such fully literary genres as the English novel or the Horatian ode, but rather a kind of phraseological patois formed by a combination of diverse elements.[19]

The original poem is remarkable for its rough texture and its unique assemblage of motley literary constituents. Pound emphasised this aspect of the poem in his remarks on it in 'I Gather the Limbs of Osiris', claiming to have 'given evidence that fine poetry may consist in elements that are or seem to be almost mutually exclusive' with his translation.[20] Thus 'The Seafarer' anticipates the rhapsodic qualities of modern literary jargoning, the capacity to federate diverse elements that so intrigues Gilles Deleuze. One crucial feature of this assortment is that the poem has an already-embodied relationship with literary tradition – it is archaic per se, quite apart from Pound's tinkering with antiquated language. This will prove to be a decisive discovery for Pound, as we shall see in Chapter 7.

Campbell finds an exponentially greater proportion of poeticisms in the first thirty-eight lines than in the last sixty, which he takes to be an indication that more than one style – and consequently more than one author – is discoverable in the text we now have. It is a polyvocal text. The concentration of these effects in the first lines can readily be appreciated in the statistical summary Campbell provides: '20 formulaic hemistiches, or one for each 1.9 lines; 18 exclusively poetic words; 13 hapex legomena', as well as no exclusively prosaic words. 'Those passages which several generations of modern readers have valued as truly great poetry', Campbell concludes, surely with Pound and his defenders in mind, 'are those which contain the highest incidence of poetic conventions'.[21] This is remarkable in the context of Pound's struggle with convention, and suggests an abiding interest in poeticisms despite the radical departure his famous/notorious translation would seem to entail. The most precious part of the poem roughly corresponds to what Pound designated as the first section of three, 'The Trials of the Sea'.[22] For Campbell, these oddities are the result of an oral poet elaborating a wealth of traditional phrases into his own expressive shape: their unfamiliarity for the intended audience is conditional upon their survival as expedient metrical paradigms in the poet's – and the tradition's

– memory. This is exactly the sensibility that the modernists cultivated. The disorientation, the feeling of being out of place in one's own language, arises from the assiduity of the poet's labour and his fluency in traditional literary jargons.

As if to consolidate the poetic density of this section of the original, Pound strews his first description of the poem's seabirds with an array of poeticisms:

> Hung with hard ice-flakes, where hail-scur flew,
> There I heard naught save the harsh sea
> And ice-cold wave, at whiles the swan cries,
> Did for my games the gannet's clamour,
> Sea-fowls' loudness was for me laughter,
> The mews singing all my mead-drink.
> Storms, on the stone-cliffs beaten, fell on the stern
> In icy feathers; full oft the eagle screamed
> With spray on his pinion.[23]

The alliteration, Pound's typically grave spondees, and the consonantal congestion and resolution, make this among the noisiest seas, these the noisiest birds, in English literature. In fact, a strong case can be made that these lines derive prosodically from Pound's experiments with Swinburne as much as from a direct encounter with the Anglo-Saxon. De Nagy's analysis of Pound's leaning on Swinburne's metric already points in this direction: 'alliteration is one part of the double principle on which Swinburne's verses are composed', he explains: 'the accent laid on the stressed syllables of the – mostly anapestic-spondaic – verses is extremely heavy and produces a certain "blurring" of the unstressed ones'.[24] The compound words add to the elements' irresistible effect – the Seafarer's language congeals into craggy, tight-knit structures and succumbs under the force of the 'ice-flakes', 'hail-scur' and 'ice-cold' waves around him, his language seeming to ossify and freeze in its very utterance. Janet Bately observes that this first section of the original is written largely in the past tense, further heightening the sense of stagnancy by delineating only completed events and by emphasising the habitual nature of certain of the actions.[25] The poet supplies a memorable figure for this stagnation: in line five, the Seafarer's body is viewed as the embattled keel of a vessel trapped in sheets of deadening ice, and the linguistic contraction develops the metaphor. Not only is his person encrypted, his language is too.

This torpid state is alleviated only by the shrieks and cries of a chorus of skirling seabirds. Interestingly enough, this is one point in the translation where Pound departs from his controversial policy of acoustic fidelity to the original. The Anglo-Saxon word used of the swan's sound is, in fact, 'song'. As we will continue to note, Pound typically refers to bird-sound not in a musical or effusive way, but as a hideous crying, just as it appears to the Seafarer. Birds rarely sing in his writing, but remain speakers of an execrable, inhuman language. In 'The Seafarer', this is the very reason for their appeal: the speaker is utterly outcast (both words mean substantially the same) from humanity. His 'living tongue' is the solipsistic speech of a friendless margin-alien. The mere fact of the seabirds' vocality registers so powerfully with the Seafarer that after the punctuation of the 'swan's cries', he imagines each sharing in the pageantry of a 'gold-giving lord . . . like those gone':[26] the 'gannet's clamour' seems to him the vociferation of his fellows at sport, the 'sea-fowls' attend upon this sport with earnest jocularity, and the mews' brimming cries supply the toast. Foley identifies this passage as an example of the 'joy in the hall' *theme* or *cluster*, found in much Old English verse.[27] He argues that

> there can be no doubt that the poet is employing this paradigm to convey a sense of desolation and loss, and he is doing so in a brilliant and affecting manner by making the fullest use of an element of traditional diction . . . For the Seafarer poet, master of his medium, the cluster offers a way of evoking or 'accessing' a system of values at once ephemeral and uncontemporary.[28]

The Anglo-Saxon 'Seafarer' anticipates the modernist notion of literature as an assemblage of traditional texts brought to bear upon the present by the agency of the poet. The notion of controlling 'access' to these traditional texts, and hence to experiences and even values themselves, is the necessary concomitant of the lyrical opacity Pound discovered in Villon and Cavalcanti, among others. Moreover, Foley realises that this heterogeneous and even fragmentary strategy provides a valid indication of 'desolation and loss' experienced by the speaker. This is one of the most telling ways in which 'The Seafarer' becomes a modern poem: it suggests the directions in which poetic form and diction may have to go to accommodate the desolation of a modern waste land.

The poet must slough off that part of language which is habitual and automatic and rely on sense and the imagination to negotiate an authentic relationship with such a world, and this is exactly what we see in the Seafarer's fantasy. However, at just the moment when this illusion reaches its apex, where the seabirds seem to provide some comfort with their 'singing', the vision proves to be unsustainable:

Storms, on the stone-cliffs beaten, fell on the stern
In icy feathers; full oft the eagle screamed
With spray on his pinion.[29]

The sea eagle proves the loudest and keenest of seabirds, and its scream provides a concrete and frightening crescendo to the first movement of the poem. Pound seems to be relying (as is his customary practice) on the earliest usages of his language here: the word 'scream' initially refers to a high-pitched, piercing noise that is expressive of pain, or other sudden emotion; it is also etymologically related to 'weep'.[30] In Old English, moreover, the word is already used in a special sense for the cries of certain birds. His translation therefore works, much as the original poem works, by inviting informed readers to consider the philological sense of the language in addition to the contemporary and habitual senses; supplementing the meaning in a recondite and condensed fashion, it offers 'access' to an unfamiliar but still significant realm of meaning. At the same time, of course, this word is aptly onomatopoeic, and so claims our attention as jargon in the manifold sense.

Although we may read this first sequence of the poem as a literal depiction of the Seafarer's voyaging, the keel/body metaphor established in the first few lines lends itself to figurative interpretation. When the Seafarer again encounters these central and highly evocative sounds and images, at any rate, his feet are firmly planted on the ground.[31] As he harkens to the seabirds that reach his native shores in springtime, 'longing comes upon him to fare forth on the water':

> Bosque taketh blossom, cometh beauty of berries,
> Fields to fairness, land fares brisker,
> All this admonisheth man eager of mood,
> The heart turns to travel so that he then thinks
> On flood-ways to be far departing.
> Cuckoo calleth with gloomy crying,
> He singeth summerward, bodeth sorrow,
> The bitter heart's blood.[32]

The part of the poem focusing thus on 'the Lure [of the sea]' makes up what Pound terms the second section.[33] If Pound's jargon captures the maritime suffering of the Seafarer in the first section, it is equally capable of articulating his longing to return to sea in the second.

Another thing that comes across vividly in this section is Pound's consistency in employing archaic forms of English in order to inflect the language with an appropriate degree of outlandishness. The 'eth' ending adheres particularly (though not exclusively) to the speech of the birds here: they 'calleth', 'singeth', 'bodeth', etc. Pound uses this suffix consistently for the Old English suffix *að*, and in effect allows the birds to address a modern English speaker in a familiar, yet strange and portentous, manner. The same cries that both horrified and strangely comforted the speaker while seafaring make him long to return to those bittersweet maritime tribulations:

> On earth's shelter cometh often to me,
> Eager and ready, the crying lone-flyer,
> Whets for the whale-path the heart irresistibly,
> O'er tracks of ocean.[34]

In fact, the symbolism ties the first two sections of the poem thematically: like this avian messenger, the speaker's yearning is the same whether on land or at sea. Furthermore, the parallel between these passages suggests that Campbell's statistics are open to another, fascinating, interpretation. Campbell omits discussion of these central lines in the second section of the poem, where the birdcalls are mentioned for the last time, because they do not appear consistent with the diminished reliance on poeticisms that dominates that section of the poem. This feature may be explained by an alternative hypothesis; namely, that the dense use of poeticisms is designed primarily to complement and indeed approximate the birds' jargon in these crucial scenes.[35] These severe sounds come closest to lyrical expression in the far-flung world of the Seafarer.

Alliterative verse is an ideal medium in which to explore this overlapping of the two primary senses of jargon. Pound's success in the poem is in no small part due to his dexterous handling of this form, as T. S. Eliot pointed out in 'Ezra Pound: His Metric and Poetry'. Eliot claims that Pound attains the same 'rough, stern beauty of the Anglo-Saxon':

> It is not a slight achievement to have brought to life alliterative verse: perhaps *The Seafarer* is the only successful piece of alliterative verse ever written in modern English; alliterative verse which is not merely a clever tour de force, but which suggests the possibilities of a new development of the form.[36]

As Eliot was quick to realise, Pound's example of alliterative verse was one of the factors that contributed to the demise of traditional accentual syllabic form in the twentieth century. The medial caesura of the Old English line in the first place allowed Pound '[t]o break the pentameter' line.[37] Having done so, the alliterating rhythmical phrases that are the basis of Anglo-Saxon prosody, free of the requirements of metrical feet and the usually iambic gambol of accentual-syllabic verse, lend themselves to free-verse composition as much as to alliterative application, and this may be what Eliot has in mind here when he notes that Pound's experiment presents 'the possibilities of a new development of . . . form'. By 1917, when Eliot published this essay, Pound had already made a first draft of 'Three Cantos of a Poem of Some Length' that exhibit these tendencies; his subsequent revisions make good on the promise.

In the passages detailing the cries of the birds, the consonantal alliteration is elevated to greater onomatopoeic heights by the concentration of vowels that, in several lines, are almost as central prosodically as the consonants. Ordinarily in Anglo-Saxon verse, of course, vowels rhyme with each other; in practice, this amounts to a more or less incidental effect, the greater part of the labour falling on the selection of stressed consonants. In Pound's translation of 'The Seafarer', however, vowels are arranged meticulously and suggestively. To try to illustrate this, I have underlined the primary (structural or prosodic) alliteration that, strictly speaking, only falls on stressed syllables, and italicised what I perceive to be secondary vowel alliteration in the lines below:

> *Sea*-fowls, loudness was for m*e* laughter [l. 21]
> Cuckoo calleth with gloomy crying [l. 53]
> *Eager* and ready   the crying lone-flyer [l. 62][38]

In these examples, the vowel-clusters function with similar structural integrity, and regulate the line as palpably, as the consonants. Again, this probably has everything to do with Pound's ongoing study of Cavalcanti and the complex verse forms of the troubadours, and very little to do with Anglo-Saxon. The arrangement is more particular than would arise on the assumption that all vowels rhyme with each other, and Pound evidently discriminates, for instance, between the hard *e* sound in the first line, the long *oo* sound in the second and the *y* (or *ai*) sound in the third example. Doing so, he impressively refutes the mistaken belief that only the two stresses in the hemistich matter in Old English alliterative verse. This is more than mere pedantry: Pound needs the gamut of vowel sounds to articulate and discriminate the cries of the seabirds around him and to accommodate it to the rasping, screeching sound of the Seafarer's frigid language. He needs this range to achieve such an intense jargon. When 'the vowel and consonantal melody or sequence seems truly to bear the trace of emotion which the poem . . . is intended to communicate', Pound writes in 'The Serious Artist', we really are dealing with genuine poetry, and not some inferior thing.[39] What makes this verse-composition poetic is precisely the articulation of subject matter and emotion, supplied by prosodic features like this.

Ford Madox Hueffer may well have been pleased with the sensual and aural qualities of the poetry he helped inspire, but he could not have foreseen how critical Pound's earlier impulse towards the conventionally poetic and arcane would be in this endeavour. Pound would not be made into a Realist, now or subsequently, but in this translation he discovered that the relationship between language and the world from which it draws veracity is complicated and reciprocal. He escaped being 'trapped, fly-papered, gummed and strapped down' by the conventional language of his contemporaries by subjecting himself to the more rigorous (and intrinsically poetic) limitations of minutely conceived and more intensely imagined situations. A decade later, Pound was still more convinced of this fact, writing to Felix Schelling, for example, that 'all that is left is exiled, driven in catacombs, exists in the isolated individual, who occasionally meets one other with a scrap of it concealed in his person'.[40] The Seafarer's experience of exile becomes the archetypal literary position in modernism, in opposition to the idea of an easy fellowship of speakers sharing pedestrian thought in a comfortably collective language. Furthermore, the lesson of 'The Seafarer' suggests that for poetic language to become meaningful and quick, it must pass through a more precarious state, tottering between meaning and banality, music and silence.

Notes

1. Pound, *Selected Prose*, p. 462.
2. See p. 101, n. 23. Pound routinely associates provincialism ('which rewards not the best work . . . but the best local work') with elite culture ('Pastiche, The Regional', *The New Age* 12; qtd in Stock, *Life of Ezra Pound*, p. 225).
3. Cf. Stock, *Life of Ezra Pound*, pp. 143–4.
4. Pound, *Selected Prose*, p. 462.
5. Pound, *Letters*, p. 178.
6. Pound, *Selected Prose*, p. 41.
7. Qtd in Robinson, 'The Might of the North', p. 199.
8. Froula, *Guide*, p. 35.
9. Pound, *Poems and Translations*, p. 236; ll. 1–8.
10. Kenner, *Pound Era*, p. 92.
11. Foley, 'Genre(s) in the Making', pp. 702–3.
12. John C. Pope, 'Second Thoughts on the Interpretation of "The Seafarer"', p. 79.
13. In his prefatory note to 'The Seafarer', Pound refers to the poem as 'the finest of the Old-English lyrics', and he continued to esteem it greatly, writing in 1934 that 'there are passages of Anglo-Saxon as good as paragraphs of the Seafarer, but I have not found any whole poem of the same value' (Pound, *ABC of Reading*, p. 52).
14. Foley, 'Genre(s) in the Making', p. 683.
15. Pound, *Selected Prose*, p. 41; cf. 'Utter', *Oxford English Dictionary*.
16. To my knowledge the term occurs only one further time in Pound's verse, in Canto LXVIII, where it is associated with foreign language and incomprehensible, because unclear, language: 'here again the french jargon / not one clear idea what they mean by / "all authority"' (Pound, *The Cantos*, p. 396).

17. Grieve, *Early Poetry and Poetics*, p. 38.
18. Campbell, 'Oral Poetry in *The Seafarer*', p. 91.
19. Foley, 'Genre(s) in the Making', p. 693.
20. Pound, *Selected Prose*, p. 26.
21. Campbell, 'Oral Poetry in *The Seafarer*', p. 94.
22. Pound, *Poems and Translations*, p. 1275, n. 236; 1.1.
23. Ibid. pp. 236–7; ll. 18–25.
24. De Nagy, *Pre-Imagist Stage*, p. 77.
25. Bately, 'Time and the Passing of Time'.
26. Pound, *Poems and Translations*, p. 238; l. 83.
27. The term was introduced, however, by Jeff Opland in 'Beowulf on the Poet'.
28. Foley, 'Genre(s) in the Making', p. 691.
29. Pound, *Poems and Translations*, p. 237; ll. 23–5. These lines include an interesting crux: Pound's proffering of 'Stern' has been regarded variously as a howler and meet poetic licence. Many translators prefer *tern*, the seabird. The fact of the matter seems to be that there is little consensus about the original – as Margaret E. Goldsmith has argued, 'even at the time when scientific bird-study begins [c. 1660s] there is considerable obscurity round the nature of birds who go by that name in England' ('The Seafarer and the Birds', p. 233). Fred C. Robinson's essay '"The Might of the North": Pound's Anglo-Saxon Studies and "The Seafarer"' remains the best account of these controversial cruces, and Robinson is both staunch and persuasive in defending the thesis that 'Pound's version is the product of a serious engagement with the Anglo-Saxon text, not of casual guessing at Anglo-Saxon words and of passing off personal prejudices as Anglo-Saxon poetry' (p. 220).
30. 'Scream', *Oxford English Dictionary*.
31. Though interesting in itself, the admission of a possibly different speaker at this point does not change my argument about the diction and style of the poem.
32. Pound, *Poems and Translations*, p. 237; ll. 48–55.
33. Ibid. p. 1275, n. 236; 1.1.
34. Ibid. p. 238; ll. 61–4.
35. Pound's effect is analogous to what White calls the 'intentional variation of melody' in Greek drama, settling on a lyric style that is 'singularly appropriate to the sentiment expressed'. Cf. Appendix, pp. 197–201.
36. Qtd in Sullivan, *Ezra Pound*, p. 74.
37. Pound, Canto LXXXI, *The Cantos*, p. 538.
38. Pound, *Poems and Translations*, p. 236; p. 237; p. 238.
39. Pound, *Literary Essays*, p. 51.
40. Pound, *Letters*, p. 181.

Chapter 6

Pound Among the Nightingales: From the Troubadours to a Cantabile Modernism

In his seminal essay 'Vorticism', Ezra Pound asserts that 'there is a sort of Poetry where music, sheer melody, seems as if it were just bursting into speech'.[1] This peculiar image of the latent and potentially explosive musicality in poetry, and the understanding of lyric art that underpins it, derives from the lyric tradition, and perhaps most immediately from a Cavalcanti sonnet that Pound had translated shortly before writing this essay in 1914. In Pound's translation of Cavalcanti's sonnet VIII, the suitor-speaker is left dazzled and dumb by the splendour of his beloved. His stupor is interrupted, however, by a mysterious noise: 'there's a deep voice heard whose sound in part / Turned into words', he proclaims.[2] This strange sound remains awkwardly, paralysingly inarticulate in Cavalcanti's poem, although it clearly relates to the speaker's preverbal, emotional reaction to his lady's sublime presence and the attendance of Amor. Late medieval Tuscan and Provençal suitors are well accustomed to this experience of incapacitating vision and the faltering language that struggles to make it known. Their nascent conception of language gives rise to an understanding of poetry as sound, or indeed music, 'bursting into speech', and Pound made increasing use of this idea, first in his translations and then in his own verse. He famously termed this kind of poetry *melopoeia* following Aristotle and Coleridge: a more respectable term, perhaps, than the algebraic-sounding 'cantabile values' – the formal features that register when a poem is spoken, chanted or sung – that he previously recognised in Cavalcanti and Villon.[3]

As he sought to understand and perfect melopoeic expression, Pound turned increasingly to Arnaut Daniel and the troubadours. Like many of the poets that interested Pound, Arnaut Daniel often poses substantial discursive obstacles for his own readership by emphasising the aural aspects of poetry. He is, not surprisingly, drawn to the archetypal symbol for poetry considered as music: birdsong. Although we may well have expected an arch-modernist of Pound's stature to scrupulously avoid this pre-eminent Romantic symbol, Pound's study of Arnaut's poetry made him more acutely aware of its technical (rather than thematic) importance to Arnaut's craft, and of its impressive range of non-Romantic associations. In fact, bird symbolism and the kind of poetry it represents in Arnaut's corpus prove to be decisive influences in the direction Pound's mature, modern work would take, drawing him increasingly towards the hieratic style he would later perfect.

Birdsong features ubiquitously in troubadour verse. Often, Provençal poets explicitly ascribe language to birds: they are intensely interested in ornitho-logie. Pound would have known this, having descanted on 'a theme by Cerclamon' (*sic*) in his 'Langue d'Oc' sequence.[4] As this series also demonstrates, the troubadours responded fervently to the Greek myth of Tereus, Procne and Philomel, and to the bird symbolism it imparted to Western literature.[5] As Pound reminds us in Canto IV, the troubadours had their own updated version of this myth. They are also among the first lyricists to single out the nightingale for special attention. The avian genius of Western European poetry has a fascinating philological history that helps explain why it became the pre-eminent literary bird during this period. In French, the term for nightingale, *rossignol*, has been an idiomatic expression for a tool that opens something locked since the fourteenth century, where it first appeared in criminal slang. The nightingale, in this usage, stands clandestinely for something like a skeleton key. This philological eccentricity has sometimes been traced to three generations of cryptologists named Rossignols who were appointed to the French court, the first and most famous of whom was named Antoine (1600–82). David Kahn, an authority on cryptology, thinks this etymology is mistaken:

> This particular usage of the term rossignol appears as criminal argot in police documents as early as 1406 – almost two centuries before the cryptologist [Antoine Rossignol] was born. Since the word also means 'nightingale,' it may be possible that the thieves adopted it as slang for a picklock because its nighttime solos of clicks and rasps were music to their ears.[6]

More likely, the famous family of cryptologists inherited the name, or claimed it, because of some previous furtive association. The startling fact remains, however: the nightingale was deployed in this codified, subterranean manner in both criminal and literary fraternities since around the time of Villon, and its song has featured as a code or cipher in literature ever since.

T. S. Eliot appears to have been aware of this quirk in 'Sweeney Among the Nightingales' where, in the closing lines, the songbird seems to license his reversion to literary jargon to intimate the main character's doom. Pound was aware of this special meaning too, as the opening 'Alba', in 'Homage à la Langue d'Oc' suggests:

> When the nightingale to his mate
> Sings day-long and night late
> My love and I keep state
>   In bower,
>   In flower,
>   'Till the watchmen on the tower
> Cry:
>   'Up! Thou rascal, Rise,
>   I see the white
>   Light
>   And the night
>   Flies.'[7]

This poem, and indeed each of the poems in the homage sequence, implicates the 'rascal' speaker in some clandestine activity, subject (along with the dawn) to the watchman's discovery, and (therefore) associates him with the furtive nightingale. This is an important poem in Pound's oeuvre. As Stuart McDougal notes, it anticipates the experiments with line length and typography that will make up the fundamental formal features of *The Cantos*.[8] On a more basic level, the clusters of sound and image evident here are typical of Pound's modernist poetics; they result from a decade spent studying the poets of Provence, Arnaut Daniel in particular.

Pound's special relationship with the birds of Provence, and with the nightingale, begins much earlier than this sequence. His translation of Bernart de Ventadorn's 'Quant L'Herba Fresq el Fuel Apar' (published in 1913) anticipates his 'Homage' and has a number of remarkable features. In the first place, it begins with an explicit yet puzzling reference to Philomel. Here is the opening of the poem (with the subsequent lines to follow):

> When grass starts green and flowers rise
> Aleaf in garden and in close
> And philomel in dulcet cries
> And lifted notes his heart bestows . . .[9]

Philomel is depicted as a pained *stil novisti* here, but it is Pound's addition. Ventadorn refers merely to the nightingale, *rossinhols* in Provençal. The change of pronoun demonstrates Pound's fluency with a bizarre Provençal lyric convention, what he referred to in the *Spirit of Romance* as the 'inexplicable address to the lady in masculine'.[10] Here, the symbol of the nightingale applies to the speaker as well as to the beloved, as though it were a perennially pertinent cipher, a poetic skeleton key.

Such gamesmanship underscores the essentially secretive and musical nature of much Provençal poetry, and suggests how important myth and symbol are for the emergence of its gamut of meanings and concomitant discursive subtleties. This is evident in the central irony of the poem. The disparity between the beauty of the nightingale's song and the dolorous-ness of its occasion is already incipient in the earliest literary treatments of the Tereus, Procne and Philomel myth, but this disparity becomes keener in troubadour verse and in Ventadorn's lyric. Pound notices that the irony is characteristic of the period, and makes frequent use of it, writing, for example, in 'From Syria': 'ne'er have I heard said this thing: / "He sings who sorrow's guise should wear"'.[11] The impertinence of song in dolorous romantic circumstances is so bittersweet that the irony becomes almost expected in poetic treatment of nightingales, and birds more generally. Pound, however, is capable of extracting an important *technical* lesson from this evocative theme. The birds' paradoxically 'dulcet cries' come to embody the mellifluence, urgency and essential inarticulateness of poetic speech for him, and he artfully demonstrates these conflicting, opaque properties in the ensuing lines of his transla-tion. The sentiment, and the composite handling of the quatrains, is muddled somewhat by the stoic repetition of certain key words, as in the second quatrain:

> Joy I've in him and in the flowers joy,
> E'en joy in me have I yet more employ,
> Hath joy in her in whom my joy is cast,
> She is such joy as hath all joys o'erpast.[12]

The epanalepsis here – 'joy' occurring initially and terminally in all but one of these lines – is cumbersome, it impedes the sense of the poem and suspends the fluency established in the first quatrain. To be successful, lyrical expression must arise out of this epistemological rigor mortis, and come partly through.

The word 'joy' assumes a basically onomatopoeic function in the poem, as though the cry of the nightingale had 'caught in the unstopped ear' of the lovesick poet-speaker.[13] The delight of the speaker is so overwhelming that it very nearly obliterates the discursive meaning of the stanza, and the voice of the poet, as we are told directly in the next quatrain:

> I love her so and so her prize,
> I fear her and such thoughts oppose
> That my poor words dare not arise,
> Nor speech nor deeds my heart disclose.[14]

Because of his high estimation of his beloved, the suitor's language has become frustrated and dislocated. The birds of this poem symbolise the struggle towards lyricism in the face of confounding experience. The poem ends, therefore, on a note of defeat:

> And yet she knows the depth of my annoy
> And, when she will, she will her grace employ;
> For God's love, Love, put now our love to test
> For time goes by and we here waste his best.[15]

If the enthralled poet is unable to force his language or deeds to adequate expression, he learns something profound about the limits of dull sublunary lovers' love in this failure, and salvages his poem.

Stuart McDougal deprecates Pound's syntactical distortion and lexical duplication here as inorganic and infelicitous: for him, words are repeated 'simply for padding' and couched in 'forced . . . inversions'.[16] He fails, however, to acknowledge that these strategies are crucial to the poet's melopoeic and thematic aims. What abundantly survives the overburdening of thought and language in this poem – Love and Will – are technical concepts in troubadour verse. This jargon enshrouds the poet's heart in secrecy, though it serendipitously forces another matter to a head, and necessitates the transformation of this secular poem into a religious meditation. To his credit, McDougal recognises that the poem's claim to our attention is musical: Pound has subordinated other matters 'to his desire to reproduce the rhyme scheme and musicality of the original', and the result is that 'his verse achieves a greater flexibility and naturalness', and even a more 'modern' language.[17] Even in this somewhat sceptical account, then, frustration of the poet-speaker's thinking and linguistic fluency results in the heightening of his lyrical powers. This is precisely the paradox symbolised by the nightingale in Western literature, and its lesson was well known to the lover in Provençal and Tuscan poetry.

When Pound refers to birds and their song in his early poems, a similar expressive anxiety is usually present. The poem 'From Syria', translated from the Provençal of Peire Bremon (included in the 1909 edition of *Personae*, though not subsequently retained) begins with a conventional invocation of birdsong as an analogue for poetic art:

> In April when I see all through
> Mead and garden new flowers blow
> And streams with ice-bands broken flow,
> Eke hear the birds their singing do;
> When spring's grass-perfume floateth by

Then 'tis sweet song and birdlet's cry
Do make mine old joy come anew.[18]

The poem was dropped by Pound, and has been justly censured by critics for, as McDougal puts it, 'pouring old wine in old bottles'. Pound, that is to say, adopts 'Pre-Raphaelite medievalisms' and other poeticisms somewhat arbitrarily.[19] If McDougal's judgement is fundamentally correct, it is nonetheless a little quick; as this stanza also demonstrates, the hackneyed quality of some of the more mechanical devices can be invigorated, and indeed modernised, by melopoeic means. We should note the anti-Romantic nature of the description, for instance: here is no nightingale singing 'of summer in full-throated ease', but a diminutive wee songster struggling to find his voice.[20] Pound energises his image by furnishing a poetic equivalent for the sound of the birds. The 'birdlet's cry' disrupts the easy atmosphere of the first three lines beginning with the transitional 'Eke' (meaning 'also', 'moreover'). This word, of medieval origin, is employed for its onomatopoeic qualities, and it stands out severely coming as it does immediately after the mellifluous 'blow' / 'flow' couplet of ll. 2–3. The surprise is registered by a concomitant syntactical contortion and an accumulation of compound words. 'Bursting out' in this way, the poem retains a capacity to surprise the reader and present its object in relatively fresh terms.

This early poem already exhibits the technique of balancing the (often awkward and shrill) sonic and discursive aspects of language, a tactic that would prove, eventually, after practice and reconsideration of the formal and dictional problem, to be even more fundamental to Pound's translations from the Provençal of Arnaut Daniel. Birdsong is a constant feature in Arnaut's poetry, where it typically embodies the *type* of verse that the poet aspires to. Pound comes to adapt this metapoetic bird symbolism to codify and hone his own technique. His critics have failed to respond to this crucial influence despite a timely reminder from Hugh Kenner who remarks:

> Four separate times Pound has cited and praised these instances [of Arnaut's imitation of bird sounds] in no case eliciting much show of response. Have his readers supposed he was dusting gadgets in a language museum?[21]

To underestimate the importance of Arnaut's technical influence on Pound is to misunderstand the technical accomplishments of Pound's most revered poetry. Thomas Grieve, an otherwise reliable authority on the early verse, argues, 'Pound's rigorous attention to form shuts out the interference of immediate influence. The result is that in these poems [he means especially the Canzoni, though the point may be taken in general] the signature is of craft, not of personality.'[22] While Pound does successfully escape the orbit of Yeats and Browning in his Tuscan and Provençal poems, it seems unreasonable to restrict the purview of poetic influence to thematics. For Pound, poetic craft is personal in proportion as it is taken seriously.

By 1911, Pound had translated all of Arnaut's poetry. The story of his evolving manuscript until its eventual publication in a revised form and in fragments, between 1918 and 1920, rivals that of Joyce's *Dubliners* for poor luck with publishers and general mishap. His perseverance in the task, however, comes to resemble the dedication of the speaker in the poems to his lady. He seems to say, with Arnaut's lover in 'Canzon: Of the Trades and Love':

> Though this measure quaint confine me,
> And I chip out words and plane them,
>   They shall yet be true and clear
> When I finally have filed them.
> Love glosses and gilds them knowing
>   That my song has for its start
> One who is worth's hold and warrant.[23]

His Arnaut translations, beginning with this pledge to do his object justice in 1911–12, coincide with his most revolutionary and influential writing, in the volumes *Cathay* (1915), *Lustra* (1916–17) and *Hugh Selwyn Mauberley* (1920), and with his redoubled critical efforts to establish a truly modern literature at the end of the decade. Perhaps as a result of the success of these epoch-making volumes, Pound's Arnaut Daniel translations, especially the latest ones, have been comparatively neglected, although they share several conspicuous technical features with the more famous poems of this period. At their best, these translations are among Pound's finest early achievements because of their dexterous lyricism and because of their systematic and definitive enumeration of what we might call Pound's *trobar clus*: they are the epitome of his early style and utilise almost all of the technical lessons he had wrested from literary tradition beginning with 'Hilda's Book'. The lyricism of these poems is often a source of difficulty and obscurity, as in *The Cantos*. Characteristically, Pound exulted in these qualities, remarking that, for example, 'if ever an art was for a few highly cultivated people it was the troubadour poetry of Provence'.[24] He also pointed out as early as 1913 that the etymon of the word *trobar* is the verb 'to find', as if to suggest their intermediary role in his attempt to discover a language and form capable of expressing the modern world, and the necessity that this language should be incisive, pliable and lyrical.[25] Indeed, in these poems, Pound begins to make and successfully employ the 'language to think in' that had eluded him in 1910.[26]

When Pound eventually published his version of Arnaut in *Instigations* (1920) he commented literally and precisely on the jargonish aspects of the troubadour's style. In the very first paragraph he recommends Arnaut's judicious mimicry of bird-sounds for their superlative melopoeic quality:

> Here are some of his canzos, the best that are left us; and he was very cunning in his imitation of birds, as in the poem *Autet*, where he stops in the middle of his singing, crying: 'Cadahus, en son us,' as a bird cries, and rhyming on it very cleverly, with no room to turn about on the words, 'Mas pel us, estauc clus,' and in the other versets. And in *L'aura amara*, he cries as the birds in autumn, and there is some of this also in his best poem, *Doutz brais e critz*.[27]

The emphasis is technical rather than thematic here: birdcalls instruct the poet in matters of cadence and rhyme (exemplified by the concentrated *-us* rhyme Pound singles out here). In 1934, when Pound comes to discuss Arnaut Daniel again, he returns to the example of 'L'aura amara' and again emphasises the technical lesson of birdcalls. Arnaut

> made the birds sing IN HIS WORDS; I don't mean that he merely referred to the birds singing – . . . he kept them at it, repeating the tune, and finding five rhymes for each of seventeen rhyme sounds in the same order . . . having done that he constructed another perfect strophe, where the bird call interrupts the verse . . . That again for six strophes WITH the words making sense.[28]

The qualifications here contain the important points. First, birds are not viewed simply as inspirational subjects; their songs are the equivalent of poetry and exhibit all the accoutrements of the poet's art. Second, the correspondence between poetry and birdsong is so complete – the melopoeia so inculcating – that it renders the communicative content of the poem almost incidental to its achievement.

Pound began to learn these lessons by translating many of Arnaut's own sounds and images into English, eventually with great skill. He takes care to retain and indeed emphasise the direct connection between birdsong and poetic style, as in the opening of 'Doutz Brais e Critz':

Sweet cries and cracks
and lays and chants inflected
By auzels who, in their Latin belikes,
Chirm each to each, even as you and I
Pipe toward those girls on whom our thoughts attract;
Are but more cause that I, whose overweening

Search is toward the noblest, set in cluster
Lines where no word pulls wry, no rhyme breaks gauges.[29]

In his introductory notes, Pound singles out this poem as Arnaut's finest, noting among other things its diversity of tone. This is a key lesson. The poem's systematic exposition of the different linguistic possibilities open to the poet makes it a suitable vehicle for Pound to explore the eclectic and inclusive aesthetic sensibility he shared with Arnaut. This begins with the parallel between the birds' chirming and the poets' piping in this stanza, and develops into a contrast between the intimacy and accuracy of the speaker's lovemaking and the 'blathered bluster' of other potential suitors' rhetorical boasting and rumour-mongering. Poetic language is thereby seen to have a direct, immediate relationship with the object it names and expounds: its aim is true and intimate knowledge, though it may appear furtive to the inexperienced.

The birds glimpsed in the first 'verset' (as Pound terms these stanzas) occasion and aurally augment this sense of lyrical variety. Their songs are celebrated for their 'cries and cracks / and lays and chants inflected', and include a whole spectrum of musical sound from the percussive to the harmonic. The suggestion that birds' chirming resembles Latin underscores the musical variegation, and recalls Pound's definition of melopoeia as words in their emergence from noise. Human meaning is constituted not in absolute or provincial terms, but across an emotive and basically acoustic spectrum or gradient encompassing Latin and Provençal, as well as more barbarous tongues. If this concept of nascent communication is common to Cavalcanti and Pound, it is, properly considered, Arnaut's poetic signature. The troubadour is, after all, most famous for Dante's celebration of his vernacular achievements in the *Commedia*, where he alone is permitted to speak in his native Provençal. Dante knew that '*il miglior fabbro*' cultivated a polyglot aesthetic, and Pound did too. This was no doubt one of the things that drew him to Arnaut Daniel in the first place, as he calls attention to this aspect of the troubadour's art regularly, noting, for instance, that 'by making songs in the *rimas escarsas* he let into Provençal poetry many words that are not found elsewhere and maybe some words half Latin'.[30]

Pound's critics have sometimes recognised this aspect of Arnaut's legacy. In his study *Ezra Pound's Medievalism*, Georg Gugelberger observes, 'polyglotism indeed is a particular medieval phenomenon due to the linguistic peculiarity of the Middle Ages. Pound knew the history of polyglot literature well enough and acknowledged its sources.'[31] For Gugelberger, the value of polyglotism is both political and lyrical:

Dronke in his study of the medieval lyric pointed out that 'the lyric poetry of these centuries (800–1300) is to a striking degree international.' It is precisely this internationalism that Ezra Pound tried to rejuvenate via his medieval studies. The true function of this bilingualism or polyglotism is rhythmical.[32]

On this understanding, the most arresting feature of multilingual poetry is not the world views it comprehends nor the parochialism it helps overcome, but the emphasis it places on sound. We see this above all in Pound's mature use of barbarisms, which contribute to the tone and spirit of a given poetic utterance even if they are neither fully integrated nor denotationally transparent. The symbol of the bird in Arnaut's poetry epitomises this view: it presents a babelised view of human language and extols the polyglottal voice as the most poetic. Pound, too, will claim this register as his own.

Pound begins to experiment with a much more radically polyglottal voice in his translations of Arnaut's poetry, initially as a means of responding to Arnaut's alien lexicon and the metapoetic bird symbolism that accompanies it. In his eventual translation, the poem 'Autet e Bas Entrels Prims Fuoills', begins in the following way:

> Now high and low, where leaves renew,
> Come buds on bough and spalliard pleach
> And no beak nor throat is muted;
> Auzel each in tune contrasted
> Letteth loose
> Wriblis spruce.
> Joy for them and spring would set
> Song on me, but Love assaileth
> Me and sets my words t'his dancing.[33]

There are three inspirational forces in this poem: spring and its epitome, birdsong, on the one hand, and Love on the other. These influences pull the poet in subtly different directions and make their presence felt in different poetic modes. The musical style of 'Doutz Brais e Critz', which carefully mimics birdsong to achieve its lyrical effect, is modulated and intensified by the overwhelming spirit of Love in this poem, remaking the music into a sprightly dance of words. The heightening effect of Love on the poet's music, manifest in the intensity created by adjacent and proximal repetition and modulation of sound, leaves the besotted speaker 'no room to turn about' on his words, and with no opportunity to embellish or rhapsodise.[34] The experience speaks through him in its own language, faltering though it is. The poem is 'set in cluster', and it becomes dense and opaque; its musical and rhythmical properties exert their priority and make the sense more difficult to fathom immediately or directly, and the utterance becomes more jargonish in the process.[35] In combination with the alien language, the effect is of the speaker being completely infused with Love and the understanding it brings: he delights in the delicious minutiae of this fresh world for their own sake and for the insights he gains through them.

Pound picks up on a perceived tension between 'song' and 'words' in his critical comments on Arnaut's poetry, suggesting that Arnaut's lyrics are 'not literature' properly considered 'but the art of fitting words well with music'.[36] He deals with language as though it were a stock of acoustic phrases or intervals to be combined in evocative – but essentially musical – ways: 'the rhythm set in a line of poetry connotes its symphony', he had determined already in 1910.[37] Literature, unlike Arnaut's art, incorporates other disciplines (rhetoric, for example) and admits a clearer prose sense than do these lyrics; nor is 'literature' so dogged in pursuit of sonic texture as to compromise sense or the style of the period (without which contemporary literature, according to Pound, must fail). He explains the distinction in a 1922 letter to Felix E. Schelling:

> The Troubadour was not worried by our sense of style, our 'literary values', he could shovel in words in any way he liked . . . The Troubadour . . . was not worried about English order; he got certain musical effects because he cd. concentrate on music without bothering about literary values. He had a freedom which we no longer have.[38]

The conventional rules that govern language, from grammatical issues to questions of taste and decorum, are seen to be less important than the 'musical effects' that the choice and arrangement of language may achieve. Pound now has a firm critical as well as poetic agenda, and he seeks increasingly to escape from the obligatory style of his contemporaries through carefully contrived diction and prosody and to recapture for modern verse Arnaut's medieval liberty. As usual for Pound, freedom comes only from discipline and discernment, as his steady progress on Arnaut's music gradually attests.

The troubadour proscription of 'literary values' is evident, above all, in Arnaut Daniel's alien lexicon. The 'explosiveness of his sound patterns and the uniqueness of his diction', to borrow a description from Pound scholar and translator of Arnaut's corpus, James Wilhelm, have been routinely observed in Arnaut scholarship since the Monk of Montaudon chastised his 'foolish words that nobody understands' in the 1190s.[39] These features were also well noted by the eminent poets of succeeding ages. Dante admires Arnaut's vocabulary in *De Vulgari Eloquentia* and Petrarch notes *'suo dir strano e bello'* – 'his strange and beautiful speech' – in *The Triumph of Love*. Pound responds to Arnaut's vocabulary in similar terms:

> The sum of the charges against Daniel seems to be that he is difficult to read; but a careful examination of the text shows that this is due not so much to obscurities of style, or to such as are caused by the constraints of complicated form, and exigency of scarce rhymes, but mainly to his refusal to use the 'journalese' of his day, and to his aversion from an obviously familiar vocabulary.[40]

Pound always sympathised with poets who attempted to slough off the staid literary habits of their contemporaries. His trouba-lore must be considered quite in keeping with his earlier aesthetic sympathies, his fascination with Romantic and Celtic language, his admiration of Swinburne and Browning, etc. Again, this is precisely how he defends it: 'the experimental demonstrations of one man may save the time of many – hence my furore over Arnaut Daniel', he writes in 'A Retrospect' (1918), '– if a man's experiments may try out one new rhyme, *or dispense conclusively with one iota of currently accepted nonsense*, he is merely playing fair with his colleagues when he chalks up the results' (emphasis added).[41] As this statement suggests, the benefit of escaping from habitual forms of expression is not simply an aesthetic virtue for Pound, but a service to clear thinking.

Much of the language that Pound eventually settled on to approximate Arnaut's 'foolish words' derives directly from the unique lexicon of Scots poet Gavin Douglas; it is consequently nearly as impossible to understand as Arnaut Daniel's.[42] Douglas's sixteenth-century translation of *The Aeneid* was much admired by Pound.[43] Utilising Bishop Douglas's Chaucerian Scots for his translations constitutes a daring attempt to avoid anything that sounded too contemporary; a preference for adroit rather than outré diction, to use Thomas Jackson's key distinction.[44] We can see this clearly in the range of terms applied to Arnaut's bird images: 'Auzel' for bird, 'Chirmes' or 'wriblis' for warbles, 'Perk' for perch, 'Pleach' for an intertwined bough or hedge, 'Quihitter' for twitter, etc. When Pound recalls the term 'auzel' later in Canto CX ('"What! What!" says the auzel here, / "Tullup" said that bird in Virginia, / their meaning?'), he seems to delight precisely in the impediments this lexicon poses to a modern – and American – audience.[45]

Aggregating all of the outlandish words in just these two 'versets' demonstrates the centrality of Douglas's jargon in Pound's development, however dubious critics have been about his success here. For Donald Davie, for instance, the result is not happy . . . What first strikes the reader is the extraordinarily indiscriminate diction of these versions: in order to get onomatopoeic and rhyming words, Pound has to let his diction veer crazily from colloquial slang to bizarre archaisms recall[ing] Browning at his worst.[46]

It must be remembered that Pound did not share the orthodox critical misgivings about Browning, and in a poem like 'Mesmerism', it becomes clear that these perceived deficiencies, the miscellaneous pneumatic forms of speech (his 'ecstatic pants') especially, were in fact particularly esteemed by Pound.[47] It cannot be denied, however, that in reverting to Douglas's Middle Scots we see Pound rejecting the conventional poeticisms of his day only to establish an even more obscurely derived lexicon. The value of Douglas's Middle Scots for Pound consists precisely in the fact that it is less familiar and less euphonious than the conventional poetic language of Georgian England. Since we tend to respond actively to new forms of expression and habitually to familiar expressions and clichés, Douglas's language is therefore more capable of the striking onomatopoeic defamiliarisation that Davie notices, and arguably more vital, since it forces the reader to conceive of its object without relying on the crutch of habit. Pound evidently hoped that his translations, like their originals, would 'charm . . . by being not too unfamiliar': it was a question of striking the authentic balance.[48]

Pound defends his practice in precisely these terms. In 'A Visiting Card' (1942), he even extols the exigency of sending one's reader to a glossary, citing 'Gavin Douglas's *Eneados*, done half a century earlier, in a Scots dialect that no one can read today without a glossary', as an example of a literary work whose appeal derives in no small part from the measured outlandishness of its language.[49] One response to this uncomfortable aspect of Pound's style has been to observe its efficacy as political statement. Having objected to the language on poetic grounds, Donald Davie settles on just such a reading:

> Whatever esteem we have and should have for Gavin Douglas's translation of the *Aeneid*, we can hardly believe that the Philadelphian Ezra Pound was any more at ease than most of us with Bishop Douglas's sixteenth century Scots. And some of Pound's many tributes to Douglas admit as much. Pound's championing of Douglas had much to do with a polemic, in itself just and timely, against the presumed and unearned superiority of metropolitan English over the dialects of the British Isles, and of the English-speaking world. At any rate it should not surprise us that when Virgil most startlingly irrupts into Pound's *Cantos* (rather late – it is in Canto 78), he should be heard speaking in the Caledonian accents of Gavin Douglas.[50]

Pound's linguistic inclusiveness, in this view, is a means of challenging staid convention and the elitism of the London salons. For all Pound's affirmed difficulties with Douglas, however, when he devotes most critical space to him in *ABC of Reading*, he makes light of these concerns by focusing on the sonic aspects of the language: 'Go slow', he cautions, 'manissis = menaces, the key to most of the unfamiliar-looking words in the sound. Don't be afraid to guess.'[51] The cultural ramifications of exploring non-standard English are therefore only part of the reason Pound turns to Douglas, the greater part being poetic, even epistemological.

For Pound, poetry involves a language that subtly hinders and therefore enriches comprehension, imposing semantic, metrical, mythical and syntactical obstacles. The demand for a glossary, far from being a sign of effete, scholastic abstraction, is precisely what ensures that poetry remains in 'the language of exploration' that he recommends in 'Vorticism'.[52] The best explanation of what Pound means by this is given much later, in Canto XCVI:

> If we never write anything save what is already understood, the field of understanding will never be extended. One demands the right, now and again, to write for a few people with special interests and whose curiosity reaches into greater detail.[53]

Pound's source for this prose caveat is one Charles du Fresne Du Cange (1610–88) who, according to Terrell, was a 'scholar and lexicographer who did basic glossaries of both medieval Greek and Latin'.[54] The poetry that Pound regards most highly is often specialised, and seems to demand translation and gloss. Because of its demand for a glossary, Douglas's language has the advantage of rendering the 'precise psychology, embedded in a now almost unintelligible jargon', that Pound sought in his earlier translations.[55] In Douglas, far from 'shovel[ing] ... in words in any way he liked', Pound finally unearthed a genuine alternative to the medievalism popularised by Morris and Rossetti.

Pound's approach to poetic diction is nothing if it is not catholic and jargonesque. The strangeness of words like 'auzel', 'wriblis' or 'spalliard' derives as much from their 'cantabile values' or melopoeic properties – their sonic and prosodic texture – as their semantic denotations. The sonic features of the language cause it to obtain and adhere more precisely to its referent than the more prosaic and familiar alternatives open to the poet. Bird and poet alike speak in a strange and difficult language that makes up for its lack of discursiveness in a language that is more pithy because it seeks a direct (and mimetic) relationship with both the poetic object and the speaker's orientation towards it. The language does not rely on a series of predicates to gradually get its bearings, but apprehends the object speculatively in its sensual immediacy.[56]

Arnaut provides the clearest exposition of this aesthetic of jargon in 'Chanson Doil Mot Son Plan e Prim'. Here are the first two stanzas of Pound's translation:

> A song where words run gimp and straight
> I'll make for buds flaunt out their state,
> And tips dilate
> With floral sheen
> Where many a green
> Leaf cometh forth for viewing,
> While 'neath dark shade
> In grass and glade
> I hear the birds are construing.
>
> In copse I hear their chirp debate,
> And lest any man me berate
> At Love's dictate
> I file and preen
> And cut words clean
> And cease not him pursuing.
> Spite his aid
> I do not evade
> Whate'er spites he be brewing.[57]

The poet's act of composition is described by a sequence of birdlike actions, culminating in the actions of filing, preening, cutting and cleaning at the heart of this second stanza. The result is a trim and orderly song whose words get precisely to the point; by attending to the matter diligently, moreover, the poet avoids censure for failing to do fit obeisance to Amor. In order to constitute poetry, the *Langue d'Oc* must be subjected to an act of hygiene that purges the debris of staid literary habit and conventional sonority, very often paring it down to the aural quintessence before 'construing' the language anew, refashioning it by incremental articulation of its sounds. Thus when Hugh Kenner famously describes Imagism as a combination of 'specifications for a technical hygiene' and a 'doctrine of the Image', he is consciously observing its consistency with Arnaut's avian aesthetic.[58]

Pound took Arnaut's advice to 'file and preen / And cut words clean' quite literally – not as a vague injunction to take pains over the language one employs as a poet and translator, but as a summons to direct and control every aspect of every word, from its linguistic denotations and connotations to the arrangement of its letters and sounds, even, as we have seen, if this involves significant departures from ordinary practice. We can really appreciate the superabundant control of Pound's eventual translation of Arnaut's 'Chanson' only by comparing it with his already accomplished version of 1911, which has none of the limpidity of the quoted example.[59] Hugh Kenner provides an astute evaluation of Pound's technical debt in this regard. He argues that Arnaut 'expects us to take pleasure in the separation, not the blending, of syllables, and in sound relieving, not prolonging, sound', and that he thereby suggested a language capable of disturbing the sonorities of Georgian poetry to Pound, a modern language that 'seems to welcome separations. Its words clip, bounding the clear distinct syllables modern French has slurred . . . to make English words new meant to make them more separately audible.'[60] The two stanzas from 'Chanson Doil Mot Son Plan e Prim' illustrate this gradually acquired Danielian effect of bounding similar short sounds in squat little lines of verse to create a babbling loquaciousness. For Arnaut, the resulting poetry is a spruce, eccentric jargon with jolts and glitches that capture the trilling and chatter of birds in a natural and pleasingly obtrusive way. Pound uses the same strategies to fine effect in his Imagist phase, making individual words stand in relief like 'petals on a wet, black bough'.[61]

These stanzas also demonstrate that Arnaut's conception of poetry as jargon relies on a musical approach to poetic form. Most of the troubadour lyrics that attracted Pound utilise *coblas unissonantis*, demanding that the poet replicate the form set in the first stanza precisely in subsequent stanzas, including the rhyme sounds. The scope of this device depends on the nature of the stanza employed. In 'Doutz Brais e Critz' the stanzas are regular, 'set in cluster / Lines where no word pulls wry, no rhyme breaks gauges'.[62] The effect of these stanzas is fluency and sincerity, the ability to make 'meaning / Stand . . . without screen'.[63] In 'Chanson Doil Mot Son Plan e Prim', on the other hand, Arnaut elects to write in lines of varying length, focusing our attention on the sounds even more completely, especially on the internal and terminal rhymes. Pound singles out just these features in his introduction:

> The songs of En Arnaut are in some versets wholly free and uneven the whole length of the verset, then the other five versets follow in the track of the first, for the same tune must be sung in them all, or sung with very slight or orderly changes.[64]

The constant, subtle modulation of a finite and often restrictive set of sounds enhances the music of poetic language. The problem is compounded in the act of translating a metrical composition, but the prospect of intense aural concentration is thereby redoubled in recompense, if these examples are anything to go by. In this way the poet, slowly and meticulously, over many years, arrives at an equivalent of the bird-language from which he draws his inspiration and acquires his technique.

Another noteworthy feature of the above description of Arnaut's conception of form is the qualified use of 'free'. Pound recognises the simultaneous formal demands of the internal contrapuntal rhyme and the *coblas unissonantis* (using the exact same rhymes in the exact same lines of each stanza), and although he replicates this with extraordinary skill, he also acknowledges a certain flexibility and spontaneity within the stanzas themselves. Around this time, most people interested in poetry in London were busy taking sides on the issue that undoubtedly became the age's most drastic legacy: the legitimacy of *vers libre* in English. For Pound, there was no question at all of free verse in English. Freedom in verse is a relative and not an absolute prosodic phenomenon. One might escape the beat of the metronome by discovering the fluid cadences of Dante or Arnaut, by writing accentual rather than accentual-syllabic verse, but this freedom invariably entailed subjugation to other and usually foreign prosodic demands.[65] In fact, Pound was drawn to Arnaut in part because he presented a fluid alternative to accentual-syllabic verse in English: 'he bears to the technique of accented verse of Europe very much the same relation that Euclid does to our mathematics', he wrote in 'I Gather the Limbs of Osiris'.[66] To his essay on 'T. S. Eliot', Pound later appended a definition of prosody that defies critics who find the definitive metric in Chaucer and Milton: 'prosody is the articulation of the total sound of a poem'.[67] This point is of paramount importance. By this time he had learned all about 'articulation' of sound – in the double sense of clear enunciation and deliberate joining or fashioning together – from Arnaut Daniel. Indeed, whenever Pound discussed *vers libre* he returned to heterometric analogues like these stanzas of Arnaut's to illustrate Eliot's point that 'no *vers* is *libre* for the man who wants to do a good job'.[68] Another favourite example was the Greek Chorus.[69] For him, writing verse involved exploring the possibilities for organising the 'total sound' of a poem; since there is copious precedent for heterosyllabic verse in Western literature, and since the writers Pound most admired used such a prosody, this would be the basis of his own mature work.

Making the cadence and (in the most literal sense) the sound of language the basis of poetic organisation changes much about poetic composition. For one, it makes rhythm a spontaneous and organic phenomenon again, forever banishing the image of the poet pacing his garden, ten steps one way, ten steps the other, muttering his nascent verses.[70] This has the additional virtue, in the context of Arnaut's pervasive bird imagery, of actually corresponding to the avian method of composition, which we might accurately describe with the Old Occitan term *permutatio*: a relatively short initial phrase is elaborated into an endless series of semblances, giving the song an overall rhythm and the bird a signature call. The poetic possibilities of this jargoning are most impressive when most concentrated, for example in the opening of 'L'Aura amara'. Pound's translation of this poem is a capstone achievement, and demonstrates just how far he has come imped on Arnaut's wing. Here is part of the first stanza:

> The bitter air
> Strips panoply
> From trees
> Where softer winds set leaves,
> And glad
> Beaks
> Now in brakes are coy,
> Scarce peep the wee
> Mates
> And un-mates.[71]

This passage clearly echoes Pound's 'Langue d'Oc' sequence. He has effectively harnessed what Kenner terms Arnaut's 'intricate refusal of prettiness': he does not succumb to the 'ambient mellifluousness' that has usually accompanied Romantic depictions of birds and that dominates the verse of Tennyson and Swinburne.[72] The rhythm created by the *permutatio* of like sounds, as well as that enforced by the cadence of the language (which is largely iambic here, except in the monosyllabic lines and in l. 7) dexterously recreates the sounds of the (natural and poetic) original. Between the plosive articulation of these lines ('glad / Beaks'; 'wee / Mates') and the rich assonance ('panop*ly*', 'tr*ees*', 'l*ea*ves', 'b*ea*ks', w*ee*', 'gl*ee*s', etc.) these lines threaten to burst into sustained song at any moment.

Although this translation is quintessentially melopoeic, and powerfully suggestive of the poetry to come, Pound recognised these modernist principles before he had in fact written much modern poetry.[73] In 'I Gather the Limbs of Osiris' (1911), he thought of Arnaut already in these terms:

> At a time when both prose and poetry were loose-jointed, prolix, barbaric, he, to all intents and virtually, rediscovered 'style.' He conceived, that is, a manner of writing in which each word should bear some burden, should make some special contribution to the effect of the whole. The poem is an organism in which each part functionates, gives to sound or to sense something – preferably to sound *and* sense gives something.[74]

Pound encountered and countered each of these maladies in his own time: to loose-jointedness he offered absolute rhythm and an uncompromising, Danielian insistence on craftsmanship; to prolixity he offered the doctrine of Imagism; and to barbarism he proposed a polyglot literature capable of overcoming parochialism and ranging over a multiplicity of literary periods and styles.

In order to assess the contribution of Pound's melopoeia to modernism in more particularly literary-historical terms, we can turn to T. S. Eliot's comments in *Ezra Pound: His Metric and Poetry*:

> Mr Pound has more recently insisted . . . on the importance of a study of music for the poet. Such a relation between poetry and music is very different from what is called the 'music' of Shelley or Swinburne, a music often nearer to rhetoric (or the art of the orator) than to the instrument. For poetry to approach the condition of music (Pound quotes approvingly the dictum of Pater) *it is not necessary that poetry should be destitute of meaning.* (Emphasis added)[75]

T. S. Eliot encouraged the idea that Pound's melopoeia involved the Paterian aesthetic conjunction of sound and sense but did not abandon objectivity and precision in its presentation of real objects. In fact, Eliot seems to elaborate on Pound's critical assessment of his own poetry here. In the essay 'Vers Libre and Arnold Dolmetsch', Pound claims: 'Poetry is the composition of words set to music. Most other definitions of it are indefensible or metaphysical.'[76] This is the kind of poetry he discovered in Arnaut Daniel. The qualification he appends to this definition is, however, more memorable: 'I do not mean', he says, 'that words should be jumbled together and made indistinct and unrecognisable in a sort of onomatopoeic paste.'[77] This is a brilliant satirical account of the worst in Shelley and Swinburne – two poet's poet's poets, to adapt John Ashbery's phrase – and it is also an acute assessment of the problematic aspect of Paterian aesthetics that I began with in the Introduction to this volume.[78] Arnaut's distinction lies in finding those words and manifesting those objects that are latent in the music. To claim that poetry constitutes jargon – in the extended sense of the word encompassing the ancient and modern aspects of the term – is not to claim that it is nonsense or that it enthusiastically courts meaninglessness but, on the contrary, to insist that it is more meaning-full than straightforward prose, and meaningful in more ways than prose.

Notes

1. Pound, *Gaudier Brzeska*, p. 82.
2. Pound, *Poems and Translations*, p. 200.
3. Pound, *Literary Essays*, p. 167. Demetres Triphonopoulos pointed out the

traditional weight of the term in his reading of an early manuscript draft of the present text, as well as Pound's likely acquaintance with an essay partly dealing with the concept that accompanies Coleridge's *Biographia Literaria* in Shawcross's 1907 edition.

4. According to Stuart McDougal, the third poem in the sequence derives from a poem by Cercamon entitled 'Quant l'aura doussa s'amarzis'. The opening of the poem, in McDougal's literal translation, reads:

> When the sweet wind becomes bitter
> And the leaf falls from the branch
> And the birds sing in their language
> And I here sigh and sing. (McDougal, *Troubadour Tradition*, pp. 133–4)

5. Birds and bird-symbolism appear to have been at the forefront of Pound's thinking between 1912 and 1918. Although I concentrate on the lyric tradition of Western Europe here, the birds of Cathay are as ubiquitous as those of Provence. As 'Sennin Poem by Kakuhaku' (from *Lustra*) demonstrates, Pound was capable of treating birds both *melopoeically*, as we shall see here, and *phanopoeically* or Imagistically. The poem offers as fine an Image as Pound produced:

> The red and green kingfishers
>   flash between the orchids and clover,
> One bird casts its gleam on another. (Pound, *Poems and Translations*,
>   p. 299; ll. 1–3)

6. Kahn, *Codebreakers*, p. 160; fn.
7. Pound, *Poems and Translations*, p. 515.
8. McDougal, *Troubadour Tradition*, p. 126.
9. Pound, *Poems and Translations*, p. 1127; ll. 1–4.
10. Pound, *Spirit of Romance*, p. 92.
11. Pound, *Poems and Translations*, pp. 95–6; ll. 18–19.
12. Ibid. p. 1127; ll. 5–8.
13. Ibid. p. 549; l. 10.
14. Ibid. p. 1127; ll. 9–12.
15. Ibid. p. 1127; ll. 13–16.
16. McDougal, *Troubadour Tradition*, p. 32.
17. Ibid. p. 32.
18. Pound, *Poems and Translations*, p. 95; ll. 1–7.
19. McDougal, *Troubadour Tradition*, p. 19.
20. Keats, *Complete Poetical Works*, p. 183.
21. Kenner, *Pound Era*, p. 87.
22. Grieve, *Early Poetry*, p. 88.
23. Pound, *Poems and Translations*, p. 1121.
24. Pound, *Letters*, p. 102.
25. Pound, *Literary Essays*, p. 95.
26. Ibid. p. 194.
27. Ibid. p. 109.
28. Pound, *ABC of Reading*, pp. 53–4.

29. Pound, *Poems and Translations*, p. 495; ll. 1–8.
30. Pound, *Literary Essays*, p. 109. He says elsewhere that 'Arnaut had been, however, to a monastic school: he knew some Latin . . . His Latin was, let us say, no better than mine' (Pound, *Poems and Translations*, p. 1123).
31. Gugelberger, *Ezra Pound's Medievalism*, p. 30.
32. Ibid. p. 30.
33. Pound, *Poems and Translations*, p. 487; ll. 1–9.
34. Pound, *Literary Essays*, p. 109.
35. Pound, *Poems and Translations*, p. 495.
36. Pound, *Literary Essays*, p. 112.
37. Pound, *Poems and Translations*, p. 194.
38. Qtd in Sullivan, *Ezra Pound*, p. 91.
39. Wilhelm provides a helpful glossary of these 'foolish words' in his edition, Daniel, *Poetry*, pp. 119–26.
40. Pound, *Spirit of Romance*, p. 25.
41. Pound, *Literary Essays*, p. 10.
42. There is perhaps a slight difference of degree, since Pound thinks Douglas's language is basically recoverable, as we shall see, whereas Daniel's meaning is often viewed as having become lost, as in Canto XX when Pound inquires about the famous Danielian crux, 'noigandres', and associates it with palpable silence, with 'Sound: as of the nightingale too far off to be heard' (*The Cantos*, p. 90). The same is often true for the sound in language, even poetic language: its music is difficult to fix or to trace as I have been attempting to do here; 'but', as Pound's Cavalcanti would have it, ''tis felt, I say' (*The Cantos*, p. 178).
43. Richard Sieburth provides a glossary of Pound's borrowings from Douglas (Pound, *Poems and Translations*, pp. 1300–1).
44. See p. 75.
45. Pound, *The Cantos*, p. 800.
46. Davie, *Studies in Ezra Pound*, p. 46.
47. Pound's attitude to Swinburne is another example of this general tendency; see, for example, de Nagy, *Pre-Imagist Stage*, p. 72.
48. Pound, *Poems and Translations*, p. 1124.
49. Pound, *Selected Prose*, p. 324.
50. Davie, *Studies in Ezra Pound*, p. 272.
51. Pound, *ABC of Reading*, p. 117.
52. Pound, *Gaudier Brzeska*, p. 88.
53. Pound, *The Cantos*, p. 679.
54. Terrell, *Companion*, vol. II, p. 604.
55. Pound, *Literary Essays*, p. 54.
56. Although the basic understanding of language is Platonic, these terms are Hegelian. Hegel draws a distinction between 'predicative thought' and 'speculative thought' in the 'Preface' to his *Phenomenology of Spirit*. Pound's advocacy of a method of 'luminous detail' amounts to something like Hegel's speculative method. See p. 6; p. 12, n. 16.
57. Pound, *Poems and Translations*, p. 481; ll. 1–18.
58. Kenner, *Pound Era*, p. 186.
59. A. David Moody's assessment of the initial translations seems correct to me: 'the translations of Arnaut published in the *New Age* are strictly studies

in technique, matchless for their sound, the way they reproduce the notes of
the original, but not of the first importance as poetry' (Moody, *Ezra Pound:
Poet*, p. 171). In their initial form, the first two stanzas of the 'Chanson
Doil' read:

> I'll make a song with   exquisite
> Clear words, for buds are blowing sweet
> Where the sprays meet,
> And flowers don
> Their bold blazon
> Where leafage springeth greenly
> O'ershadowing
> The birds that sing
> And cry in coppice seemly.
>
> The bosques among   they're singing fleet.
> In shame's avoid my staves compete,
> Fine-filed and neat,
> With love's glaives on
> His ways they run;
> From him no whim can turn me,
> Although he bring
> Great sorrowing,
> Although he proudly spurn me. (Pound, *Poems and Translations*,
>   p. 1118)

60. Ibid. p. 86; p. 85.
61. Ibid. p. 287.
62. Ibid. p. 495; ll. 7–8.
63. Ibid. p. 496; ll. 53–4.
64. Pound, *Literary Essays*, p. 110.
65. Cf. 'Alexandrine and other grammarians have made cubby-holes for various
    groupings of syllables; they have put names upon them, and have given
    various labels to "metres" consisting in combinations of these different
    groups. Thus it would be hard to escape contact with some group or other;
    only an encyclopedist could ever be half sure he had done so. The known
    categories could allow a fair liberty to the most conscientious traditionalist.
    The most fanatical *verslibrist* will escape them with difficulty' (Pound, 'T. S.
    Eliot', *Poetry* 10 [1917], p. 421. Qtd in Sullivan, *Ezra Pound*, p. 80).
66. Qtd in Sullivan, *Ezra Pound*, p. 27.
67. Ibid. p. 80. It is again worth noting that Robert Bridges published *Milton's
    Prosody, with a Chapter on Accentual Verse and Notes* in 1893, which
    refuted George Saintsbury's thesis that *Paradise Lost* utilises extra-metrical
    syllables profusely. Bridges countered that Milton used poetic elision exten-
    sively and that, with a few reasonable rules governing this process, each
    line in the poem could be understood to conform to the stricter demands
    of accentual-syllabic verse. Thus the Milton of the early twentieth century
    became the champion of unflinching iambic verse of the sort that Pound
    most hoped to escape.

68. Qtd in Sullivan, *Ezra Pound*, p. 80.
69. Cf. 'If the earnest upholder of conventional imbecility will turn at random to ... almost any notable Greek chorus, it is vaguely possible that the light of *vers libre* might spread some faint aurora upon his cerebral tissues' (Pound, *Literary Essays*, p. 93). See Appendix for a not quite random Greek chorus.
70. William Hazlitt provides this famous description of Wordsworth composing (qtd in Burke, *Philosophy of Literary Form*, pp. 9–10). Pound thought Wordsworth a 'dull sheep', perhaps with an eye on this pastoral pacing back and forth (Pound, *Letters*, p. 90).
71. Pound, *Poems and Translations*, p. 489; ll. 1–10.
72. Kenner, *Pound Era*, p. 89; p. 87.
73. A striking later example occurs in Pound's 1951 translations of the Italian poet Saturno Montanari:

> A swallow for shuttle, back,
> forth, forth, back
>   from shack to
> marsh track;
>   to the far
> sky-line that's fading now.
> A thin song of a girl plucking grain,
> a child cries from the threshing floor. (Pound, *Poems and Translations*, p. 1116)

74. Pound, *Selected Prose*, p. 26.
75. Qtd in Sullivan, *Ezra Pound*, p. 72.
76. Pound, *Literary Essays*, p. 437.
77. Ibid. p. 437.
78. See pp. 2–3.

Chapter 7

Beyond/Formulated Language: The Function of Intensity in *Cathay* and *Lustra*

The poems Pound composed during and after World War I respond to the challenge posed by Ford Maddox Hueffer, and exhibit none of the lavish chicanery of his earlier work. In *Lustra*, he introduces these new poems with aplomb:

> Here they stand without quaint devices,
> Here they are with nothing archaic about them.[1]

We have seen this phrase before. At the end of Chapter 4, we caught Pound 'Ponder[ing] . . . in silence o'er earth's queynt devyse'.[2] The repeated phrase, minus the earlier orthographic flourish, signals the discrepancy between his poetic style in 1908 and 1916. The Celtic Twilightisms, the Anglo-Saxon inflections, the trouba-lore – all are banished from these volumes. It has been customary practice, almost since their publication, to remark the straightforwardness, plainness and simplicity of these poems; if we look more closely at Pound's new poetry, however, it becomes obvious that their greatly esteemed simplicity is only one aspect of their achievement. A corresponding and proportional difficulty – an opacity, as I have been employing the term – exists in these volumes too. *Cathay* and *Lustra*, that is to say, retain many of the jargonish aspects of Pound's earlier poetry. In these volumes, he seeks to supercharge ordinary language with intensity and precision, first by turning towards more intimate and personal expression while scrupulously disdaining public and political discourse, and second, by concentrating on the pictorial – or *phanopoeic* – qualities of the presentation. By adopting a more laconic and epigrammatic register, the poet hoped to steer his art beyond the platitudes of 'formulated language', and to pose an epistemological and ideological challenge to the ordinary, habitual speech of his day.[3]

Fundamentally, Pound owes the discovery of an enduring practicable alternative to his earlier, more turgid style not only to Ford Maddox Hueffer, but also to the great T'ang Dynasty Chinese poet Li Po (called Rihaku in Japanese) and to the critical efforts of the orientalist Ernest Fenollosa. Pound considered Rihaku to be an extremely traditional poet. He discovered in him an author, not unlike himself, who was a 'great "compiler"', gathering together, 'weeding out', and 'revising' the best traditional material available to him.[4] Despite the impression that Pound's first instalment of Chinese poetry scorns the erudition and ostentation of his earlier work, Rihaku offers Pound anything but an alternative to the role of sophisticated poetic intermediary he had been developing. In a stark attempt to call attention to this aspect of Chinese poetry, Pound published a short companion essay to *Cathay*, entitled 'Chinese Poetry', that observes the coexistence of simplicity and difficulty in Chinese poetry, and suggests that his own latest volume responds to each of these tendencies. In *Cathay*, we find him at the familiar tasks of gathering, sifting, 'weeding' and 'revising', but these traditional poetic functions appear in a new light in this volume, and eventually constitute a genuinely modern way of being traditional.

The famous simplicity of *Cathay* can be easily illustrated with reference to any number of poems from the volume, perhaps most readily the charming 'River Merchant's Wife: A Letter'. This poem details the tribulations of a young married woman whose husband is abroad. Initially the speaker, who is still a girl, struggles to come to terms with her affection for her husband, being young and 'bashful'. By the end of the poem she no longer struggles, and her fondness finds expression in plain, austere ways until, in the last line, she asks simply for notice of his return, that she may come to greet him 'as far as Cho-fu-Sa'.[5] Here are 'two small people, without dislike or suspicion', and the language of their correspondence is consequently lacking in guile and sophistication (quite the opposite, in fact, of Pound's own epistolary style).[6] Despite her youth, and the foreignness of the first stirrings of adult emotion, the speaker is acutely aware of her circumstances and emotional development, and also capable of pithy self-expression, as in the following lines:

> At fifteen I stopped scowling,
> I desired my dust to be mingled with yours
> Forever and forever, and forever.[7]

The simple device of repetition – of denying the speaker more copious lyrical expression – reveals her condition delicately and poignantly, especially in its pluralisation of 'forever', which magnifies her anguish and underscores her pleasing lack of philosophical sophistication. For the speaker of the poem, love means the simple reassurance of a mortal goal; of not finding herself, at the close of her life, eternally alone. Pound's new linguistic abstemiousness amounts to an exercise in disciplined characterisation here, with much the same concentration as the skirl he devised for his Seafarer or the constriction of his ornithological courtesans. As his subject is more naive, so is his language more basic, rudimentary and direct. Like 'The Seafarer', too, this poem proffers the speaker's song-of-herself in her own language, her own emotional 'journey's jargon'.[8] The speaker in this poem is simpatico, and the apparent difference between the two modes is down to the more ordinary circumstances of her lot in life. This also explains, in part, Pound's esteem for Li Po: 'One cannot consider Rihaku as a foreigner', he explains, 'one can only consider him human.'[9]

In many ways, then, this apparently new style cultivates personae like the others: the mannerisms are simply the appropriate ones for his particular subject. Pound is quick to laud the straightforward sort of poetry epitomised by 'The River Merchant's Wife: A Letter', but he always insists on viewing it as a kind of special case; its rare beauties are born of obstinate stock:

> Nearly everyone who has written about Chinese has mentioned the existence of . . . short, obscure poems. In contrast to them, in most rigorous contrast, we find poems of the greatest vigour and clarity. We find a directness and realism such as we find only in early Saxon verse and in the Poema de Cid, and in Homer, or rather in what Homer would be if he wrote without epithet.[10]

The difficulty of Chinese poetry is its most distinctive feature for Pound and his generation: only against the background of its general obscurity do its signal charms, 'vigour and clarity', emerge fully and distinctly. At the macro and micro level, as we shall shortly see, Chinese poetry is a literature of contrasts for Pound; and his analogies, therefore, are telling: 'The Seafarer' (there is no doubt he chiefly means these particular 'early Saxon verse[s]' given the prefatory note to *Cathay* and its inclusion as the penultimate poem in the volume) is celebrated not for the difficulties it presents most contemporary readers, but for the very same 'directness and realism', 'vigor and clarity' that readers are much more comfortable ascribing to 'The River Merchant's Wife'.

This overlooked essay draws more attention to the difficult poems than to those that posterity has better remembered, and suggests that Pound's readers have not been entirely correct in assuming that the volume as a whole presents a critical, epoch-making volte-face. This reading makes Pound's inclusion of 'The Seafarer', and his remarkable insistence on its integrality to the volume, something of an anomaly when in fact it presents a vital clue to his aesthetic attitude in this crucial period. In his essay on 'Chinese Poetry', Pound tried to explain the complementarity of these apparently different kinds of writing, and to reconcile his audience to the apparent contradiction between the sort of poetry he was known for and was continuing to write, and the new simplicity he was then introducing:

> The first distinction between Chinese taste and our own is that the Chinese *like* poetry that they have to think about, and even poetry that they have to puzzle over. This latter taste has occasionally broken out in Europe, notably in twelfth-century Provence and thirteenth-century Tuscany, but it has never held its own for very long.[11]

In the context of Pound's earlier poetry, and given his simultaneous and ongoing reworking of Arnaut Daniel's *trobar clus*, it should be clear that lyrical difficulty is central to Pound's modernising effort even in *Cathay*. He evidently hoped to prepare an audience for the kind of poetry that has to be thought about and puzzled over. Although the simplicity, 'vigor and clarity' of his Chinese translations have drawn the most critical commentary, it remains nevertheless true that these esteemed qualities are founded upon the kind of lyrical opacity that, for Pound, always makes poetry what it is.

To emphasise the mutuality of these two aspects of Rihaku's art still further, Pound prints an example of such a puzzle-poem, an epigram entitled 'The Jewel Stairs' Grievance', immediately following 'The River-Merchant's Wife: A Letter' in *Cathay*. He distinguishes it from the simpler 'River Merchant's Wife' by eagerly explicating its subtleties (he resisted the temptation to subject the 'naïve beauty', 'gracious simplicity and completeness' of the latter to impertinent arcane analysis).[12] Here is the poem, followed by Pound's exegesis, both in their entirety. It illustrates the kind of difficulty that inhabits Pound's poetry of this period and offers an instructive example of the kind of lyrical demands it makes upon the reader:

THE JEWEL-STAIRS GRIEVANCE

The jeweled steps are already quite white with dew,
It is so late that the dew soaks my gauze stockings,
And I let down the crystal curtain
And watch the moon through the clear autumn.

I have never found any occidental who could 'make much' of that poem at one reading. Yet upon careful examination we find that everything is there, not merely by 'suggestion' but by a sort of mathematical process of reduction.

Let us consider what circumstances would be needed to produce just the words of this poem. You can play Conan Doyle if you like.

First, 'jewel-stairs,' therefore the scene is in a palace.

Second, 'gauze stockings,' therefore a court lady is speaking, not a servant or common person who is in the palace by chance.

Third, 'dew soaks,' therefore the lady has been waiting, she has not just come.

Fourth, 'clear autumn with moon showing,' therefore the man who has not come cannot excuse himself on the grounds that the evening was unfit for the rendezvous.

Fifth, you ask how do we know she was waiting for a man? Well, the title calls the poem a 'grievance.'[13]

Pound exults in the routine failure of his cultured acquaintances to fathom this poem, which apparently legitimises his schoolmasterly exegesis (in the case of 'The River Merchant's Wife', this would have been impudent, he says). His criticism poses as a sort of necessary decoding of the poem's lyrical jargon, hence the scientific, deductive tone and the repetition of 'therefore'. Although the language of the poem is drawn from ordinary speech, it is charged with the utmost emotional significance, in part because of its careful understatement. It shares this feature with 'The River Merchant's Wife': the words on the page seem pregnant with circumstance and emotion, and evoke some sense of their own inevitability. The reader, like the poet, must become adept at whittling common expressions down to their salient dramatic essence and emotional pith to appreciate this art.

Crucially, however, this is not a new demand upon Pound's readership: he explained the method of his Browningesque dramatic monologues to W. C. Williams in almost the same terms at the outset of his career.[14] The same skills are required in the more famous and ostensibly simpler poems too: in 'The River Merchant's Wife', for example, where the speaker's 'hair was still cut straight' across her forehead (my favourite example: she is too young for any investment in her appearance or to have to submit to conventional gendering); being 'called to, a thousand times [she] never looked back' and, at fifteen, 'desired her dust to be mingled' with her absent husband's 'forever and forever, and forever': each of these details presents an intense 'reduction' of circumstance into a kind of lyric kernel that allows the reader to appreciate exactly the course of emotional development of the young woman by inference and extrapolation only.[15] Ordinary facility with the language is, as Pound points out gleefully, incapable of revealing the full significance of the poem; only 'careful examination' of diction and tone – exactly the sort of thought process that the poet is already fluent in – can realise the situation hinted at in the epigram. His method, as Thomas Jackson explains, 'requires the total exclusion of all elements of expression and "content" which do not function immediately in the delineation of the crucial moment'.[16] T. S. Eliot remarks that the vertiginous quality of much modern poetry is often

> caused by the author's having left out something which the reader is used to finding; so that the reader, bewildered, gropes around for what is absent, and puzzles his head for a kind of 'meaning' which is not there, and is not meant to be there.[17]

This kind of dilatatory extrapolation is often required in twentieth-century poetry; rarely, I think, before *Cathay*. The proper effort, exemplified by Pound in this excerpt, begins with the detail that the text provides. It asks: what circumstances would be needed to produce just the words of this poem? What particularities does its formula comprehend?

Even in this supposedly simple state, then, poetry persists in asking special things of its readers; it behaves in a stubborn and surreptitious manner, and gives the bounty of its meaning meagrely, and yet profusely, all at once. Pound's most doctrinaire explanation of his new style takes this into consideration, and occurs in the context of his editorial advice to Harriet Monroe of *Poetry* magazine. In one letter he insists that

> Poetry must be *as well written as prose*. Its language must be a fine language, departing in no way from speech save by a heightened intensity (i.e. simplicity). There must be no book words, no periphrases, no inversions . . . There must be no interjections. No words flying off to nothing . . . There must be no clichés, set phrases, stereotyped journalese . . . Nothing that you couldn't, in some circumstances, in the stress of some emotion, actually say. Every literaryism, every book word, fritters away a scrap of the reader's patience, a scrap of his sense of your sincerity. When one really feels and thinks, one stammers with simple speech.[18]

At first glance these proscriptions would appear to obliterate the poet's previous efforts, and for the reader who has followed Eliot's advice and sought to understand Pound's poetry chronologically, this is bound to come as a surprise.[19] It implicitly renounces much of his earlier output as bookish and fake, and we find Pound, in editing subsequent editions of *Personae*, making the point explicit by leaving some of his most preposterous inventions to defunction. But the proscriptions are a little misleading; are, perhaps, designed to whittle down *Poetry*'s weekly mailbag to the more interesting and modern specimens; they certainly do not apply to the master-poet. Pound's emphasis is not on verisimilitude exactly, although it is crucial to try to present, as far as possible, 'actual' circumstances and emotions, what one might 'really' feel and think. His aim is not ordinary speech but something that differs from it, if only 'by a heightened intensity'. The language of poetry, moreover, is to be a 'fine' language: used here (rather adroitly) to mean 'free from foreign or extraneous matter, having no dross or other impurity; clear, pure, refined'.[20] Just because Pound was sceptical of what he terms the 'stilted traditional dialect . . . [the] "language of verse" unused in the actual talk of the people, even of "the best people", for the expression of reality and emotion', does not mean that he had suddenly become a realist.[21] As one contemporary reviewer noted of *Cathay*, 'his verse is not ordinary speech, but he aims at the illusion of ordinary speech'.[22] This is especially true of a poem like 'The River Merchant's Wife'.

We need to remember that for Pound, 'the common word is not the same as the mot juste, not by a long way'.[23] The truly modern aspect of his new style cannot be understood simply by invoking these dogmatic proscriptions of bookish language and affectation. Modern poetry is defined and differentiated from prose not by these restrictions, but above all by virtue of its greater 'intensity' for Pound.[24] Despite a slight and uncharacteristic vagueness, Pound clearly viewed this as a precise term rather than a fuzzy, impressionistic notion. His seminal essay, 'Vorticism', first published in *Blast* and later reprinted in *Gaudier Brzeska: A Memoir*, tries to be clearer about the matter (but does not quite succeed):

> Vorticism is an intensive art. I mean by this, that one is concerned with the relative intensity, or relative significance, of different sorts of expression. One desires the most intense, for certain forms of expression *are* 'more intense' than others. They are more dynamic. I do not mean that they are more emphatic, or that they are yelled louder.[25]

Poetic intensity is, first, not a question of amplitude or volume for Pound (*Cathay* and *Lustra*, in fact, seem calculated to demonstrate that intensity can be achieved quietly or resoundingly, respectively).[26] By stressing the 'relative significance' of a given utterance, rather, he indicates that poetic speech is a matter of the relationship between language and life. The poet strives to capture a remarkable experience, and to present this experience in the most vital way possible, essentially continuing the experiment in poetic articulation that enjoyed so much success in his translation/adaptation of 'The Seafarer'.

Just as he believed that 'certain forms of expression are "more intense" than others', Pound held that some experiences – 'a moment of song, self-analysis, or sudden understanding or revelation', for example – are undergone more directly and authentically, and are therefore lived more intensely, than others.[27] These emotional experiences, A. David Moody reminds us, are quite as necessary for Pound's verse as they are for, say, William Wordsworth's. Moody adeptly ventriloquises Pound's miscellaneous remarks on emotion and poetic intensity, producing the following précis:

> The pre-requisite is intense emotion ... 'There must be intense emotion before language simplifies itself to the point of Imagism'. The greater the emotional energy, the greater the compression and 'the austerity or economy of the speech'. Emotion is 'the fusing, arranging, unifying force'. It is the primary energy; it 'causes pattern to arise in the mind'; it is an organizer of form in the poem; it creates that 'vortex or cluster of fused ideas ... endowed with energy' which is what Pound meant by 'the Image'.[28]

Language that taps these rich currents is always to be preferred over language derived from habitual (passively undergone) experience, which only serves to muddle and mute the life that gives it being.

Throughout his earlier career, Pound discovered and championed authors that would consolidate this perspective, but in the war years Remy de Gourmont seemed to him to be the chief proponent of this no-nonsense attitude. His systematic avoidance of prescribed and mechanical expression was not so much a stylistic preoccupation as an epistemological necessity. Pound hoped that by harnessing this impulse he could sustain a more rigorous inquiry about the world. In 'Vorticism' he explains:

> When I find people ridiculing the new arts, or making fun of the clumsy odd terms that we use in trying to talk of them amongst ourselves; when they laugh at our talking about the 'ice-block quality' in Picasso, I think it is only because they do not know what thought is like, and that they are familiar only with argument and gibe and opinion. That is to say, they can only enjoy what they have been brought up to consider enjoyable, or what some essayist has talked about in mellifluous phrases. They think only 'the shells of thought,' as De Gourmont calls them; the thoughts that have already been thought by others.[29]

The emphasis is distinctly on the *res* rather than on the *verba* here. Pound 'knows what thought is like' and his explicit aim is now clear thinking. The ad hoc qualities of language, in the Picasso example for instance, are what give it purchase on experience and make it apt. Expressions that pre-exist are too static and worn to articulate much about actual experience, especially new experience. Henceforth, poetry must aim at forging original perceptions and conceptions; it must make thought (a)new.[30]

This understanding of language derives from Nietzsche, who held that 'metaphor, for the authentic poet, is not a figure of rhetoric but a representative image standing concretely before him in lieu of a concept'.[31] Pound had been working out the implications of this point of view at least since 'The Seafarer', whose benumbed, stiffened language anticipates the clumsy candour of the river merchant's wife. He found an eloquent defence of this approach in Ernest Fenollosa's essay, 'The Chinese Character as a Medium for Poetry', about which I will shortly have much to say. For Fenollosa, 'Languages to-day are thin and cold because we think less and less into them.'[32] Only occasionally, 'when the difficulty of placing some odd term arises' or in translation, do we 'attain for a moment the inner heat of thought'.[33] Pound – ventriloquising Fenollosa here – considers language as the vehicle of intellection; language is necessary although not sufficient for the constatation and conveyance of genuine thought. While cliché makes up the bulk of ordinary language, it serves only to blunt and abstract it, so that its content is ultimately reduced to a banal, mechanical and self-reflexive procedure devoid of vitality. Poetic intensity, on the contrary, is achieved by writing about vital experience without conventionalising it, by realising this 'inner heat of thought'. This heat, it may be supposed, arises when words genuinely encounter circumstance: an inevitable surface friction occurs when the two ways of being collide or align.

The chief consequence of refocusing his effort in this way via Fenollosa was Pound's increasing estimation of what he termed 'frankness' in poetry, a notion that he traced, in his obituary for Remy de Gourmont, to the poet's *French*-ness (a detail that, incidentally, confirms Pound's constant state of vigilance when it comes to etymological detail).[34] That de Gourmont writes 'frankly', Pound explains,

> does not mean [that he writes] 'grossly'. It does not mean the over-emphasis of neo-realism, of red-bloodism, of slums dragged into the light, of men writing while drugged with two or three notions, or with the lust for an epigram. It means simply that a man writes his thought, that is to say, his doubts, his inconclusions as well as his 'convictions', which last are so often borrowed affairs.[35]

Frank writing is characterised by an uncertainty about the human capacity for definitive conclusion and scepticism about deeply held personal beliefs. The latter are too often the result of the kind of short-circuiting of the thought process that Orwell will describe so well in 'Politics and the English Language', a kind of automatic thought lacking in necessary friction, whereas in fact, as Pound told Harriet Monroe, 'when one really feels and thinks, one stammers with simple speech'.[36] We can see, in 'The River Merchant's Wife' and throughout *Cathay*, how Pound applies this philosophy. Doubts, anxieties, moments of naivety – these are the human qualities that really convey. Such thoughts have 'the property of life. They [are] immersed in the manifest universe [and] not cut out, put on shelves and in bottles' in Pound's understanding;[37] or, in Fenollosa's terms, they remain 'as flexible as possible, full of the sap of nature'.[38] Both prefer to consider poetic language as fundamentally inchoate and nascent rather than dictionarial; a function of its election and arrangement rather than absolute, sovereign and unambiguous.

In 'The Jewel Stairs' Grievance' the suppressed details appear to be unknowable – until, that is, the ingenious critic joins the dots. The poem poses many similar problems as the Anglo-Saxon 'Seafarer'. On 'first reading', neither seems to supply the details necessary for comprehension and both display – even flaunt – an oblique attitude towards their ultimate subject matter. This manner is justified on the basis of maintaining an authentic relationship with the experiences depicted in the poems. Since other aspects of experience ordinarily supplement language – sensory and emotional aspects, for example – poetic diction must be chosen to bring these fundamentals to consciousness. Stammering intellection provides one way of achieving the quick, authentic quality Pound had been seeking since 1911, and it suggests a deep distrust of all too-confident pronouncements and protestations. Hesitation is a significant feature of poetic language, as has often been comprehended in exclusively prosodic terms; for Pound, however, the caesura demands larger scope, and comes to certify language's lyrical potential to mean in a quite ontological sense.[39]

That language might fail to signify, at least immediately, is often Pound's point of departure in his most powerful and characteristic verse. He realises that the capacity to reach 'beyond the existing categories of language' demands that the reader's patience may be strained occasionally and sometimes systematically frustrated.[40] This confounding of semantic priority leads, eventually, to the increasing importance of visual presentation in Pound's poetry. With Imagism, Pound discovered an alternative *type* of clarity, and his diction becomes more terrestrial because it becomes ancillary to experience. Pound discovered that he could most surely rely on the reader to discover his distinct poetic object when it was presented in stark visual terms. Accordingly, in 'Vorticism', he invents a 'new category of language' in which 'the image is itself the speech. The image is the word beyond formulated language.'[41]

Before considering the implications of this famous definition, it is worth dwelling a moment on the ambiguity of Pound's language here. In the poems of *Cathay*, Pound has often aimed precisely at the presentation of a strategic, curial formula for experience; his rendering of Rihaku's verse is therefore translation in a double sense, since it brings into a new language an experience that was itself concentrated into a *formula*.[42] This, positive, sense of the term is now the conventional scientific sense, of course: Rihaku, via Pound, offers 'an expression of the constituents of a compound by means of symbols', or 'a condensed tabulation'. Pound's metaphor – and during the early part of the twentieth century it is still a metaphor – foregrounds the dilatatory nature of his new experiments in poetic form. In simultaneously proscribing 'formulated language' in advancing a theory of Imagism, however, Pound deploys the word in the original, literary sense as 'a set form of words . . . prescribed by authority or custom'. Following Thomas Carlyle, Pound uses the term 'formulated' to dismiss the 'fettering conventionalities of usage' and 'mere acquiescence in tradition' in his famous definition,[43] once again seeking to steer his cohorts away from the '*lingua morta*' of his earlier verse.[44] His image therefore has the dual function of blasting the sediment of unthinking usage and of driving experience into a more crystalline form.

Precisely this considered, discustoming aspect of his poetic language is, again, what brings real experience concretely and intensely into view for Ezra Pound. Consequently, some of the habitual trappings of language may well be omitted altogether. This is evidently the case in Pound's most famous Imagist poem, 'In a Station of the Metro', where the urge for phenomenal exactitude results in a compact poem that carefully limits the impositions of grammar and syntax. The poem is essentially the same kind of epigram as 'The Jewel Stairs' Grievance'. Pound's account of the redaction of the poem even allows us to see the process he describes in 'Chinese Poetry' in reverse. He tells us exactly 'what circumstances would be needed to produce just the words of this poem':

> For well over a year I have been trying to make a poem of a very beautiful thing that befell me in the Paris Underground. I got out of a train at, I think, La Concorde, and in the jostle I saw a beautiful face, and then, turning suddenly, another and another, and then a beautiful child's face, and then another beautiful face . . . I tried to write the poem weeks afterwards in Italy, but found it useless. Then the other night, wondering how I should tell the adventure, it struck me that in Japan, where a work of art is not estimated by its acreage and where sixteen syllables are counted enough for a poem if you arrange and punctuate them properly, one might very well make a little poem which would be translated about as follows:
>
> > The apparition of these faces in the crowd;
> > Petals on a wet, black bough.
>
> And there, or in some other very old, very quiet civilization, some one else might understand the significance.[45]

'In a Station of the Metro' is, like many of the poems in *Cathay*, a poem to be thought about and puzzled over. One supposes, even, that few contemporary occidentals would have been able to make much of it at a single reading unlike, say, the following similar line in Tolstoy's *Anna Karenina*. When Levin first glimpses Kitty Shcherbátsky at the Moscow skating rink, 'there seemed to be nothing very special in her dress, nor in her pose', the narrator says, 'but for Levin *she was as easy to recognize in that crowd as a rose among nettles*' (emphasis added).[46] We must try to account for the very different effect of these two figures.

If Pound's poem is notoriously scant, the compositional circumstances it reveals are detailed and patterned: it turns on a correspondence between two dynamic images: haunting visages that flit in and out of the speaker's field of perception in the first line, and glistening petals that flutter against a dark branch behind them in the second. Ernest Fenollosa's words best describe the kind of insight Pound aims for here:

> Relations are more real and more important than the things that they relate. The forces which produce the branch-angles of an oak lay potent in the acorn. Similar lines of resistance, half curbing the out-pressing vitalities, govern the branching of rivers and of nations. Thus a nerve, a wire, a roadway, and a clearing-house are only varying channels which communication forces for itself. This is more than analogy, it is identity of structure. Nature furnishes her own clues. Had the world not been full of homologies, sympathies, and identities, thought would have been starved and language chained to the obvious. There would have been no bridge whereby to cross from the minor truth of the seen to the major truth of the unseen.[47]

Pound probably had this passage in mind during the extended period he was contemplating his experience in the Paris Underground. The juxtapositional effect of associating the dank, modern, urban underground with the quintessentially natural, Romantic image has the double effect of tarnishing the traditional beauty of the foliage and of beautifying the dingy underground scene. We are treated to a visionary moment that glimpses the paradox of modernisation: it is not so much that we discover beauty and ugliness where we least expect them but that the terms themselves are withdrawn and we discover something flashing beyond our accustomed noumenal world: we discover an 'identity of structure' in the Poundian universe, and realise that, unlike Tolstoy's simile, his poetic device 'is more than analogy'. There is no 'representative image standing concretely before him' as there is for Tolstoy's narrator,[48] and although it would be excessive to say that for the latter, 'thought [is] starved and language chained to the obvious', the association nevertheless relies on the decorative image being handy to the delighting Levin, whose thought is quite consumed by Kitty's 'adventure'.

Pound's qualifications of the epigrammatic form of the poem are equally revealing. He emphasises above all the importance of organising language: the poet, he avows, must 'arrange and punctuate . . . properly'. In 'In a Station of the Metro', the order of word and image, and the minimal punctuation, confer the requisite curial qualities. In one important sense at least, there 'is' no correspondence between 'The apparition of these faces in the crowd' and the 'Petals on a wet, black bough': the punctuation and grammar of the poem refuse to install it. Nor is there anyone (like Tolstoy's narrator) capable of positing the correspondence. Fenollosa's essay again hints at the reason why: 'sentences must be like the mingling of the fringes of feathered banners, or as the colors of many flowers blended into the single sheen of a meadow', he says; the poet's metaphors 'are only ways of getting rid of the dead white plaster of the cupola'.[49] For Fenollosa, and so for Pound, the poet cannot afford to rely on such banalities as mere existence. Shakespeare, we learn in Fenollosa's essay, scorned to employ the cupola more than any English poet.[50] Certainly, the removal of 'is' or 'is like' results in a commingling of the first and the second image in Pound's poem in a way that does not occur in Tolstoy's description.

Pound explains the effect as a 'super-position[ing]' derived from and inherent to the 'one image poem': there is in fact no correspondence posited between two discrete images, but an irresolute fusion of the two lines so as to evoke 'the precise instant when a thing outward and objective transforms itself . . . into a thing inward and subjective': the nascent moment of poetic insight itself.[51] Thing-hood itself is ancillary to this moment of intense lyrical perception. By focusing on the 'precise instant' of poetic transmogrification in this way, we can see how Pound's Image – or Vortex – differs from Tolstoy's simile: the former is intrinsic and intense in a way that the makes the latter seem an extrinsic, elective or whimsical decoration. The vibrating components of Pound's poem are composites themselves, of course, and the effect of the punctuation is both to bring them together and to keep them apart; to produce an exquisite patterning out of essentially inchoate experience – an index of the poet's involvement in, and mediation of, the circumstances, which he nevertheless demands that the reader reproduce for him- or herself. Charles Altieri suggests just how radical this phanopoeic aesthetic can be:

> Standing in and as itself, sustained by the energies of a making, rather than the beliefs or needs of a maker, the work asserts and wields human creative power . . . The work enters history by virtue of its power to resist the rule of history that all things lose their hold on the present.[52]

None of this can be achieved with a more conventional narrative, even using focalisation. This is perhaps why, after all, Pound tells the story of the poem's origin in such hypothetical terms: because of the tentative and fleeting claims to elucidating and being in the world that 'In a Station of the Metro' comprehends and re-presents. If it is true, as Fenollosa contends, that 'poetry surpasses prose especially in that the poet *selects for juxtaposition* those words whose overtones blend into a delicate and lucid harmony', then 'In a Station of the Metro' can hardly be dismissed on the basis of its brevity: it accomplishes more, in a greater variety of ways, than the equivalent acreage of syllables in *Anna Karenina*.[53]

In 'Chinese Poetry', Pound's phrase for this sort of composition is 'a sort of mathematical process of reduction'; a wonderful metaphor for the operation he describes. The poet first plots an elaborate equation for his experience, and then solves this equation by eliminating its redundant elements. He is, finally, left with a simple formula, a single, '*hokku*-like sentence' for the complex that he struggled to smuggle over into language.[54] The beauty of this process is that the equation contains the original inspirational experience, but is not limited by its phenomenal details: the equation is, at once, reality and symbol, particular and universal. The final reduction attains the mysterious indeterminacy of tentative, vanishing insight; the poem, like the formula, is always nascent, always coming into and reaching beyond manifest being. Elsewhere, Pound uses a more elaborate version of this comparison between the (Vorticist) poem and the equation in analytical geometry, ostensibly to clarify what he means by intensity in art. 'Mathematics is dull as dishwater until one reaches analytics', he contends, 'but in analytics we come upon a new way of dealing with form. It is in this way that art handles life.'[55] As relatively simple mathematical formulae delineate the essence of geometrical form and comprehend an infinite sequence of particulars, so too, 'great works of art . . . cause form to come into being' by relating their multifaceted particulars to some more universal expression. Thus, 'In a Station of the Metro' inhabits a region where correspondences and order are always emerging; like the formula, it is balanced on the edge of particular significance.[56] From this, Pound's famous definition of the Vortex follows: 'The image is not an idea. It is a radiant node or cluster; it is what I can, and must perforce, call a vortex, from which, and through which, and into which, ideas are constantly rushing.'[57] Unlike Nietzsche's metaphor, the Image does not 'stand . . . in lieu of a concept'; it does not 'stand' at all. Rather, it enables a play of perceptual and intellectual forces, now conceptual, now particular, in which, to adapt Fenollosa's marvellous phrase, we seem 'to be watching things work out their own fate'.[58]

Pound's exclusion of tense is critical to this effect, which thereby exceeds conventional metaphor precisely as conventional metaphor exceeds simile. The result is a kind of poetic shorthand, conveying in a minimal, always latent, way a maximum of experienced, manifest reality. 'Poetic thought works by suggestion, crowding maximum meaning into the single phrase pregnant, charged and luminous from within', according to Fenollosa, and 'In a Station of the Metro' aims to succeed on these terms exactly.[59] Pound does not therefore expect that his poem will reach a general audience (despite certain accessible qualities); rather, his imagined auditor is a lone and, certainly, a remote figure – a hypothetical figure, even – who may chance to contemplate its curious laconism or wonder what circumstances would be needed to produce just these words.

The Vortex, therefore, is both that 'radiant node or cluster . . . through which, and into which, ideas are constantly rushing' and a means of putting art into authentic contact with experience, before things are definitively formulated, 'trapped, fly-papered, gummed and strapped down', or otherwise committed to the taxonomic reliquary of the past.[60] It is a means of clinging to the emergent present in spite of language. Pound continually comes back to the idea that literary art has become alienated from life and that the fundamental task of the poet is to realign or rectify this relationship. His characteristic response during his Imagist phase hardly differs from his earlier response, and we soon find him returning to the same old cruces, the nature of poetic language and the viability of heightened language, on the one hand, and the legitimate lyricising potential of foreign matter, on the other. In 'A Retrospect', written just a couple of years after the letter to Monroe quoted above, the objective is still 'the living tongue', and he insists, as he had in 1911, that this is not the same thing as the 'daily speech' encountered in ordinary circumstances. He maintains that

> no good poetry is ever written in a manner twenty years old, for to write in such a manner shows conclusively that the writer thinks from books, convention and *cliché*, and not from life, yet a man feeling the divorce of life and his art may naturally try to resurrect a forgotten mode if he finds in the mode some leaven, or if he think he sees in it some element lacking in contemporary art which might unite that art again to its sustenance, life.[61]

This presents an important qualification to his earlier remarks, expanding upon what it means to 'really feel and think' and offering a familiar alternative to simple stammering. The frank artist, who feels 'the divorce of life and his art', may deviate substantially from the spoken language in order to circumvent morbid habit and achieve exactitude of expression. The frank artist may restore art to its legitimate place and rescue it from the prevailing social, cultural and linguistic conditions, what Fenollosa terms 'the anemia of modern Speech', by returning to the mode – or modernity – of traditional and temporarily forgotten figures like Rihaku.[62] As the word 'leaven' indicates, recourse to unfamiliar phrases can enliven contemporary literature by unburdening it of conventional phraseology and sententiousness. Even archaisms (which he instructed Harriet Monroe to be vigilant against in *Poetry*) may, in fact, contribute to poetry in and of the present if they can enable genuine contact with the opaque, vital essence of the illusory world. This was the hard-won lesson of 'The Seafarer'.

Pound continues to cast around thus, in the manner of Rihaku, for 'leaven' with which to unite 'art again to its sustenance, life'.[63] He finds an immediate ally in (or makes an immediate ally of) Fenollosa:

> the chief work of literary men in dealing with language, and of poets especially, lies in feeling back along the ancient lines of advance. He must do this so that he may keep his words enriched by all their subtle undertones of meaning. The original metaphors stand as a kind of luminous background, giving colour and vitality, forcing them closer to the concreteness of natural processes.[64]

This is a remarkable passage: it suggests that language can overcome its modern torpor if poets only remember their philology and their heritage. Employing words with a sense of their antecedent usages makes language more solid and palpable for Fenollosa, rather than more effete or esoteric. It enables language to come into closer contact with the world as it is. Pound concurs: 'The poet in dealing with his own time, must also see to it that language does not petrify on his hands', he adds to Fenollosa's remarks in a footnote (before claiming this as an endorsement of Imagism, which it is not). The contemporary poet has a dual responsibility, to life and to the still-living language of the past.

This situation involves an apparent contradiction, and Pound's position can only be appreciated if we remember that he absolutely believed that the clarity and directness he found himself capable of in *Cathay* was fundamentally born of the opacity of his earlier verse. Pound remains committed to an aesthetic of jargon in these poems, and their intensity and donative qualities require special poetic decoding. In order to achieve such lucidity, Pound believed, it was necessary that the poet learn to discriminate minutely in matters of diction and form, and this could only be done by exploring the full gamut of specialised languages. In the flood of 'neo-imagists' that appeared in the middle of the decade, he lamented a lack of 'the very discrimination, the whole core of significance I've taken twelve years of discipline to get'; what he took, in short, to be a lack of compass, and the disciplined style it enables.[65] The verse of his imitators is not (or is non-)significant, he says, because its manner is passively inherited and outward. This is, of course, exactly the same error that his own earlier verse exhibits. Genuine poetry requires discipline; it requires the poet to undergo an apprenticeship, to know firsthand arcane, erudite, abstract and egregious language, even if all that is learned in this way is how to weed it out (to return to the skill Pound admired in Rihaku) or concentrate it into a significant 'core'. This dedication to craft affords discrimination to the poet and allows that the intense moment can be wrought into poetry. Only thus can the vaunted simplicity of *Cathay* be obtained. 'True Ease in Writing comes from Art, not Chance', says Alexander Pope in his *Essay on Criticism*; this could almost have been written in epigraph for *Cathay*.[66]

During this revolutionary period Pound had been working assiduously on Tuscan and Provençal translations too, and he would soon be drawn to the Latin of Ovid and Propertius. He explains a consistent approach to diction in these complementary endeavours:

> The point of the archaic language in the Prov. trans. is that the Latin is really 'modern'. We are just getting back to a Roman state of civilization, or in reach of it; whereas the Provençal feeling is archaic, we are ages away from it. (Whether I have managed to convey this or not I can't say; but it is the reason for the archaic dialect.) (Anecdote: Years ago when I was just trying to find and use modern speech, old Bridges carefully went through *Personae* and *Exultations* and commended every archaism [to my horror], exclaiming 'We'll git 'em all back; we'll git 'em *all* back'. Eheu Fugaces!).[67]

If Ford Maddox Hueffer directed Pound towards the direct mode of *Lustra* and *Cathay* – towards 'the living tongue' – Robert Bridges reminds him of his earlier conviction that uncommon and unfamiliar terms may indeed become vital under the right circumstances. Roman and Provençal poetry are both *historically* remote from modern sensibility, Pound acknowledges here, but that is beside the point. The crucial difference is that his Provençal poems require archaic forms of English because they have an inexorable relationship with the past built into them, like 'The Seafarer'. They are traditional in the etymological sense: in their striving after ancient mysteries and forgotten lore, in their accumulation and handing down of the wisdom of the generations. When the poet or translator deals with Imperial Rome, or T'ang Dynasty China, however, he is dealing with ideas and words that are articled (in different ways) to the immediate concerns of their present. There is, as Pound had claimed of the poems of *Lustra*, 'nothing archaic about them'.

Pound's advice about resurrecting a 'foreign mode' requires his readers to recognise, in suitable traditional poetry, an intractable concern with the present, with their own present.

This, after all, is the etymon of the word 'modern'. In order to understand why writers of the Roman Decadence seem to Pound so much more contemporary than many twentieth-century authors, it is necessary only to discern that both ages are bound up in their own modernity. The poems in *Cathay* are also caught up in their present; their speakers are, however, more squeamish about public matters that they, unlike the Roman citizen, cannot influence. Having established that other ages are also concerned with their own modernity, other aspects of their contemporaneity present themselves. For example, Pound is able to point out to one protégé that 'the Roman poets are the only ones we know of who had approximately the same problems as we have. The metropolis, the imperial posts to all corners of the known world.'[68] This is the kind of 'leaven' Pound hoped to discover in the past, which he hoped was distinct from 'collecting old coins', as Eliot put it: a way of looking at and thinking about contemporary institutions and attitudes.[69] The difference lies in the necessity of first discovering a historical age that has a comparable, and yet distinct, *mode*: an appreciation of, or an obsession with, its own modernity.

There is another salient quality about the Latin poetry Pound most admired: the frankness he found in Rihaku and Remy de Gourmont, and, for that matter, in W. B. Yeats. Pound and Yeats were both sceptical of what they perceived to be a Victorian over-reliance on rhetoric in poetry, and Pound credited Yeats with having 'once and for all stripped English poetry of its perdamnable rhetoric. He has boiled away all that is not poetic . . . He has made our poetic idiom a thing pliable, a speech without inversions', adding that 'the poetry which I expect to see written during the next decade or so, it will, I think, move against poppy-cock, it will be harder and saner, it will be what Mr. Hewlett calls "nearer the bone"'.[70] By the middle of World War I, Pound was seeking a poetry that dodged 'perdamnable rhetoric' and was encouraged by the precedent of Rihaku, Propertius and Ovid. In these comments, moreover, Pound associates the avoidance of rhetoric with a 'living tongue': a plain and pliable, hard and sane form of speech that is, again, not to be equated directly with the spoken tongue. The error he hoped to avoid is the supervening conceits of overtly political language, what we today term 'spin'.

In 'Vorticism', Pound offers a memorable and useful definition of rhetoric that also helps explain his increasing reliance on direct presentation in the visual medium. 'The "image" is the furthest possible remove from rhetoric', he writes, where 'rhetoric is the art of dressing up some unimportant matter so as to fool the audience for the time being'.[71] The objective of rhetoric, Pound contends, is present utility, which is always diametrically opposed to the objective of literature, which he famously defines as 'news that STAYS news'.[72] This dichotomy allows us to appreciate how the poems of *Cathay* further his exploration of the 'living tongue'. A poem such as 'The River-Merchant's Wife: A Letter' concentrates on the plainest human matters: 'emotions with the charm of direct impressions', to quote Fenollosa.[73] It staunchly refuses to gossip or to broach public matters, preferring more intimate, immediate and thinkable subjects, in the sense outlined by de Gourmont.

In both 'Song of the Bowmen of Shu' and 'Lament of the Frontier Guard' we are consequently given a bottom-up view of martial life. The private soldiers struggle to understand the necessity of war and the desolation that it brings. In the latter poem, the speaker is unwilling to, or incapable of, blaming the powers of the realm whose frontier he guards, despite

> sorrow, sorrow like rain.
> Sorrow to go, and sorrow, sorrow returning,
> Desolate, desolate fields,
> And no children of warfare upon them,
>   No longer the men for offence and defence.[74]

War's ravages make nonsense of nominal, rhetorical categories like 'offence and defence', while obliterating the very names of history's famous protagonists (and of the historians themselves). Here, the repetition functions much as it does in 'The River Merchant's Wife: A Letter', producing a node of intensity that places the speaker in a dynamic relationship with his physical and emotional circumstances. In 'Song of the Bowmen of Shu' the matter is still more delicately balanced:

> There is no ease in Royal affairs, we have no comfort.[75]

This juxtaposition of perspective implies a lack of contact and understanding between the decision-makers and those charged, unto death, with implementing and defending these decisions.

The passage that best sums up the ideological critique of politics and war in *Cathay* is, however, two short, simple lines from 'South-Folk in Cold Country':

> Hard fight gets no reward.
> Loyalty is hard to explain.[76]

The very mechanism of allegiance that makes war possible, perhaps even heroic, is directly called into question, and the laconic quality of these lines anticipates Pound's more vitriolic and famous condemnations of war in 'Hugh Selwyn Mauberley' and Canto XVI.[77] As A. David Moody explains, Pound

> is intent . . . on implicating the condition of the empire in the condition of the individual poet. There may be then a further relation, between Rihaku's China and the British Empire in 1914. In both there were barbarians to be fought off, by soldiers having a hard time at the front; in both there was a lack of enlightened direction from the ruling class at home; and in both the arts, including the art of government, were in their usual decadent state.[78]

On this understanding, poetry represents an opportunity to transgress established discourses, by either shunning or contesting the official language and its ideological implications. In this, 'Pound's situation as a poet was after all quite like Rihaku's.'[79] After all, it is not only poetic language that is opaque: routine language, and perhaps especially habitual political language, comes to work in quirky, furtive ways; its meaning often eludes the ordinary user and undermines his or her explicit interests and intentions. Pound seeks an alternative to such double-speak in lyrical intensity, in poetry.

Reaching 'beyond formulated language' by cultivating intensity in the various forms examined here is finally what guarantees that poetic communication will prove significant rather than platitudinous, and it becomes an increasing obligation for Pound. The Chinese poems of *Cathay* and the most desultory blastings of *Lustra* refuse to compel the muse to serve public or political discourse, sometimes defiantly so. 'Hating rhetoric and undeceived by imperial hog-wash' like the Chinese and Roman poets he admired, Pound had determined not to be deceived, not at any cost, by the rampant and destructive patriotism that marked the early twentieth century, and for that he would need to 'feel . . . back along the ancient lines of advance' explored by other poets who found themselves in approximately the same circumstances.[80] 'And that', says Pound, also in Canto XVI, 'was the revolution . . . / as soon as they named it.'[81]

Notes

1. Pound, 'Salutation the Second', *Poems and Translations*, p. 266; ll. 7–8.
2. Pound, 'Masks', *Poems and Translations*, p. 45; l. 14.
3. Pound, *Gaudier Brzeska*, p. 88.
4. Pound, 'Chinese Poetry', p. 55.

5. Pound, *Poems and Translations*, p. 252; l. 30.

6. Ibid. p. 251; l. 6.

7. Ibid. p. 251; ll. 11–13.

8. Ibid. p. 236.

9. Qtd in Moody, *Ezra Pound: Poet*, p. 303.

10. Pound, 'Chinese Poetry', p. 57.

11. Ibid. p. 55.

12. Pound, 'Chinese Poetry', pp. 94–5.

13. Ibid. pp. 55–6. An abbreviated version of this same exegesis accompanies the poem in *Personae*.

14. Cf. 'I catch the character I happen to be interested in at the moment he interests me, usually a moment of song, self-analysis, or sudden understanding or revelation . . . the rest of the play would bore me and presumably the reader' (Pound, *Letters*, pp. 3–4).

15. 'The phrase "my Lord, you"' presents another discriminating example of this technique, as Demetres Tryphonopoulos suggests in a generous early reading of the present manuscript: 'English unlike other languages has no honorific form – so Pound invented one.'

16. Jackson, *Early Poetry*, p. 27.

17. Eliot, *Use of Poetry*, p. 151.

18. Pound, *Letters*, pp. 48–9.

19. Pound often erected chronology to a methodological principle too. He advises Iris Barry, for example, that 'it is best to go at the thing chronologically, otherwise one gets excited over an imitation instead of a discovery' (Pound, *Letters*, p. 90).

20. 'Fine', *Oxford English Dictionary*.

21. Pound, *Selected Prose*, p. 461.

22. *Times Literary Supplement*, 16 November 1916; qtd in Stock, *Life of Ezra Pound*, p. 196.

23. Pound, *Gaudier Brzeska*, p. 115.

24. Pound, *Letters*, pp. 48–9.

25. Pound, *Gaudier Brzeska*, pp. 90–1.

26. He talks of seeking an audience in 'some very old, very quiet civilization' for 'In a Station of the Metro', surely with China in mind (*T. P.'s Weekly*, 6 June 1913; qtd in Stock, *Life of Ezra Pound*, p. 136).

27. Pound, *Letters*, pp. 3–4.

28. Moody, *Ezra Pound: Poet*, p. 227.

29. Pound, *Gaudier Brzeska*, p. 87.

30. A. David Moody's vibrant reading of Canto IV draws attention to the radical promise of this way of conceiving of the poetic task: 'a special kind of meaning . . . is generated . . . in the spaces between the things that are said. Being unstated, it is generally only in the mind of the reader, and is therefore necessarily individual. Moreover, the canto does not lay down what is to be thought, but simply what is to be experienced and then thought about or contemplated. With luck it will generate new meaning free from received ideas and conventional sentiments. Perhaps it should not be thought of as "meaning" at all, but rather as an energizing of the mind to see things in relation to each other and so to develop an original way of conceiving the ready-made world' (Moody, *Ezra Pound: Poet*, p. 365).

31. Nietzsche, *Birth of Tragedy*, p. 55; §VIII.
32. Pound, *Instigations*, p. 379.
33. Ibid. p. 371.
34. The word 'acquired the sense of "free" because in Frankish Gaul full freedom was possessed only by those belonging to, or adopted into, the dominant people' ('Frank', *Oxford English Dictionary*).
35. Pound, *Selected Prose*, p. 417.
36. Pound, *Letters*, pp. 48–9.
37. Pound, *Selected Prose*, p. 418.
38. Pound, *Instigations*, p. 146.
39. This idea has a rich post-Romantic genealogy, from Hölderlin's reading of Greek tragedy to Mallarmé's 'Crisis in Poetry', for example.
40. Pound, *Gaudier Brzeska*, p. 88.
41. Ibid. p. 88.
42. Cf. p. 152.
43. 'Formula', *Oxford English Dictionary*.
44. Sutton, *Pound, Thayer, Watson and The Dial*, p. 71. We find the same sense governing E. M. Forster's famous analysis of two-dimensional, 'flat' characters in novels not long after Pound's renunciation of formulated language: 'they are constructed round a single idea or quality' – the character's 'formula' which 'can be expressed in one sentence', for Forster (*Aspects of the Novel*, pp. 67–8; cf. also p. 73, p. 78). For Forster, as for Pound, the aim is to transcend what can be formulated in a 'flat', unsurprising way.
45. Pound, *T. P.'s Weekly*, 6 June 1913; qtd in Stock, *Life of Ezra Pound*, p. 136.
46. Tolstoy, *Anna Karenina*, p. 28.
47. Pound, *Instigations*, p. 377.
48. Nietzsche, *Birth of Tragedy*, p. 55.
49. Pound, *Instigations*, p. 386.
50. Ibid. p. 384.
51. Pound, *Gaudier Brzeska*, p. 89.
52. Altieri, *Painterly Abstraction in Modern American Poetry: The Contemporaneity of Modernism*, p. 300; qtd in Stauder, 'Beyond the Synopsis of Vision', p. 209.
53. Pound, *Instigations*, p. 387. Wallace Stevens's poem 'Artificial Populations' offers an interesting coda to this comparison, and can be read as a meditation on Pound's famous breakthrough:

> the Orient and the Occident embrace
> To form that weather's appropriate people,
> The rosy men and the women of the rose,
> Astute in being what they are made to be.
>
> This artificial population is like
> A healing-point in the sickness of the mind:
> Like angels resting on a rustic steeple
> Or a confect of leafy faces in a tree—
>
> A health—and the faces in a summer night. (Stevens, *Selected Poems*, p. 315)

54. Ibid. pp. 86–9.

55. Ibid. p. 91.

56. 'The Chinese Written Character' again supplies the original of this meta-phorical description: Cf. 'Chinese notation . . . is based upon a vivid short-hand picture of the operations of nature. In the algebraic figure and in the spoken word there is no natural connection between thing and sign' (Pound, *Instigations*, p. 362).

57. Pound, *Gaudier Brzeska*, p. 92.

58. Pound, *Instigations*, p. 363.

59. Ibid. p. 383.

60. Pound, *Selected Prose*, p. 462.

61. Pound, *Literary Essays*, p. 11.

62. Pound, *Instigations*, p. 379.

63. Pound, *Literary Essays*, p. 11.

64. Pound, *Instigations*, p. 378.

65. Pound, *Letters*, p. 48.

66. Pope, *Alexander Pope*, p. 29.

67. Pound, *Letters*, p. 179. He recalls this anecdote in Canto LXXX (*The Cantos*, p. 527). Pound's remarks in *The Spirit of Romance* are also rel-evant to the distinction he makes here: 'the living conditions of Provence gave the necessary restraint, produced the tension sufficient for the results . . . a tension unattainable under, let us say, the living conditions of imperial Rome' (*Spirit of Romance*, p. 97).

68. Pound, *Letters*, p. 90.

69. This becomes the orthodox modernist position on tradition and the individual talent. As T. S. Eliot explains in his 'Introduction' to Pound's *Selected Poems* (1928), 'Pound is often most "original" in the right sense, when he is most "archeological" in the ordinary sense. It is almost too platitudinous to say that one is not modern by writing about chimney-pots, or archaic by writing about oriflammes. It is true that most people who write about oriflammes are merely collecting old coins, as most people who write about chimney-pots are merely forging new ones. If one can really penetrate the life of another age, one is penetrating the life of one's own' (Sullivan, *Ezra Pound*, p. 103).The modern poet, that is to say, will often have to rely on unfamiliar diction in order to reorient a stodgy reliance on either tradition or mere novelty in order to 'penetrate the life' of the age. Eliot picks up several themes from Pound's own earlier defence of archaism and barbarism here, especially the notion that historically remote language may be immediate, precise and poetic (and even the only available means of thinking at all about the modern world). In fact, Pound copyedited the text and would have ample opportunity to suggest or insist upon some of these nuances (Stock, *Life of Ezra Pound*, p. 209).

70. Pound, *Literary Essays*, pp. 11–12.

71. Pound, *Gaudier Brzeska*, p. 83.

72. Pound, *ABC of Reading*, p. 29.

73. Pound, *Instigations*, p. 376.

74. Pound, *Poems and Translations*, p. 254; ll. 17–21.

75. Ibid. p. 249; l. 11.

76. Ibid. p. 259; ll. 10–11.

77. In Canto XVI especially we find the same plain groundling grumblings and juxtapositional undercurrents of *Cathay*: cf. 'they called him a swashbuckler. / I didn't know what it was / But I thought: This is pretty bloody damn fine'; 'I can hold out for ten minutes / With my sergeant and a machine-gun. / And they rebuked him for levity'; etc. (Pound, *The Cantos*, p. 70; p. 71).
78. Moody, *Ezra Pound: Poet*, p. 267.
79. Ibid. p. 267.
80. Pound, *Letters*, p. 150; *Instigations*, p. 378.
81. Pound, *The Cantos*, p. 75.

Envoi: 'Not of One Bird But of Many'

Writing for Pound's twenty-first-century listening audience, Margaret Fisher tolerantly explains that '*The Cantos*, one of the 20th Century's most influential poems, bears a title that could be translated as "The Songs" – though it never is.'[1] From the foregoing perspective, this may well seem a regrettable critical oversight; and yet Pound's art, as we have seen, often obtains precisely by such opacity as his title, in its untranslated form, effortlessly secures. His poem begins by scrambling the logopoeic and melopoeic propensities of its first words, beckoning the jargon that will ensue from its first precarious instalment. Significantly, Canto I revisits the alliterative cant of 'The Seafarer' in an effort to ground the poem at once in the dual traditions of Homeric Epic and Anglo-Saxon lyric (which is, for Pound, coterminous with Rihaku's effort to reconstitute the literature of China's Classical period, and the difficult art of Provence). The long poem therefore offers a 'Draft of XXX Cantos' in several decisive ways: a 'modern phonetic spelling of DRAUGHT', according to the *Oxford English Dictionary*, the word 'draft' is a 'drawing down', 'drawing off'; a 'detachment, or selection . . . from a larger body'. It is first used in the robust sense, as of a plough's pulling of a load, or 'the act of drawing a net for fish, or for birds'.[2] Evidently, the poet does not simply hand over some provisional or propaedeutic work in his 'Draft', hazarding what he will deliver only later but (as Pound has it in his very early poem 'The Lees') proposes to drink directly, as it were, from the muse's bowl, 'the lees / Of song wine that the master bards of old / Have left'.[3] The promise of the title is that the poet's song – a lyrical and unbounded, jargonish effusion, in which the bird-like poet can 'whirr his heart out, joyously' – will be traditional in the special modern sense Pound discovered during his apprenticeship.[4]

Ezra Pound proceeds to do exactly this – to 'whirr his heart out, joyously' – for the next half century.[5] We have exceptionally fine testimony from A. David Moody (via Daniel Albright) that Pound's preoccupation with birdsong lasts a lifetime. On the penultimate page of *The Cantos*, among the fragments he left incomplete, Pound relates an extraordinary story recalled from his summer journeying in France in 1912. As Moody relates the story,

> He was in Allègre ('the joyous') by 2.15, and it was in a field near there that he experienced something so intensely that he made a note of the exact moment, 'July 16/4.04 P.M.'—it was apparently 'a field of larks' that made him think of some troubadour singing of nightingales, and which he would recall in the last fragments of his *Cantos*.[6]

Thus his very last efforts reveal the poet drafting in the manifold sense he announces with the publication of his first instalment of his 'Songs' in 1930. This drafting was always central to his view of poeting; his perennial method. In placing 'The Tree' first in his oeuvre, he announced as much:

> 'Twas not until the gods had been
> Kindly entreated and been brought within
> Unto the hearth of their heart's home
> That they might do this wonder thing.[7]

The spirit of casting about for, invoking and federating, literary experience is the one constant in his long career as a poetic jargoner. Nevertheless, the experience to which Moody draws our attention, alluded to in these 'Notes for CXII et seq.', may with some justice be described as the liminal moment in his fulfilling this trajectory: Pound's pilgrimage to Hautefort, Montignac, Malemort, etc. allowed him to 'enter arcanum', his original jargonish enthusiasms and strait troubalore leading him, surely, to the more speculative and polyvocal method of *The Cantos*.[8]

The birds of *The Cantos* deserve special attention, more than can be allocated in a volume such as the present one. In this same, very late fragment, the poet again situates us at the onset of his great endeavour when, 'for one beautiful day there was peace':

> Brancusi's bird
>   in the hollow of pine trunks
> or when the snow was like sea foam
>   Twilit sky leaded with elm boughs.[9]

Constantin Brancusi's *Golden Bird* was completed in 1916 and Pound published an essay on the sculptor in *The Little Review* of autumn 1921. In it, Pound claims that 'Brancusi has set out on the maddeningly more difficult exploration toward getting all forms into one form; this is as long as any Buddhist's contemplation of the universe or as any mediaeval saint's contemplation of divine love.'[10] Looking back on some 116 cantos, it is obvious that Pound shares this 'maddening', 'difficult' and arcane ambition. His essay also suggests why the next lines should appear so similar to 'In a Station of the Metro': in Brancusi's sculpture, we access 'form free from all terrestrial gravitation; form as free in its own life as the form of the analytic geometers'.[11] Invoking Brancusi's *Golden Bird* at this moment, Pound reminds his reader of the formal insights that make his epic possible in the first place. 'A man hurls himself toward the infinite and the works of art are his vestiges, his trace in the manifest', Pound says: if he does not succeed in fully compassing the pure flight, it is not for want of concentration.[12]

At its most lyrical, Pound's epic soars beyond the constraint of poetic gravitation and achieves the same indubitably pure form as Brancusi's *Bird*. Even readers that are prepared to write off *The Cantos* as a whole (as indeed was Pound himself on occasion) are often quick to laud their favourite passages: the seething magnetism of Canto XLV; Pound's ultimate accomplishment of what he had once taken to be impossible in Canto XXXVI, his superlative translation of 'Donna Mi Prega'; the incomparably lyrical culmination of Canto LXXXI; or more idiosyncratic passages such as the visionary incantation at the centre of Canto XC. As his critics recognise, the effect is formal and rhythmical: the rhythms 'focus our attention, drawing into themselves, not a knowledge made up of discriminations of degrees, kinds and essences, but a kind of knowledge for which rhythm lends a topology but for which no grammar is possible or even desirable'.[13] Ellen Stauder's difficulty here illustrates the substantial problem of discussing Pound's jargoning in strictly discursive, or even prosodic terms, but her reading is characteristically judicious: the rhythms *are* the meaning. The rhythms are precisely how Pound drafts the poetic and prosaic past into the ambivalent light of contemporaneity: the rhythms are the warp of his melody: are *The Cantos*, his songs. The force of his absolute form is, like gravity, somewhat inversely proportional to the measures of traditional metrics – but it can thereby lead to extraordinary, exorbitant effects, as a comet teeming past a sun.

This is the truly vital significance of Pound's later jargoning. As he allows in his early Cavalcanti essay, 'sound does not require a human being to produce it. The bird, the phonograph sing'.[14] So, in *The Cantos*, we find

    Confusion of voices as from several transmitters, broken
      phrases,

And many birds singing in counterpoint/In the summer
    morning.[15]

The most incontrovertible signature of his jargoning is not the melody
itself – the rhythm, in Pound's terms – but its warp: voices are muddled,
transmissions scrambled, so that the contrapunto reveals, chiefly, a
multitudinous swarm of source-signals and shifting frequencies. We are
forced to reckon not only with an inexhaustible storehouse of prosodic
improvisation, but also with other opacities: sundry languages sing,
literary debris sings, glosses sing, letters sing, abbreviations, hieroglyphs
and ideograms sing, signs sing. Pound's jargoning, like the birds', is not
circumscribed by the narrow range of post-Romantic sentiment that
usually gives rise to bird symbolism in literature, but embraces a full
range of living experience in an equivalent variety of voices, tones and
registers, as he learned to during his lyrical apprenticeship. As Alan
Powers reminds us,

> to call bird sounds 'song' is to project a relatively narrow range of human
> activity. For birds, what we call their 'songs' are more often curses and
> threats, defiance or concession, arrests and apprehensions, or even weather
> bulletins and realty leases. We simians do not tend to 'sing' upon being
> stopped for speeding; a bird would. Nor do we 'sing' when a deadly enemy
> approaches our home to steal and possibly eat our offspring.[16]

Remarkably, tellingly, the only ornithological scenario among these
examples which Pound does not succeed in setting in a canto, or song,
is 'being stopped for speeding': he drafts or makes a distinct locutor for
each of the other circumstances.

    The temptation to limit this explication to these melopoeic features of
The Cantos crucially misses the dual aspect of jargoning incipient in the
poetic tradition and Pound's increasing awareness and cultivation of *le
mot juste*. From the very beginning of his career he was absorbed by the
play of the word on the page, which would be, often enough, otherwise
unsounded and unacknowledged in his verse. *The Cantos* are the culmination of this multifaceted interest in the corporeality of *logos*. 'There
are two kinds of written language, one based on sound, and the other
on sight', writes Pound, and both are integral to his opus.[17] Surprisingly,
critics have often discovered an almost prosodic significance in the
latter. Ellen Stauder explains:

> The visual figures, such as the hieroglyphs, have a double effect. They stop
> the flow of language and yet they are almost always redundant; that is, Pound
> nearly always gives us a gloss for his Chinese characters so their meaning, at
> one level, obviates the need for these signs. But at another level, the signs are

their meaning in a way that no discourse, i.e., no grammar or syntax, can specify. Indeed, the importance of these signs lies in their materiality which can be displayed, even translated, but never fully so.[18]

The Chinese characters, which Pound famously believed Henri Gaudier Brzeska could sight-read due to some innate ability or his training as a sculptor, may serve in a purely formal way for Pound's less gifted readers, and as a sign, at least, of their own indicativity. Not only do they interrupt the poem in a caesural manner, they punctuate it and give full play to certain of its macro-rhythms. The play of these devices is not totally different from Pound's dexterous prosodic time-*sign*aturing and, for Stauder at least, it *sign*ifies in the same way: to 'emphasize precisely the otherness of experience'.[19]

Instead of making time known to sight, like crotchets on a stave, these foreign characters make sight available in time: they pose their significance on a prosodic datum. Like musical notes, these characters do not transliterate. They exist at the interstices of the 'two *kinds* of written language' that Pound draws our attention to (emphasis added).[20] They are one of the interlanguages of *The Cantos*, rather than one of its languages: a node or 'vortex, from which, and through which, and into which, ideas are constantly rushing'.[21] Assimilation into Pound's jargon, that is to say, does not in any way imply homogenisation: its rhythms are constituted between different kinds of things as well as between things of similar ilk; its meaning aggregates but does not totalise, very much like 'In a Station of the Metro', and the aim is the same partial, partible and participative vision and revision of its miscellaneous subjects.

Among the poem's strange codes and ciphers, the musical note, as transcribed upon the staves of Canto LXXV and elsewhere, offers a singularly arresting example of Pound's poetic jargon: one of its auxiliary languages or interlanguages. Pound takes the word 'auzil', meaning bird, direct and intact from Arnaut. Might this appropriation refer directly to the auxiliary nature of his *ornitho-logie*? The *Oxford English Dictionary*, unfortunately, does not provide any guidance in this instance. It would seem commonsensical to suppose that while a musical score might have some designable musical purport, it can have no discursive, rationalisable meaning. What is the sense of a sign with no discursive meaning? What is the mere reader (and not the hearer) to make of it? Pound's critics have been up to this challenge too: they point out that Pound seems determined to undermine the transparent signification that we might ordinarily suppose to reside in musical notation. Rather than presenting an ideal basis for performance, the canto insists on its own piecemeal constatation in time. As Ellen Stauder describes it (following the lead of Pound's own music criticism), 'What we see, and what we have the potential for hearing, is Janequin's "Chant des Oiseaux" rendered in Gerhart Münch's handwritten transcription for violin and piano of Francesco da Milano's lute transcription of Janequin's choral setting.'[22] The canto remains meaningful by virtue of its selection and transmission – in formal terms, that is – and foregrounds the vital drafting of the whole undertaking. In this instance, as Stauder goes on to show, this is even more drastic than we have so far supposed:

> the Janequin transcription does not simply re-write the same piece for a different instrument; in making use of the chromatic possibilities inherent in the lute, da Milano more radically transforms the original and in so doing releases for hearing a more archaic music that was in the original but was unsounded, unheard, even by da Milano himself.[23]

The redaction enables a kind of paradoxical, or even impossible, authenticity here; it allows Pound and his contemporaries to perceive the secret life of music that has lain quietly dormant for centuries, literally sepulchred in its own surviving.[24]

Pound was intrigued by the mode – the relative modernities – of Rihaku and Propertius, let us recall, and the first part should not surprise us here. But that the very means of art's enduring should in effect amount to a kind of temporary silencing or nullification is a more remarkable insight, a compelling realisation of Nietzsche's aphorism, in *The Gay Science*, that 'the living is merely a type of what is dead, and a very rare type'.[25] Certainly, Pound's successful drafting requires that he should fish 'by obstinate isles' and that he should now and again resurrect an unremembered author.[26] In this dialectical understanding of tradition, and in the constatation of an epic poem that routinely insists not merely on the act of poetic transmission but on the interruption that alone makes tradition possible, Pound escapes the orbit of his predecessors, however. For Browning, famously, 'poets know the dragnet's trick, / Catching the dead, if fate denies the quick': Pound will have none of this Manicheanism.[27] Instead, his *mode* of being historical resembles Giorgio Agamben's tradition of the immemorial, where philosophical knowledge is presented as 'a dialectic of memory and oblivion, unconcealment and concealment, *alētheia* and *lēthē* . . . a memory that, in its very taking place, forgets itself [and where] what must be grasped and transmitted is . . . oblivion as such'.[28]

Like his plenteous commentary on Arnaut Daniel, Pound's own explanation of Canto LXXV offers no explication at all, but its enthusiasms and emphases are telling:

Clement Janequin wrote a chorus, with sounds for the singers of the different parts of the chorus. These sounds would have no literary or poetic value
if you took the music away, but when Francesco da Milano reduced it for
the lute, the birds were still in the music. And when Münch transcribed it
for modern instruments the birds were still there. They ARE still there in the
violin part. That is why the monument outlasts the bronze casting.[29]

Tradition, on this understanding, is ancillary and vehicular to the
miracle that is transmitted thereby. This is why its temporary silencing
is only one of the ways by which genuine art survives and succeeds.
The same is true of art that is true of the human spirit in W. B. Yeats's
brilliant self-elegy:

A brief parting from those dear
Is the worst man has to fear.
Though grave-digger's toil is long,
Sharp their spades, their muscles strong,
They but thrust their buried men
Back in the human mind again.[30]

Janequin's birds – Pound's birds – are the indelible symbolic datum of
The Cantos, not only 'part of the fabric of interruptions and plurality
that suggest the spontaneity of lyrical-musical form', but the lyrical-
musical stuff that underwrites its ability to *make* sense (not meaning) in
the first place.[31]

As Margaret Fisher has only lately revealed, the jargon of *The Cantos*,
epitomised by Canto LXXV, has a conspicuous analogue in Pound's
musical output. His first opera, Fisher contends, sounds 'like a test
conducted in the laboratory of someone obsessed with the relationship between words and music'.[32] His listeners, who have often been
readers of his poetry, are drawn to the prosodic aspects of his compositions in this medium too. Charles Amirkhanian writes, for example,
that 'the transparence of his prosody – the setting of texts to musical
lines – achieves with distinction his goal of illuminating the sounding
language and emotional expression of the authors whose work he set'.[33]
Just as Pound's lexical approach to music in Canto LXXV involved a
model of tradition that surpasses Browning's (or Morris's or Rossetti's)
straightforward immersion in the past, so too his auditory arrangement
performs a dialectical drafting of history into the contemporary moment
while simultaneously archaeologising the present. In Fisher's appraisal
of *Le Testament*, Pound's second opera,

Because the music had a medieval flavor in a foreign language, and the spoken
words a modern sound in a familiar language, Pound was able to bring past

and present time together in one aural space . . . Pound's intent was not to paint a picture of fifteenth- and twentieth-century lives, but an audiogram of one fifteenth-century voice cutting through numerous twentieth-century voices.[34]

Pound relies once again on a range of idiolects, registers, voices and interlanguages that essentialise the partability of his score. We find him reversing the traditional paradigm that discovers an archetypal poetic speech in the song of birds: instead, he teaches music how to jargon in the cant of the ages, reverse-engineering the composite lyric strategies he wrested from tradition so as to stuff the song of his ancient progenitors with so much talk.

As Fisher demonstrates, Pound's trials of radiographic form occur in the context of important technological innovations that allow language to appear in a light that, if not unique, is certainly rare in the aesthetic milieu whose tutelary spirit is Nietzsche's symbolic 'statue of a god without a head'. In directing our attention to the analysis of Pound's contemporary, Rudolf Arnheim, she allows us to see exactly what radio had to offer poetry, and vice versa. Arnheim explains how

> It is difficult at first for most people to realize that, in the work of art, the sound of the word, because it is more elemental, should be of more importance than the meaning. But it is so. In radio drama, even more forcibly than on the stage, the world is first revealed as sound, as expression, embedded in a world of expressive natural sounds which, so to speak, constitute the scenery. The separation of noise and word occurs only on a higher plane. Fundamentally, purely sensuously, both are first and foremost sounds, and it is just this sensuous unity that makes possible an aural art, by utilising word and noise simultaneously . . . It should be realized that the elemental force lies in the sound, which affects everyone more directly than the meaning of the word, and all radio art must make this fact its starting-point.[35]

This could be 'Ezra Pound Speaking' (as the poet famously began his notorious radio speeches). The epistemological revitalisation that radio promised had implications that reached far beyond radiophonic usage: in particular, it offered Pound's generation a means, however temporary, of glimpsing Nietzsche's capitated statue once more.

For Fisher, Pound seems to have provisionally considered that 'radio alone . . . yields appropriate conditions for releasing the music in language: namely, a performing space at once empty and dimensionless, from which words can emanate free of any material associations'.[36] This is probably only partly true: he was after all working on *The Cantos* all along, in substantially the same terms. Pound was also acutely sensitive to what he continually referred to as the divorce of words from music, the very condition that Nietzsche diagnoses so splendidly, and beyond which the Appendix to the present volume tentatively ventures. Whatever else the startling imposition of Canto LXXV is, it is *not* unprecedented; however arresting Pound's jargoning may have appeared to his first audience, it must after all be regarded as a distinctly traditional way of being modern or, it may be, vice versa.

Jargoning continues to offer poets a way of enervating language and causing new sounds and meanings to be uttered well into the twenty-first century, and Pound's labours in this direction are cardinal to the vitality of this poetic mode. When the poetic world was concerned largely with crepuscular and mellifluous sound, he helped poetry realise a fuller and more ranging song. His call, as Edwin Morgan writes of the starlings in Glasgow's George Square, is distinctive and urgent:

> There is something to be said for these joyous messengers
> that we repel in our indignant orderliness.
> They lift up our eyes, they lighten the heart,
> and some day we'll decipher that sweet frenzied whistling
> as they wheel and settle along our hard roofs
> and take those grey buttresses for home.
> One thing we know they say, after their fashion.
> They like the warm cliffs of man.[37]

So I hope in the foregoing study of Pound's early aesthetic, for all the foreignness, abstraction and stubborn erudition (mostly Pound's, I hope) to account for a delightful and humane kind of poetry. As A. David Moody cogently summarises, 'nothing poetic is alien' to Ezra Pound. In this same Poundian spirit I trust not to have deciphered but, on the contrary, and rather more plainly, to have come to know his myriad voices somewhat the better, to have become more comfortable with his still strange jargoning.

Notes

1. Fisher, 'Ezra Pound: Composer', p. 14.
2. 'Draft', *Oxford English Dictionary*.
3. Pound, *Poems and Translations*, p. 8; ll. 8–10.
4. Ibid. p. 8; l. 6.
5. Assuming Pound began 'drafting' *The Cantos* in 1915 (cf. Moody, *Ezra Pound: Poet*, p. xv).
6. Moody, *Ezra Pound: Poet*, p. 192.
7. Pound, *Poems and Translations*, p. 14.
8. Pound, *The Cantos*, p. 823.

9. Ibid. p. 821.
10. Pound, *Literary Essays*, p. 442.
11. Ibid. p. 444.
12. Ibid. p. 441.
13. Stauder, 'Crystal Waves', p. 103.
14. Pound, *Literary Essays*, p. 151.
15. Pound, *The Cantos*, p. 436.
16. Powers, *BirdTalk*, p. 45.
17. Pound, *ABC of Reading*, p. 20.
18. Stauder, 'Crystal Waves', p. 93.
19. Ibid. p. 107.
20. Pound, *ABC of Reading*, p. 20.
21. Pound, *Gaudier Brzeska*, p. 92.
22. Stauder, 'Without an Ear of His Own', p. 262.
23. Ibid. p. 263.
24. For Pound, this was an enduring way of thinking about history. In one of his radio speeches he complains that America endures history as a kind of deliberate nullification of the past: 'Can't go back before Gettysburg, the very names are forgotten now. Names we, the men of my time, grew up on, but we WERE being taught to forget. Or rather the WHOLE of the history was aimed at FORGETTING. It was top dressing, a monotony of military encounters, done with music and banners, to KEEP the nation's mind OFF the causes—off the REAL causes' (Pound, *Ezra Pound Speaking*, p. 75). Some of this is clearly anticipated in *Cathay* – see pp. 159–61.
25. Nietzsche, *Gay Science*, p. 109.
26. Pound, 'Hugh Selwyn Mauberley', *Poems and Translations*, p. 549.
27. Browning, *Sordello, Book the First, Works of Robert Browning*, vol. I, p. 180; ll. 35–6. Pound's 1966 foreword to the *Selected Cantos of Ezra Pound* proffers 'the following lines from the earlier draft of a Canto (1912)' as 'the best introduction to the *Cantos*', drawing inordinate attention to the importance of Browning's dragnet metaphor:

> Hang it all, there can be but one 'Sordello'!
> But say I want to, say I take your whole bag of *tricks*,
> Let in your quirks and tweeks, and say the thing's an art-form,
> Your Sordello, and that the modern world
> Needs such a *rag-bag* to stuff all its thoughts in;
> *Say that I dump my catch, shiny and silvery*
> *As fresh sardines slapping and slipping on the marginal cobbles?*
> (I stand before the booth, the speech; but the truth
> Is inside this discourse—this book is full of the marrow of wisdom.)
>   (Pound, *Selected Cantos*, p. 1; emphasis added)

28. Agamben, 'Tradition of the Immemorial', pp. 105–6.
29. Pound, *ABC of Reading*, p. 264.
30. Yeats, 'Under Ben Bulben', *Poems*, pp. 375–6.
31. Stauder, 'Without an Ear of His Own', p. 268.
32. Fisher, 'Ezra Pound: Composer', p. 30. My hunch is that she (consciously or unconsciously) intends an echo of Hugh Kenner's remark about Pound's

cribbing Arnaut Daniel's bird symbolism: 'Have his readers supposed he was he was dusting gadgets in a language museum?' (Kenner, *Pound Era*, p. 87).

33. Amirkhanian, 'Lost and Found Pound', p. 10.
34. Fisher, *Ezra Pound's Radio Operas*, p. 96.
35. Qtd in Fisher, *Ezra Pound's Radio Operas*, p. 72.
36. Fisher, *Ezra Pound's Radio Operas*, p. 100. In spectacular Poundian fashion, Fisher is here quoting Elissa Guralnick drawing upon Louise Cleveland's reading of music in Beckett.
37. Morgan, 'The Starlings in George Square', *Second Life*, p. 34.

Appendix: 'Barbarians and Dark Words of God': Poetic Jargon in Greek Drama

By the eighth century BCE, Greek society had become unprecedentedly cosmopolitan. The Dark Age ended with a population explosion and general increase in human activity and interaction, evident in the increased number of burials, in the quantity and diversity of relics deposited at oracular and religious sites, and in a resurgence of figurative art that increasingly depicts multiple human figures engaged in communal and municipal tasks.[1] From Homer and Thucydides we learn of a world bound by unlikely alliances in war and unlooked-for enmity in peace. Yet despite – or perhaps because of – this new, bustling contact, many scholars have sought to understand Greek society by emphasising important divisions within that society; the perceived distinction between Greek and non-Greek, or barbarian, is the most important among these distinctions.

Timothy Long argues that the advent of Greek ethnography (which begins in the 'very late 6th century', around the time of the Old Comedy of Aeschylus and Sophocles, with Hecataeus of Miletus's map and periegesis) represents 'a gigantic expansion of Greek knowledge of foreign cultures'.[2] The impressive array of ethnographic titles he adduces demonstrates the expansiveness and thoroughness of this new knowledge.[3] It seems likely that Athenians admitted a distinction between Hellene and non-Hellene (indeed the development of ethnography would seem to be predicated upon it), but that they were also capable of distinguishing degrees of foreignness in a way that corresponds with their burgeoning ethnographic capabilities. Athenians had, for instance, two distinct words by which a foreigner might be known: *xenoi* and *barbaroi*, suggesting both the importance of the distinction and its flexibility. They employed the former term for their non-Athenian neighbours, while the latter term typically specifies a still more remote origin, ethnicity or nationality.

Thucydides is perhaps first among early authors to discuss the

Hellene–barbarian distinction in a systematic way. He points out that despite its ubiquity in his own day, the distinction had not been universally observed in the past. He says that Homer declines to use the term *barbaroi*, reasoning that this was because, until the Trojan War, 'the Hellenes were not yet known by one name', and had as yet undertaken no collective action, obviating the need for any dichotomy whatsoever.[4] Strabo, writing some four hundred years later, objects to Thucydides' argument in two interesting ways: first, he notes that Homer does in fact employ the adjectival form in his description of 'the Carians, of barbarian speech', and that he could not have done so had the word *barbaroi*, along with the concept it implies, not been current and available; he also suggests that Homer does indeed conceive of the Hellenes collectively in a phrase he twice repeats, 'Hellas and mid-Argos'.[5] Strabo's insight is illuminating because it introduces an important nuance to the discussion. He recognises that the term *barbaroi* may function as a marker of a particular type of speech, or to specify an origin somewhere vaguely beyond 'Hellas and mid-Argos', and a correspondingly different sense of identity. Often, it means both at the same time.

Thucydides, in restricting himself to the social and geographical sense of the word, is insufficiently alert to what Strabo considers to be the real basis of the antithesis: spoken language. For Strabo, the Hellene–barbarian distinction originates as the Hellenes come to terms with unfamiliar speech. He conjectures that 'the word barbarian was first uttered onomatopoeically in reference to people who enunciated words only with difficulty and talked harshly and raucously, like our words "battarizein," "traulizein," and "psellizein" [stutter, lisp, speak falteringly]'.[6] Assuming an acoustical origin for the term *barbaroi*, and a linguistic basis for the Hellene–barbarian distinction, allows Strabo to question the historical authorities on the matter, and re-evaluate the prevailing opinion of his own day.[7] Only subsequently did the word attain its familiar sense as a derisive term for a foreigner, and Strabo insists the Greeks 'misused the word as a general ethnic term, thus making a logical distinction between the Greeks and all other races'. Presumably, Thucydides did not acknowledge the Hellene–barbarian distinction because he thought of it in the modern sense, as a 'general ethnic term'.

To distinguish between Hellenes, foreigners and barbarians indicates that the ancient Greeks were sensitive to the variegated make-up of their society and alert to the inconstant capabilities of its various factions to communicate effectively with each other. The term barbarian, at least initially, admonishes incomprehensibility rather than immorality, and it does not transparently indicate or vilify ethnicity or national origin. Timothy Long singles out language as 'the first criterion' in any such distinction, a fact that is signally demonstrated by a curious literary detail: the 'Greeks usually find the closest parallel to barbarian speech in the inarticulate twittering of birds' – hardly an obvious vehicle for cultural denigration.[8] This is evident above all in Greek drama. Of the many references to birds and their song in Greek literature, the overwhelming majority of them are to be found in passages dealing with foreigners, *xenos* and *barbaros*. Long insists that 'not only are all barbarian languages like the twittering of birds, so also is any dialect but Attic'.[9] A closer examination of the matter reveals that bird symbolism often carefully articulates essential differences between languages and the characters that speak them. Bird symbolism in Western literature thus begins as a means of describing and comprehending the outsider's position in Hellenic society. It marks a linguistic (and not an ethnic or moral) difference and – this is the vital point – does not quite reduce its subject to the status of a non-communicative, unintelligent and unintelligible object. In some important respects, the application of bird symbolism and the status of the barbarian has demonstrably positive connotations, implying insight and power that exceeds that of ordinary Athenians.

Athenians were genuinely interested in esoteric knowledge, as their ethnography is quick to demonstrate. The bulk of this material serves to introduce and explain strange weather patterns and geographical features; to describe exotic creatures: lions and tigers, crocodiles, hippopotami, and unusually strange birds such as cranes, peacocks and phoenix; to detail foreign customs like 'burial practices, methods of sacrifice, oath-taking, prophecy, diet, gods, clothing, warfare, and customs involving marriage and sexual intercourse'; and most interestingly, to explain unknown words.[10] It was surely intended that this knowledge be put to good use, and interest in it demonstrates that Athenians were fundamentally open to new and different ideas about the world they inhabited, and willing, at least in theory, to grant equal or superior insight to others. Their habitual assumption was that knowledge is inextricably bound up with language, and that they could enrich their understanding by incorporating the *logos* of other cultures into their own world view.

Birds, and their songs, were among the most meaningful esoteric phenomena beholden to the Greeks, as the ubiquitous practice of augury demonstrates; they enabled Athenians to conduct their lives in ways that might please the gods. In order to appreciate the significance of any Hellene–barbarian distinction in Greek society, and of bird symbolism in Greek literature, it is necessary to look at examples of this way of describing and thinking about foreigners in some detail. Aeschylus's *Agamemnon* provides several. Here, the stranger Cassandra arrives with Agamemnon from the Trojan War. She is a curious prize: Clytaemnestra proposes to put her to work almost immediately as a house servant, as would have been routine employ for those prisoners of war who were not simply put to death.[11] Her real import, however, is immediately and forcibly impressed upon the Chorus and the audience in the series of apocalyptic visions that she then pronounces. Her entrance is concealed from the audience until the fateful moment when Agamemnon steps down onto the opulent tapestries laid by Clytaemnestra in ostensible welcome for him. Agamemnon discovers her to the audience, and immediately pronounces her a barbarian, but cautions his followers to treat her with respect and dignity.[12] She is exotically dressed in the sacred regalia of Apollo, so as to warrant Agamemnon's pride in her as 'the gift of the armies, / flower and pride of all the wealth we won', as well as Clytaemnestra's caution.[13] Agamemnon himself, perhaps inadvertently, inclines the audience to see her as a semi-civilised conjuror from afar, by clearly promulgating a dichotomy between the Hellene and barbarian in the moments before Cassandra's spectacular unveiling. He insists, first, that he does not merit Clytaemnestra's gawking reception since he is not 'some barbarian *peacocking* out of Asia' in patent contrast to his prize (emphasis added).[14] Cassandra's attire immediately forces Clytaemnestra to acknowledge her threat, however, and the Chorus Leader to recall her 'fame as a seer' and consequently rebuke her: 'no one looks for seers in Argos'.[15] She is by all accounts conspicuously out of place in Argos.

Though Cassandra's appearance foregrounds her foreignness for the other characters in the play, and for the audience, her language is more decisively (and correctly) barbarian. If Agamemnon makes no reference to her speech when he first introduces her, this is because she has been and will remain perfectly silent for some time. In all, she maintains silence for 301 lines (after her concealed introduction, that is), even refusing to respond to Clytaemnestra when she is enjoined to come along to her doom.[16] Clytaemnestra is right to interpret Cassandra's silence as hostile. She recognises that this silence is a communicative act as she reveals in a fascinating exchange with the Chorus Leader that details the full extent of her suspicions:

LEADER
  It's *you* she is speaking to, it's all too clear.
  You're caught in the nets of doom – obey
  if you can obey, unless you cannot bear to.
CLYTAEMNESTRA
  Unless she's like a swallow, possessed
  Of her own barbaric song, strange, dark.
  I speak directly as I can – she must obey.[17]

The bird symbolism is obviously apt because of Cassandra's dramatic silence (swallows are far from renowned as songbirds), but the image insinuates that something much more sinister is afoot than a simple lack of understanding between the two characters. Clytaemnestra suspects that Cassandra's divinatory ability, rather than her foreign status, is responsible for her self-absorbed demeanour, and is frightened of the revelation it promises to yield. If we are in any doubt about exactly what Clytaemnestra suspects, she provides clarification a few moments later: 'she's mad', she suggests, 'her evil genius murmuring in her ears'.[18] Apollo, that is to say, is speaking to her.

If Clytaemnestra's anthropolatry were not enough to damn them all, she here equates the god's inspiration to the babblings of madness.[19] The gods, it seems, speak a language that is a 'strange', 'dark', 'evil . . . murmuring'. Before Cassandra even begins to speak she is allied with the gods as a purveyor of an exotic and dangerous barbarian language. Clytaemnestra contrasts her own precise and clear Greek to Cassandra's silent speech, and the theme is taken up by the Chorus Leader: Clytaemnestra is 'all too clear', while Cassandra persists in her obscurity with 'signs' and 'riddles'.[20] The Hellene–barbarian distinction operates in *The Oresteia*, then, with an important dramatic function.

If Cassandra is a barbarian in the 'general ethnic' sense current by Strabo's time, it is her language that marks her as such. In both its silent and ecstatic form, it is crucially different from any dialect that the other characters recognise. The Leader of the Chorus initially treats her merely as the speaker of a foreign tongue: 'I think / the stranger needs an interpreter, someone clear', he says, insisting that the communicative impasse can be overcome by a sufficiently sympathetic and dexterous translator.[21] Clytaemnestra dismisses this explanation immediately in her paranoia, and the Leader comes to see the extent of his difficulties when Cassandra speaks: 'I can't read these signs; I knew the first', he says, 'still lost. Her riddles, her dark words of god – / I'm groping, helpless'.[22]

There is no question of Cassandra's speech being entirely mortal for the Chorus Leader; it is infused with some other opaque matter. Her language is characterised as a torrent of indelible signs, 'words, more words . . . endless words'; as comprising 'a seer's techniques'. The effects of this language are as precisely rendered: it produces 'hurt' and 'terror', extreme physiological or psychological reactions, but it also provides access to 'truth'.[23] As the Chorus Leader begins to realise, this kind of language markedly differs from what might be expected of a 'general ethnic' barbarian:

CHORUS LEADER
But you amaze me. Bred across the sea,
your language strange, and still you see the truth
as if you had been there.
CASSANDRA
                              Apollo the prophet
introduced me to this gift.
CHORUS LEADER
A *god* – and moved with love?[24]

If the Chorus Leader is to fathom Cassandra it will be otherwise than by acquiring a knowledge of her vocabulary and grammar. Understanding, in this instance, is made possible by the act of empathy that the Chorus Leader initially proposes. In the torrent of sound that she produces, 'terror and the truth' present themselves forcefully and ineluctably, and the task awaiting the exegete is but to make himself open to these forces as they appear. It is not an impossible hermeneutical task to understand her, merely a different one; as the Leader says: 'I'm no judge, I've little skill with oracles, / but even I know danger when I hear it'.[25] Cassandra's meaning is not fundamentally a discursive one, but an imaginative, poetic one.

* * *

The attempt to empathise with Cassandra's situation and her plea leads both Leader and Chorus to another bird (and song) that epitomises the kind of brutal suffering Cassandra envisions for Atreus's heirs and for herself: the nightingale. The story of the rape of Philomel is perhaps the bloodiest and most gratuitously violent myth that was known to the Greeks, and it figures prominently here in *The Agamemnon*. Briefly, the story is as follows: Philomel and Procne are sisters, daughters of Pandion, King of Athens. Tereus, King of Thrace, wins Procne as his wife for service rendered to her father in battle. When, some time later, Tereus returns to Athens to escort Procne's sister to Thrace, the north-ernmost city in Greece, he becomes besotted, rapes her, cuts out her tongue and imprisons her in a fortress or deep forest. She manages to communicate her whereabouts and her suffering to Procne by means of an elaborate tapestry conveyed by a servant, and, disguised as a bacchant, Procne manages to find her. Together they plot revenge on Tereus. Procne stabs her own son Itys to death, depriving Tereus of an heir, and the sisters then serve son to father in some homely dish, reserving the head for postprandial presentation to him, at which point Tereus realises what has happened and makes for his revenge on the sisters.[26]

The gods then intervene, changing each character into a bird: Tereus into a (traditionally quarrelsome) hoopoe, Procne into a nightingale and Philomel into a swallow. The hoopoe and the swallow make sense as symbolic expressions of the violent traits Tereus demonstrates in the tale, and of the glossectomised Philomel respectively (the swallow is not much of a songbird, its cries are stifled twitters). Procne's transformation into the nightingale is usually explained by the mournful quality of the nightingale's song; in this guise she reputedly laments her lost son though she herself put him to death.

Immediately after the Chorus have attributed the strangeness in Cassandra's speech to Apollonian inspiration (and distinguished it as a torrent of emotive yet indecipherable words) and just before they begin to understand the import of what she is saying, they turn to this myth in their attempt to follow and comprehend the transition from silence to horrific communication:

LEADER AND CHORUS
   Mad with rapture – god speeds you on
     to the song, the deathsong,
  like the nightingale that broods on sorrow,
    mourns her son, her son,
  her life inspired with grief for him,
  she lilts and shrills, dark bird that lives for night.
CASSANDRA
  The nightingale – O for a song, a fate like hers!
   The gods gave her a life of ease, swathed in her wings,
  no tears, no wailing. The knife waits for me.[27]

From this exchange, and the pathos that it evokes (Cassandra's fate is even more gruesome than Procne's who, though destitute of her son, escapes human grief by metamorphosis), the Leader and Chorus become capable of the empathy that can alone equip them for the agony of Cassandra's song. Finally, they understand:

LEADER AND CHORUS
  What are you saying? Wait, it's clear,
  a child could see the truth, it wounds within,
     like a bloody fang it tears –
    I hear your destiny – breaking sobs,
     cries that stab the ears . . .

  You cannot stop, your song goes on –
  some spirit drops from the heights and treads you down
     and the brutal strain grows –
   your death-throes come and come and
    I cannot see the end![28]

The swallow and nightingale images are complementary – two halves of a *symbolon* – and a correct interpretation of Cassandra's behaviour and speech require this recognition. At first, the vanquished Trojan is victim merely: she has suffered the violence of defeat and is cast in the bonds of slavery, reduced to a person without a voice, like Philomel. This in itself is insufficient to rouse the Chorus to sympathy or to presage the tragedy that is about to take place. Then, however, through communion with the gods, she is transformed into the knowing agent of her own misery: Procne, who sacrifices her own happiness for the greater civic good (i.e., her sister's vendetta). Procne chooses revenge on her husband over what happiness might remain to her, and thus inaugurates a cycle of violence that only the gods can remedy. Cassandra, too, stands at the head of such a cycle of revenge, and it will run its bloody, purgative course through *The Agamemnon* and after. The potent combination of Procne's knowledge of the brutality of her actions and of the devastating consequences they will have for her, and at the same time her impotence to act otherwise, recommends the parallel with Cassandra, and only when they have realised the full extent of the allusion do the Chorus begin to understand her prophesies. The basis of their understanding is, then, cultural and linguistic – even literary and poetic.

This myth is an intriguing corollary to the events and characters of *The Agamemnon* for several additional reasons, but particularly because the action takes place in the northernmost province in Greece. Thracians are often reckoned to be particularly barbaric in Greek literature, and the actions firstly of Tereus, and then of the two expatriated Athenian sisters, appear calculated to suggest the horrors only Athenian civility can hold in abeyance. The myth is gratuitous on almost every count: not only does it consist of a redoubled revenge plot but each of the crimes is disproportionate even to the vile acts which precipitate them. Thus, Philomel's glossectomy would appear ample indemnity against discovering Tereus's initial violence, but the myth also insists on imprisoning her; similarly, when Itys is murdered, depriving Tereus of an heir, we might suppose that the revenge was heinous but proportionate to the extreme violence inflicted on Philomel; the myth insists on his being fed to his father. The purpose of these gratuitous extra measures is to emphasise the disparity between Athenian humanity and Thracian brutality. The discourse of barbarism serves to insinuate a general ethnic and moral difference between the two peoples while forcing them, as well as us, to question the absolute claims of such a world view. It appears rather as Strabo has indicated: a circumspect world view is the proper zeitgeist of so cosmopolitan a society. Cassandra may presage the horrors that unfold here, but they are not her doing; on the contrary, the events are deeply rooted in the house of Atreus and acutely implicate the society they are part of.

Though we are accustomed to thinking of literary comparison as being an imaginative and sometimes extraneous sort of identification, it is worth pointing out that not only is Cassandra *compared* to the swallow and the nightingale in *The Agamemnon*, she is often treated precisely as if she were one of these birds in this play. The comparison has a curiously literal dimension. The fact of her presence and her wailing for Apollo is 'a bad omen' for the chorus, and it turns out to be a correct omen; her bodily presence is 'read' just as if she were herself a bird and her song a portent of what is to come.[29] The terrifying presence that Cassandra exerts on Clytaemnestra and the audience, her too-capable transmission of those dark words of god, become even more pregnant if we consider how she literally approaches an avian condition for the other characters in the play, and how her language approximates not the speech of a foreigner, but a kind of *ornitho-logie*. She becomes comprehensible according to certain established rules that had long comprised the science of augury.

The importance of augury to Greek life is hard to overestimate. According to Leonard Lutwack, its influence is at least as old as the eighth century BCE, by which time 'Hesiod had written a treatise called *Divination by Birds*, no longer extant, which probably explained how signs could be used by farmers, sailors and rulers to avoid disaster in the conduct of their affairs'.[30] Augury derives its significance from the birds' supposed proximity to the gods, since they occupy the sky, the earthly region closest to the gods' heavenly abode; their quick, capricious movements, which seemingly belie the direction of the gods; and the strange rhythmical beauties of their song, which were readily understood to be literally inspired by the gods. Plutarch establishes this basis for the legitimacy of augury in *On the Intelligence of Animals*:

> In the art of predicting the future, the most important and most ancient part consists of bird lore. Thanks to their speed and intelligence, and to the precision of the movements with which they respond to everything impinging upon their senses, birds are the veritable instruments of divine power. It is the gods who determine the variety of their movements, and elicit from them their cries and twitterings.

He also argues that their song identifies birds as most like humans in intelligence, and distinguishes them from other animals, fish for example, which 'being dumb, are devoid of prophetic gifts. They are condemned to live in a place hated by the gods, where neither reason nor spiritual intelligence exists.'[31]

A complex and highly systematic method of interpretation, which translates the signs manifested by the birds into Attic Greek, evolved whereby soothsayers and exegetes could reveal the wishes of the gods. Most Greeks would practise augury in the circumstances of their ordinary life and according to their own talent. The signs afforded the Greek augur by birds' behaviour, feeding and song were not, according to H. W. Parke, 'like the Roman *auspica*, looked for in a particular place, after a specific ritual, but were taken as observed. Also there was no need to seek a reputed prophet to provide an interpretation.'[32] Moreover, birds were thought to convey the immortals' will not exceptionally but routinely and by default. It was even necessary to employ a different word, οἰωνῶν, a rare and poetic word, when one wanted to direct attention to a merely physical bird in Greek.[33] The ordinary Greek word for bird, *Öinos* or *Ornis*, even came itself to mean 'portent', and became applicable to anything that might offer insight into the will of the gods, so that by Aristophanes' time it was possible to generalise in a metonymical way from birds to other propitious signs.[34] As Stephen Halliwell observes, Aristophanes capitalises on this meaning in the parabasis of *Birds* when he has the Chorus Leader address the audience thus: 'You call a "bird" whatever gives you hints for augury. / A *word* can be a "bird" for you; you call a sneeze a "bird"; / Chance tokens, voices, slaves, and asses; you treat them all as "birds".'[35]

Augury, then, was merely the most ubiquitous and prestigious of the divinatory arts practised throughout antiquity, and we find some of these working in conjunction with augury in *The Agamemnon*. An involuntary action, like a sneeze or a convulsion, for example, was often thought to be portentous (based on the assumption that involuntary actions were instigated by the gods, and so might manifest their will).[36] Many of Cassandra's actions are thus pregnant with meaning, from her spectacular unveiling at the moment of Agamemnon's alighting on the blood-red tapestries, to her sudden recourse to speech and ecstatic convulsions. Her association with birds would also have been portentous, as an instance of *cledomancy* that, according to Robert Flacelière, 'was particularly concerned with the etymological meanings of words, especially of names'.[37]

Cassandra is thus understood to be an intermediary for the gods, and her actions, especially her ecstatic convulsions and pronouncements, may be referred to their will as cledons. The bird images with which the other characters describe her have a similarly ominous, but almost literal, function. The opening chorus of *The Agamemnon* begins with a prophecy for the house of Atreus. Calchas interprets the sight of two eagles attacking a pregnant hare as a sign that the war against Troy would go well, but cautioning against incurring the curse of the gods and warning of the deaths of Agamemnon and Cassandra.[38] The ominous power of their symbolism is meanwhile invested in Cassandra, and when next we hear of birds we are at the point of the fulfilment of Calchas's prophecy. To then identify Cassandra in her obstinate silence with the swallow, and subsequently with Philomel's plight, heightens the dramatic intensity at the climactic moment of the play, raising Cassandra's terror to fever pitch, and providing for the characters and audience a parallel of archetypal barbarity. But a contemporary audience would probably view such coincidences not so much as a literary allusion or conceit, but as an instance of (carefully arranged) cledomancy.

By examining the bird symbolism in *The Agamemnon*, it therefore becomes possible to discern two discrete types of foreign speech in ancient Greece: the relatively distinguished speech of those hailing from beyond 'Hellas and Mid-Argos', and the absolutely foreign speech of the gods. The former differs in no essential way from the Attic of the Tragedians, so that Strabo can (following Aristophanes and other Athenian comedic writers) even consider natives of Athens to have a barbarian speech quality in certain contexts.[39] The latter is qualitatively different from Attic Greek, an absolutely unknown and unknowable language whose closest analogue is birdsong. It amounts to something like pure *logos*, an opaque mediation between the immortal wisdom of the gods and the finite understanding of humanity.[40] It is a language nonetheless, and works 'by means of a conventional language whose grammar and laws were known', as Robert Flacelière writes, but only known to the initiated.[41] The supposition of such a language of the gods has a clear precedent if not a direct progenitor in the well-established and highly developed language that is augury. This language first took the form of symbolic and enigmatic verses, the necessary precaution of professional augurs and exegetes who would maintain their livelihood, but the same type of speech quickly becomes one of several available models for poetic speech: a poetics of jargon.

* * *

Nowhere in classical literature is a systematic poetics of jargon more clearly realised than in the play simply titled *Birds*, Aristophanes' remarkable poetic tour de force that systematically explores the comedic and literary possibilities of a huge variety of different foreign tongues. This play transforms literary symbolism concerned with birds and their songs into enchanting comedy and, by assimilating a mélange of diversely barbaric registers, challenges subsequent authors with a new type of literary art that is eager to embrace strange and exotic words, sounds and rhythms. At the same time, Aristophanes' avant-garde stylistic experiments derive from the same concerns and out of the same literary and cultural traditions that interested previous writers. The play returns to the archetypal myth of Athenian barbarism, though its action begins some time after Tereus, Procne (Prokne in the play) and Philomel's metamorphosis into birds. The former king of Thrace now lords over an empire of birds, and two Athenians, Peisetairos and Euelpides, seek out his kingdom desiring permanent escape from the litigiousness of Athenian life. They are drawn to what they perceive to be the civic excellences of Tereus's bird-kingdom: freedom from their accustomed chores and an abundance of spots in which to laze around, frequent festivals and feasts, and neighbours who are indignant only when their sons *aren't* customarily groped. This society is utopian only in the comic sense of at least not being Athens, and the Hellene–barbarian antithesis is seen to be a laughable fiction perpetrated by truants like Peisetairos for their own dubious advantage. 'Athenian anxieties about racial purity and citizenship', a leitmotif of the play according to Hubbard, 'are shown to be only a matter of convention.'[42]

The fiction does, however, remain powerfully in place throughout the play, even although the central characters strive in various ways to reject its validity. Tereus, for instance, attempts to obviate the linguistic differences between the birds and the Athenians and pleads that his new fellows 'used of course, to be barbarians once: / But I have taught them Greek since settling here with them', he says.[43] For many Greek authors, the possibility that the Greek language could be compromised by an influx of foreign tongues, become meaningless and so lose its essential relationship with the original matter it comprehended, was a real danger. Since *Birds* is the most linguistically and poetically eclectic play to have survived from this period, and Aristophanes' characters continually delight in barbarisms and exotic expressions throughout the author's work, it appears that Aristophanes is cynical about this conservative approach to language.[44] If barbarism is conventionally regarded as a threat to the social and cosmological order, Aristophanes secures his comic effect by demonstrating how it can be both efficiently and refreshingly eloquent.

The birds persist in communicating after their own fashion throughout the play, in their own highly stylised language, and are often vastly more competent and resourceful in this endeavour than the Greek characters. A particularly striking example of this occurs when Tereus implores Prokne's help in rousing his fellow birds. He carefully distinguishes her speech from that of the Athenians, describing it in terms that are remarkably consistent with those used to describe Cassandra's speech in *The Agamemnon*: her 'sacred chants' are said to be 'inspired'; a 'pure' song composed of 'liquid notes'.[45] He then himself goes on to provide a demonstration of the sort of eloquence that such a song can command, in the first of many of his attempts to render birdsong in poetry, some of the finest verse he composed.

It is vital to note in this regard how carefully the birds exploit and subvert their traditional role as the conduit of communication between mortals and gods in the play. Peisetairos' plans to thwart intercourse between the two, frustrating humanity by preventing the gods interceding in their lives, and particularly their control of the seasons, and frustrating the gods by denying them the tributary prayers and sacrificial offerings they have come to expect. The situation closely parallels that which Tiresias announces in *Antigone*: by rendering the auspices unreadable the birds may reduce the social equilibrium between gods and men to chaos (that they stand to gain from this chaos at the expense of both men and gods is a ridiculous comic addition). The birds are hypostatised as *logos* itself, and the rupture they propose in communication threatens only to replace the pedestrian wrangling of the Athenian merchants and jurors with the birds' spectacularly poetic jargon.

The birds are not the only group of barbarians in Aristophanes' comedy, however, and their song needs to be carefully distinguished from the language of the others. Offering the most tangible counterpoint to their melodious strain is the Triballian, the barbarian god who arrives at the end of the play, along with Poseidon and Heracles, to negotiate a peace between gods and birds. He is introduced to the audience and the other characters as 'much the most / Barbarian god' that Poseidon has 'ever set eyes upon'.[46] His speech, like the birds', is often merely, or primarily, phonetic, but it differs from that of the birds in that its noise is not musically enabled: he speaks only short, fragmentary utterances, with none of the exquisite form or patterning of the birds' speech. The other characters in *Birds* do not seem to understand what the Triballian says very clearly at all, but, curiously enough, his speech is no less a summons to the imagination than the birds' speech or than Cassandra's speech in *The Agamemnon*, though it works in an utterly different way. His first response, at l. 1615, is 'totally unclear' according to Dunbar, and may be deliberate and total gibberish.[47] The second and third occasions that follow 'contain some intelligible Greek', but again, there is no consensus about what the Triballian says or intends. Whatever sense is most handy to the more sophisticated characters in the play is simply inferred and assumed each time he speaks. As Timothy Long puts it: 'everyone is well disposed to any answer that can be construed as a yes.

Is the answer in itself understandable? Almost certainly not.'[48] This gives rise to an inevitable dispute between two characters both claiming the Triballian's assent to their devices, and the resulting dialogue is quite revealing:

> PEISETAIROS. The Triballian has the casting vote. Well then?
> TRIBALLIAN. Di luvvli tawli girli Princi-cinsi.
>   Di birdi handi ova.
> HERACLES [*emphatically*].
>   He votes in favour.
> POSEIDON. He doesn't vote to hand her over at all!
>   He's simply twittering on just like the swallows.
> PEISETAIROS. That means he wants her handing *to* the swallows![49]

Though far from emphatic, the import of the Triballian's response is clear enough, and Heracles is quickly satisfied: the ambassadors are to hand over Basileia, Apollo's consort, to the birds. Poseidon this time pleads that the Triballian's words convey no such thing, and dismisses them as being like the proverbially meaningless chatter of the birds, since they offer no tangible support for his own position.[50] This is an especially pointed piece of irony because we have learned that the birds are quite the most linguistically capable characters in this world, and that their song is the most meaning-full. At the same time, only in the context of its supposed affinity with birdsong does the Triballian's speech ultimately decide the matter. Peisetairos takes the nonsensical elements that have dominated the Triballian's utterances, and that he is reminded of by Poseidon, as a cledon – an unwitting indication that his own aspirations are acceptable to the gods – rather than at face value. This is blatantly contrary to the gods' own interests, and a keen illustration of the most basic dilemma of augury: once law and grammar are established, the augur or exegete becomes more authoritative than the gods themselves. Having become a bird, Peisetairos exerts control of the auspices so that he can have his own way as chief augur. Understanding becomes an unnecessary inconvenience when the interpreter becomes more powerful even than any putative author, and this is precisely the state of play as the comedy concludes, in pure festival.

This indecipherability is in patent contrast to each of the speakers that have appeared up to this very late point in the play, and also to Cassandra in *The Agamemnon*. This sort of language is entirely dependent on the immediate context in which it appears, as Long again suggests: 'only when the answer of the barbarian is crucial can he say anything decipherable'.[51] The dramatic situation entirely circumscribes the meaning that the Triballian's utterance will have. This is the kind of speech that the first human might have uttered, gesturing towards food or a natural enemy, and is, simply, part of his sensible orientation in the world, no less and no more revealing than his physical demeanour or his clothing. The bird reference is again particularly apposite, for the swallow seems chosen to suggest the basic quality of his utterance, and lack of more ambitious, lyrical articulation. The same figure, let us recall, was used of Cassandra while she remained a passive observer of Agamemnon's welcome by Clytaemnestra. The swallow is the pre-eminent symbol of the barbarian in Greek literature presumably because it seems reticent to sing like other birds, and the sounds it makes are rather noises than melodies, like the Triballian's speech in this comedy.

Aristophanes' distinction between these two forms of non-Attic utterance, the barbarian's and the songbird's, suggest that there are at least a couple of alternatives open to poets and dramatists wishing to explore the literary possibilities of considering language in this way. The Triballian's rough and ready speech is scarcely communicative, and marks him as a primitive character; indeed, it fits perfectly well with Strabo's notion of barbarian speech as difficult and harsh, marked by stuttering and lisping. Language can help orientate such a character in the world, but cannot achieve lucidity on any aspect of that world. Birdsong, on the other hand, is a more sensible medium even than pedestrian Athenian Greek. Birdsong and barbarianism are two complementary ideas, then, but they are deployed discretely and have the potential to mean different things. This is one of the reason why the comedy in Aristophanes' play does not satisfactorily reduce to satire: the strange language evinced by the birds cannot be thought of like the Triballian's, as a stilted barbarian tongue, as an enfeebled Greek, at all. On the contrary, their language *is* Greek; its strangeness is possible within the Greek language itself, and constitutes a delightful and poetic type of Greek. The Triballian, on the contrary, is a clumsy stock character; the audience can scarcely stop laughing at him long enough to sympathise with him. Despite the fact that he ought to be as adept at Greek as the birds' tutor, Tereus the hoopoe, since the name Triballian 'belonged to a Thracian tribe who became a byword at Athens for extreme savagery' according to Halliwell's footnote – despite being a *god*, moreover – he does not manage to communicate with the audience or the other characters in the play. One can only conclude from this parallel that the birds' poetic jargon is quite distinct from the Triballian's outright barbarism.

Nor is this the only group of characters in the play whose use of language marks them as peculiar. Gorgias and the sophists are introduced shortly after the Triballian, and are perhaps made to seem even more ridiculously barbarous than he is, as '*nasty* beasts who live by tongue work'.[52] This is not an uncommon view of the sophists' activities, then or now. Scott Consigny summarises Plato's view of Gorgias as 'a festive orator . . . among the class of verbal athletes who are mere jugglers of words rather than true philosophers intent on finding truth'.[53] But as more recent critics have come to realise, following G. W. F. Hegel (for whom Gorgias 'is a subjective idealist, for whom objective reality is neither knowable nor articulable in words'), the importance placed by the sophists on language may have important, positive consequences. One recent interpreter, Anthony Cascardi, summarises this position memorably, explaining that, for Gorgias,

> we are confined in a 'virtual prison-house,' wherein 'our thoughts and our existence, our mind as much as our being' is trapped within an 'obstinate, intransigent cellophane margin; we are caught in the ambiguity of not knowing being from non-being because of the opaque gossamer of words'.[54]

Cascardi appeals to the opacity of language in the sense that I have been employing throughout. Gorgias's belief in a 'prison-house' of language means, on this radical account, that all truth is fundamentally individual, local and temporary, a matter of subjective conviction, of rhetoric as much as truth per se. This appears consonant with Aristophanes' approach to language in *Birds*, an approach that emphasises diversity and attests to different degrees and kinds of language and so of knowledge. Aristophanes skilfully perverts and explodes this doctrine, suggesting that the sophists' reality is literally produced by their linguistic exercises, the result of their literary-philosophical fancy: 'All they sow and all they reap, / All that falls into their hands, / Comes to them by use of tongue.'[55]

The philosopher Socrates, depicted as a dubious mage rather than a person governed by reason, is similarly disposed of in *Birds*.[56] The figures of rhetorician and philosopher are treated with a remarkable uniformity throughout the comedy. Peisetairos in particular, whose name means 'persuader of companion(s)', and who is responsible for instigating the birds' revolt and creating Cloud-cuckoo-land, is not even exempt from the charge of sophism; the hoopoe describes him as 'a wily old fox – / Sophist and quibbler and spiv, so smooth and so subtle',[57] terms which, Halliwell suggests, would 'suit a rhetorical adept, not least one who is a product, or for that matter a purveyor, of sophistic techniques'.[58] He elsewhere exhibits

> a sharpness of debating style, an array of cosmogonical, historical, and religious lore, and a sense of how power can be wrested from the gods back to the birds, all of which give something of the character of a rhetorical politician or ambassador.[59]

It appears that the barbarian and the philosophers have similar problems with language: it separates them from the society of men that would make it properly meaningful. For the Triballian, recall, every noise he utters is put to use according to the inclinations of the other characters, and without regard for meaning. The sophists use language simply for their own profit, without regard for the truth, and even Socrates' wisdom is arcane and largely unamenable to human use on this satirical account. Aristophanes seems to advance a critique of philosophy with these gestures. He suggests that philosophy has retreated to a level of abstraction in its musings that prevents it from correctly apprehending the world as it appears to the populace, of becoming abstruse and mystical like the sacrificial rites of the old religions, of lacking transparency or humanity. Although the term did not exist for the Greeks, he basically accuses them of proliferating jargon. The charge, directed perhaps for the first time at learned language rather than merely different language, will be often repeated, and it will prove a necessary bane for the philosopher and the poet alike.

It appears that Aristophanes takes Gorgias's teachings about language and knowledge seriously on some level, as seriously perhaps as Gorgias himself, whose treatise *On That Which is Not, Or Nature*, which is known only through summaries, is thought to be an attempt to prove an impossible philosophical argument, and so an ingenious demonstration of the power of rhetoric. His reference certainly belies a familiarity with the sophists' teaching, since he seems to specifically refer to Gorgias's repudiation of popular orators who live by the water-clock or *clepsydra*, an apparatus used to limit the time of each orator in legal and political contexts.[60] Gorgias's revulsion was for external limitations on experienced reality: since truth is for him individual and temporary (i.e., based in the moment), it follows that such artificial devices could only obscure human access to truth and render it even more arbitrary that it is already.

The clepsydra stands as a particularly apt symbol for Aristophanes' poetic art in *Birds*: each speaker has his or her particularly allocated measure; an allotted time and metre in which to claim our attention. Aristophanes creates a poetic opening on experienced reality, a 'kairotic moment' such as Gorgias advocates is necessary to the acquisition of knowledge. And, as Consigny reminds us,

> Gorgias is not alone in maintaining that human beings are unable to comprehend the ultimate nature of things. Indeed, as Plato points out, this is the traditional view of many poets whom he opposes in what he calls the 'ancient quarrel' between poetry and philosophy ... and whom he specifically associates with Gorgias when he characterizes Gorgian rhetoric as poetic.[61]

If Plato's reading of Gorgias is correct, the significance of Gorgias for *Birds* lies in his levelling of all discursive language to so much rhetoric. On such a conception, the perfection and epitome of human reasoning is not truth or philosophy but poetry. In a world of nothing but opinion and rhetoric there can be no more reliable criterion for accepting or dismissing something as fact or fiction than the extent to which it is plausible and well-formed. In *Birds*, Aristophanes concludes that the most perfect expression of human thought attainable is the most copious exploration of the *form* of that thought. Moreover, he presents us, in *Birds*, with an attempt to perfect such a *logos* by bestowing upon us a purely musical language, the least sophisticated and subjective rhetoric imaginable, and the most poetic: the jargoning of the birds.

* * *

There is every reason to suppose that bird symbolism pre-dates even the earliest literary usage, going back to pre-Homeric myth. The case of Tereus, Procne and Philomel is perhaps typical in this regard: it bundles a potent store of thematic associations and hands them down to literary posterity. But this myth has another, more unique and telling reason to recommend it to poets and dramatists. By focusing on the vocal abilities of bird and human together, it supplies a unique and enduring way of thinking about poetic art. For Aristophanes, the myth results in a prosodic system obviously based on the sonic qualities that he would have been able to observe in the calls of Athenian birds. His rhythmic virtuosity and unique sensitivity to sound – bird and human – deliver a highly natural evocation of birdcalls and some of the most remarkable, stylised and unique poetry of the Attic stage. The dual capacity to render birdsong realistically and meet the exigencies of poetic form so subtly intersects with the thematic concerns of the play and produces an emphatic style that both governs the play's meaning and supplies a decisive datum of interpretation. In doing so, it provides a paradigm for subsequent literary jargonings.

Greek drama uses chanting and song (accompanied or not) to such an extent that an audience could understand the parallel between an actor's dialogue and the birdsong it dramatises without much prodding from the dramatist. Nevertheless, Aristophanes elects to foreground the musicality of his characters' voices throughout his work, and often in surprising ways. Most invitingly of all, the character most lauded for beautiful song in *Birds* – Prokne the nightingale – never even gets to speak. Her first entrance is announced by Tereus the hoopoe, who rouses her thus:

Come, nest-mate of mine, wake up from your sleep!
Issue forth all the strains of the sacred chants
In which you lament, with a mouth that's inspired,
For the child of us both, oh piteous Itys!
Let your voice thrill the air with its liquid notes,
Through your vibrant throat! For your song is so pure
As it echoes around, through the rich-leaved trees,
Till it reaches the throne of lord Zeus above,
Where Phoibos as well, golden-tressed god of song,
Hears your grief and responds on his ivory lyre,
As he summons the gods to take part in the dance.
Then is heard from above an immortal choir,
      All in unison clear,
As the gods cry in grief for your plight.[62]

This description of the nightingale's song is delightfully controlled to suggest its musicality, and when it arrives it takes the form of the aulete's (or piper's) melody, no doubt in plausible imitation of the nightingale's song.[63] Composed of 'liquid notes' – lilting and flowing phrases that suggest the sound and movement of a stream, emitted by a throat that vibrates like the reed in a wind instrument, gathering a 'pure' sound – the nightingale's song, as intimated by the aulete, is both the epitome of musicality and untrammelled by the necessity to make discursive sense. Taking Prokne's mythical glossectomy into consideration, Aristophanes seems to suggest that perfect lyricism is incompatible with ordinary, prosaic, Athenian language. We are also reminded here that birdsong involves 'inspiration', awakening the traditionally direct relationship between birdsong and the gods. As part of the 'thrilled' cosmos effected by Prokne's cry as its echoes abound in the air, the gods cannot help but respond in kind to the nightingale: Phoibos and Zeus, and then all the gods, respond with music of their own. Where the hoopoe responds in precisely the same way as the gods, by bursting into elaborate song, the mortals resort to appreciative ejaculations. All of nature is united in producing this most perfect expression of natural beauty: human, bird, god – all are members of the ensemble.[64]

Prokne is introduced for a second time by the Chorus Leader as 'the sweet-tongued nightingale, / The bird who sings just like a Muse.'[65] This comparison between Prokne and the inspirational daughters of Zeus and Mnemosyne who preside over human learning and art again impresses the divine associations of birdsong upon the audience. At the same time, the terms echo Euelpides' ecstatic reception of the piper's song: 'O Zeus in heaven! The birdy's lovely voice! / It filled the wood with a sound as sweet as honey!'[66] Both insist that the song appeals in some sensual way, and the simile 'sweet as honey' makes the specific association with taste and appetite. The terms of praise are unanimously sensual: Prokne's language is a natural language, one with a direct and immediate effect on the body, and so its charms are irresistible to the two truant epicureans who come across it. The parabasis also cements the nightingale's reputation as the most musical of birds by celebrating her 'melodious sounds', which acquire the tangibility of an elaborately woven fabric.[67] In terms of this metaphor, the lauded quality is not simply melody, but harmony and antiphony, the fitting together of discrete elements to form a more intricate symphonic pattern. The nightingale's song is composed of heterogeneous musical elements rather than a simple musical phrase or effusion.

If these hyperbolic reactions are to be taken seriously, the reason for denying Prokne actual speech is hardly a question of restricting her role. Her status as 'loveliest of all the birds', her lauded song, the most superlative among them all, entitles Prokne to a perfectly musical part. Her voice serves as an ideal that the other characters will in various ways approximate in their own speech; many other birdsongs in the play share several of the qualities just enumerated, though they cannot quite attain the fluency that allows Prokne to forego the more directly discursive modes of Attic speech. Perfect musicality is presented as an asymptote that the other birds may approach but never entirely attain: their speech remains variously proportioned admixtures of human language and mere sound. Aristophanes presents a communicative spectrum ranging from the pedestrian magniloquence of the Athenians and the absurdly pragmatic rhetoric of the ambassadors and philosophers, on the one hand, to the ecstatic music of the nightingale, on the other. Most characters in the play fit somewhere in between.

* * *

The musicality of Aristophanes' other characters is most perfectly realised in the rhythm of their language. The iterant qualities of melody, and therefore birdsong, may be readily reproduced by the rhythms of Attic verse. Since the latter is organised according to quantity, the duration of individual notes and phrases, and of course the punctual silences, can be given with some degree of fidelity (and without the automatic and overbearing rhetorical emphasis of accentual-syllabic verse). Hardly musical notation at its best, perhaps, but we may well agree with Leonard Lutwack: it is about 'all that language can do in this respect'.[68] In Aristophanes' capable hands the prosodic resources of the Attic stage and of lyrical tradition brim with melody, harmony and rhythm; he could hardly have been more explicit in this regard. The fact that

Aristophanes includes 'every major type of meter found in Attic drama, with, in addition, some rarities', provides an important clue to the type of drama we are dealing with.[69] Like Pindar's odes, for example, *Birds* seeks a formal analogue for its thematic concerns. Where Pindar's forceful and supple metric hopes to equal or surpass the extraordinary feats of the Olympians he celebrates, Aristophanes' versification provides a stereophonic spectacle befitting the pageant of plume and talon he presents on-stage. Dunbar's conclusion, that he evidently 'set out to dazzle his audience with a display of metrical and musical virtuosity', is irresistible.[70]

The variety and virtuosity of the spectacle performs two crucial and essentially musical functions in the play: first, it delineates an impressive variety of birdcalls, allowing the perceptive auditor to distinguish between bird species. Second, nimbly flitting between a great variety of metres, with all their attendant variations, enables the dramatist to subtly replicate the agile turn of phrase of the more elaborate songsters. In order to appreciate the earnestness of this effort, it is necessary first to remind ourselves that Greek audiences, or certain elements within them at least, were infinitely more attuned to the musical aspects of poetic language than moderns. By way of illustration, L. P. E. Parker notes that 'Aristophanes' contemporaries were able to recognize not only verbal allusion but rhythmic allusion, not only verbal stylistic level but musical stylistic level. This is perhaps the widest gulf between their powers of appreciation and ours.'[71] To elevate the prosodic and musical elements of the play into an important datum of interpretation is therefore both consistent with the reception the play would have met with from its original audience and with the conviction of modern scholarship; indeed, scarcely any other literary text has demanded so much attention to prosody and been so enriched thereby.

Many authors who deal notably with birdsong (perhaps especially the Romantics) are guilty of failing to mark the idiosyncrasies of the particular birdcalls they celebrate in their poetry, producing a generalised poetic trope. Aristophanes, on the contrary, distinguishes between species of birds with his prosody, couching each species' call in a discrete verse form. This effect is most impressive when it is first introduced, in the hoopoe's solo. I quote it at length:

> Hoopoopoo! Hoopoopoo!
> Ee-oo! Ee-oo! Come everyone!
> Come all my feathered friends!
> All you who live on well-sown farmers' fields,
>   You myriad flocks of barley-eaters,
>   Seed-peckers of countless kinds,

Fly quickly here, emit your mellow cries!
And all you birds that crowd in furrows
To twitter round the crumbling clods
    With such elated sounds,
Twee-twee, twee-twee! Twee-twee, twee-twee!

And all you birds of garden habitats
    Where ivy branches sprout,
You mountain species, feeders on olives and berries,
    Take wing at once in answer to my call!
        Trrrr, trrrr! Trrrr, trrrr!

And you who on the rolling hills
Gulp down shrill gnats, and you who live
In the dew-soaked plains and Marathon's lonely meadows,
    With you of mottled-wings, O francolin, francolin!
    And birds which over the sea's great swell
        Soar out among the halcyons,
Come here to learn the latest news!
Yes, every class of long-necked bird
    Must congregate around me.
    An old and wily man's arrived;
    His mind is full of new ideas
    And new the deeds he plans to do.
Come, all you birds, to hold discussion,
    Quickly, quickly, quickly, quickly!
        Tsee-tsee, tsee-tsee!
        Kee-wick! Kee-wick!
Tsee-tsee, tsee-tsee, tisisisi![72]

The most striking features of this solo are its rhythmical variety and percussive use of aural effects. These are related and are, broadly considered, aspects of the dramatist's prosody. Aristophanes was perhaps inspired to recreate such lyrical fluency by observing the many species of birds (though as far as I am aware not the hoopoe) that repeat and respond to the cries of other birds.[73] As Alan Powers observes, birds mimic either to lure other birds towards them, or, more benevolently, as a spontaneous and improvised form of communication.[74] In the case of the hoopoe's solo, both are dramatically expedient. His song, as depicted here, is akin to the North American mockingbird's, stored with a 'vast anthology of other birds' calls, done in his own timbre, sometimes with his own added microtones'.[75] Like many able mimickers, Tereus appears to have developed a lingua franca that is universally recognised by bird and human alike. The mimicry in his song is most acute to modern ears in the lines where distinct onomatopoeic expressions complement the metrical variety: the *Twee-twee*'s, *Trrrr-trrrr*'s, *Tsee-tsee*'s and *Kee-wick*'s.

This song has, in addition to its own excellences, the important dramatic function of introducing the Chorus for the first time in the play. Twenty-four species of birds are separately named by the dramatist (although there is some critical debate about their identity in modern ornithological terms), and they remain easily distinguishable on-stage by costumes (with a specified colour in most instances) and by their diverse masks.[76] The hoopoe's solo prepares the audience for this unprecedented vision of particularity by mimicking, and announcing, the several calls of each member of the Chorus in turn.[77] The impression we get of the hoopoe from this solo is of an urbane multilinguist, shifting at will between a splendid variety of dialects and jargons.[78]

The broad inclusiveness of social (and anti-social) activity depicted in *Birds* has become a well-noted interpretive crux, and Aristophanes' metrical diversity has the important function of distinguishing a rich variety of human and avian behaviour in the play. From the supreme lyricism of the hoopoe's solo and the Choral songs, to the curt repartee that predominates in the second half of the play (and in most scenes featuring human characters), Aristophanes seems to recognise, as most subsequent authors do not, that birdsong is not simply a beautiful and evocative melody, at least as far as the birds themselves are concerned. Such a notion is preposterously Romantic, perhaps, and it is in part responsible for the neglect of serious technical reflection on birdsong as a paradigm in poetic creation. As Alan Powers explains, what appears to us a beautiful lyrical effusion is, more often than not, anything but.[79] Whatever Aristophanes' poetics of jargon may be, it is not in any sense exclusively or even primarily concerned with mellifluousness. Instead, by founding his art on a range of birdcalls, Aristophanes' jargon becomes amenable to a sweeping array of occasions and many different types of expression. This is perhaps the essential thing in literary comedy: its alchemical ability to transform base animal matter (especially when it concerns humans) into entertainment of the highest aesthetic and intellectual order rests in no small part on the wide aperture of the comedic lens. The term 'jargon' presupposes that the language so described will be neither popular nor familiar, nor too narrowly traditional nor generic, but peripheral, strange, enticing and opaque at the same time. A jargonish aesthetic tends towards inclusiveness: the vagaries of sexual desire or the latest, most arcane scientific and ethnographic developments alike will serve as its subject. Poets, like the birds themselves, need only observe a simple maxim, also well stated by Powers: 'when their behavior changes, their language changes'.[80]

Critical interest in prosodic variety and inclusiveness in *Birds* has been persistent and productive in the twentieth century, beginning with

J. W. White. His theory of 'intentional variation of melody' explains that change of rhythm is often intentional and significant: the rhythm selected is often 'singularly appropriate to the sentiment expressed' in Aristophanes.[81] The examples he provides often concern psychological or emotional changes between choral strophe and antistrophe, and Parker adds compelling accounts of similar instances of metrical expressionism.[82] In general, prosody is used as a device to add contextual specificity and emotional complexity to the characters in *Birds*, and so to differentiate them. If this reading is correct, the requirement for such a double signification prevents Aristophanes from treating prosody in a more conventional and more absolute sense. He does indeed make use of certain a priori associations of particular metres in *Birds*, but in a disciplined way that prevents the play from seeming mechanical.[83] The metrical resourcefulness of the poet proves sufficient to distinguish a range of different birdcalls in the play; it helps to differentiate character and to suggest context-specific alterations within character.

Aristophanes reserves his most spectacular forms (aside from the pure music of the aulete) for the hoopoe and the Chorus, where he transforms ordinary Attic Greek into a poetry befitting its avian locutors. Significantly, the most impressive speeches these characters make contain the highest proportion of pure sounds. For extended moments in the play, language is reduced – or *heightened* in the dramatic context – to rhythm and melody, often with dazzling results, as in the hoopoe's extravagant summons to the other birds where the high concentration of merely phonetic passages is conspicuously instrumental in securing his effect. The song begins with a repeated birdcall that transitions neatly into more clearly articulated speech in l. 228. As Dunbar observes, we are prepared for this attempt to display the hoopoe's song directly by a preceding passage that reproduces his sound in similar terms: a repeated sequence of ἐποποι, here given as 'hoopoopoo'.[84] The next line begins in the same fashion with a basic, sonic usage of language; sense, however, seems to gradually assert itself.[85]

With this initial gradient between sound and sense, fittingly dubbed 'one of the most attractive features of Aristophanes' bird-language' by Dunbar, we are shown human meaning gradually emerging from avian noise.[86] We get to hear sense emerging in a casual, natural fashion here, in stark contrast to the precarious way it emerges when the other ambassadors attempt to involve the Triballian in their deliberations, for example, where the difficulty between sound and sense is surmountable only by extraordinary and unwarranted acts of inference. The effect is secured by a superabundance of onomatopoeic words, at the beginning and end of the solo especially (the names of many Greek birds are derived mimetically and onomatopoeically from their call, and Aristophanes makes the most of this happy detail).[87]

At moments like these in the play language indeed seems to be a kind of code to be made or broken.[88] To adapt a phrase from Dudley Fitts's (rather free) translation of the play, the language reveals, beyond its surfaces, 'the sparkling / Undersong' to the inarticulate utterances of the birds. The anthropomorphic focalisation offered by the particular device of transitioning from bird language to human language at the beginning of this song, and back again at the end, results in a kind of magical translation of the birds' jargon: the poetic equivalent of cinematic fairy dust. It is surely significant that Tereus should provide this himself; he is the only character with knowledge of both human and bird language since his metamorphosis ('Your mind contains the thoughts of man and bird', says Peisetairos).[89] The more spectacular achievement is that Aristophanes should succeed in having him speak both languages *at the same time*, for his noises are a realistic reminder of the hoopoe's chattering, and yet he conspires to convey a human meaning with these very utterances. His speech, throughout the play, is a complex and precarious interlanguage, different from anything actually spoken by man or bird and so more exotic; it is more refined than any regional form, neither Attic nor barbarian but artificial, context specific and non-habitual. Its capaciousness and variety represent the epitome of communicative achievement in the world of the play, and Aristophanes claims for poetry thus conceived something analogous to what Descartes (and, via Descartes, what Noam Chomsky) claims for Reason: it is a 'universal instrument which can serve for all contingencies'[90] and that 'therefore provides for unbounded diversity of free thought and action'.[91]

Crucially, Aristophanes' emphasis on the aural aspects of language in the hoopoe's solo lyric and elsewhere are quite doxological, and they complement the available contemporary aesthetic models nicely. Although more interested in epic and tragic literature, Aristotle's comments in the *Poetics* provide a useful critical framework. For Aristotle,

> diction becomes distinguished and non-prosaic by the uses of unfamiliar terms, i.e. strange words, metaphors, lengthened forms, and everything that deviates from the ordinary modes of speech. – But a whole statement in such terms will either be a riddle or a barbarism, a riddle, if made up of metaphors, a barbarism, if made up of strange words.[92]

In reserving the term barbarism for the extended use of unfamiliar terms and accommodating the occasional adoption of an obscure word or phrase within ordinary poetic practice, Aristotle allows us to appreciate just how radical the hoopoe's first song is. He also suggests that we

may distinguish legitimate poetic use of barbarism and barbarism that is
used 'improperly', or 'with a view to provoking laughter', and suggests
the effect of 'too apparent' use of any strange quality in drama is invariably 'ludicrous'. If it suits the dramatist's ends to provoke laughter, as
for example in Aristophanes' presentation of the Triballian's speech,
then it may indeed constitute expedient if not fine poetry, but overuse
of these estranging effects in epic and tragic literature are, for him, a
serious breach of poetic decorum. As so often in Aristotle, the question
is of balance: 'These, the strange word, the metaphor, the ornamental
equivalent, &c, will save the language from seeming mean and prosaic,
while the ordinary words in it will secure the requisite clearness.'[93] On
this account, the two elements of discourse, sound and sense, are seen
to be capable of more or less autonomous existence, and this is how
Aristophanes treats them in the hoopoe's first song. By dichotomising
language in this way, it becomes possible to use it in a contrapuntal,
musical fashion, now privileging the merely percussive, now emphasising the discursive element etc., weaving the two together so as to accent
different qualities of the 'fabric' depending on the context and the sense
– or nonsense – to be conveyed.

A variety of different but related types of barbarism operate in these
early invocations by the hoopoe. There are those, indeed, which appear
to shun discursive meaning deliberately and emphatically, nonsense
words and onomatopoeic expressions that enable a mimetic depiction of
the birdcall while meeting the demands of the prosody. A good example
of this first sort of poetic obfuscation is a word that Aristophanes particularly associates with the nightingale, ξουθης. This word poses an interesting problem because of its unknown meaning and etymology. Dunbar
notes that the word is 'always applied to winged creatures by contemporary poets', but conjectures that already (i.e., by the fifth century
BCE) it no longer had any precise meaning.[94] M. S. Silk argues that the
word is best thought of as an *iconym*, that is, 'a word which has lost its
denotations' but has, in this instance, maintained its associations with
'sound and/or rapid movement'.[95] Instead of *meaning*, iconyms possess
and produce what Silk describes as 'a diffuse imprecision', which 'tends
to linger, like a haze'.[96] That is to say, they clearly have much the same
function in Aristophanes' verse as the examples of nonsense words and
onomatopoeia: they infect the sense with the materiality of the language
and prioritise its sound.[97] Associating the nightingale with meaningless,
pure sound is, moreover, consistent with Prokne's portrayal in the play
by a mute character on-stage accompanied by the melody of the aulete,
the most compelling symbol of Aristophanes' dichotomous understanding of poetic art in the play. Were it not for the infallible 'identity'

between music and poetry, Prokne would seem quite as disembodied as Nietzsche's headless statue.

There are also several other less pronounced strategies that complement these powerfully sense-stymieing effects, and make for an even more tactile and less discursive kind of poetry. For instance, Aristophanes makes routine use of an often-specialised vocabulary that admits various degrees and sources of obscurity. In such instances, and there are too many to enumerate fully here, the strange term acts both as a sonic cipher that fills the utterance up with opaque matter as the characters' ontological status seems to require, and at the same time suggests – or conveys directly to those familiar with the term – something more precisely discursive. The text routinely delights in pointing out these linguistic features. One prime example, already mentioned, is the word οἰωνῶν, 'meaning "large birds" without implications of augury', which, like many words in the play, is now known to be an exclusively poetic usage.[98] Barbarisms – that is to say, word adoptions from other, foreign, languages, and especially those extended passages that Aristotle cautiously proffers to the poet – are favoured devices of this kind, and are used to imbue the passage with a rich aural texture and diminish its denotative purchase on the audience.

Barbarisms reproduce the effect of language stymieing local human understanding. Encountering a barbarism, as for example the parody of Thracian vowels that make up the Triballian's initial response to Peisetairos, one meets directly the sonic corporeality of language and the suggestion, however muted by unfamiliarity, of potentially meaningful communication.[99] Barbarisms are a summons to interpretation because they seem mysteriously to grapple with exotic knowledge, the subject of so many ethnographies (and because of the otherwise regular syntax, grammar and in this case rhythmical contexts in which they appear). They are an invitation to make sense precisely out of the unknown, and again show language in its emergence from mere noise. It is surely not surprising that writers as early as Strabo have supposed the word's origin to be onomatopoeic: what initially survives in a borrowing is not the knowledge that a word or phrase apprehends, but its hollow sound and its feeling; its very potential to mean.

A plausibly strange and melodious birdlike poetry may be produced by systematically adapting and concentrating the ordinary conventions of lyric and tragic poetry. Indeed, this may not even be a poetic conceit at all, since the practice of couching important pronouncements in the accoutrements of poetry is one of the staples of augury: 'Loxias', the ambiguous one, is the name given to Apollo in *Oedipus Rex*. Accordingly, Kenneth Dover notices that the parabasis song uses the 'vocabulary and imagery of tragic and lyric poetry to bring the birds, as part of the order of nature, into a relation with the gods which is independent of man'.[100] In order to underscore the sonic aspects of language and aid in his poetic approximation of birdsong, Aristophanes employs many other established literary devices with the same exuberance as he displays in his use of barbarisms. The most obvious and ubiquitous of these are the puns and double entendres found abundantly throughout the play that supply much of its comic force.[101] But the systematic use of such dissimulation supplies more than comedy: it enables language to function in a direct and dramatically efficient way while presenting ancillary meaning in the form of idiomatic or context-specific codes. Puns supply the literary equivalent to grace notes in music: the dramatist introduces with them an embellishment that is extraneous to the structural and thematic demands of the composition, but which the performer and audience clearly relish. These are by definition based precisely on the aural features of Aristophanes' language. By emphasising the identity of sound in divergent discursive contexts, Aristophanes allows the sound of the language to govern its importance, often singularly. The sound of language, its materiality, emerges as a primary consideration of the text, and often seems even more crucial than the sense. As Parker explains

> words, as has often been pointed out, were much more important in ancient Greek song than, generally, in that of modern Europe – and even in modern Europe comic opera is an exception. But here, in the birds' song, the words are genuinely secondary.[102]

In combination with other effects, this verbal thickening, this dissimulation, effectively allows language to approach the much greater polysemy of birdsong. The secondary meaning that emerges is, moreover, often unnoticed or misunderstood by those characters against whom the humour is directed, further impressing the audience with the sense that language is a meaningful code only within a particular dramatic or idiomatic context. The extended use of 'bird' to mean 'whatever gives you hints for augury' simply generalises this point.

Another traditional device that Aristophanes deploys in his aesthetics of jargon is the extended use of poetic compounds; there are many in the play – *Nephelokokkygia*, or Cloud-cuckoo-land – being only the most famous.[103] These are, almost without exception, 'choice and very rare compound[s]', often found exclusively in verse according to Dunbar. Neologisms, too, feature prominently in *Birds*. Compound and novel forms do not necessarily render a passage more obscure, since the articulated words or syllables may well be transparent enough in themselves.[104] Periphrasis and circumlocution are sufficient, however, to imbue the passage with density and materiality, while presenting its quotient of ideas as if for the first time. Aristophanes often urges us to consider language thus in its emergence. When the Chorus Leader notes the idiomatic usage of 'birds' for 'whatever gives you hints for augury', for example, he attests to the dynamic and associative nature of human signification whereby words come to mean things most suggestively by overextension, and by exceeding their immediate denotations.[105] Borrowing the compound epithet from epic and heroic literature makes Aristophanes' verse less prosaic, more spontaneous and more imaginative. The effect is of elaborating a relatively coarse sensible material into an unprecedented and ready new tongue. In addition to the spontaneous quality of this kind of homespun, improvisatory language, there is the impressive fact that these longer compound phrases more completely fulfil the prosodic demands of metron or line, and the result is a more perfectly musical – if less direct and grammatical – song.[106]

The basic strategy is consistent with the use of other devices in the play, and has of course received fairly systematic treatment by Aristotle who, let us recall, says quite clearly (in distinction to Ariphrades and other detractors) that 'it is a great thing, indeed, to make a proper use of ... compounds and strange words', because it 'gives diction a non-prosaic character'.[107] Aristotle is quick to point out that he does not simply mean reasonably unfamiliar words whose meanings are not precisely known by laymen, but γλωττα, 'expressions unknown in the language of common life'.[108] This is tantamount to a defence of technical language in poetry, and the terms of the debate have changed very little since Aristotle's time.[109] According to M. S. Silk, ancient scholars compiled long lists of such obscure terms. Individual authors were typically interested in different sources of obscurity in investigating such things: Aristotle seems particularly intrigued by borrowings from other dialects and tongues, Galen was more concerned with obsolete literary expressions, etc.[110] But the point of such lists is clearly to facilitate a readier understanding of the obscure term. In Aristophanes we glimpse how the two types of jargon – poetic and learned – may complement each other. He produces plausibly technical-sounding terms for the birds he lists and avoids their ordinary names (perhaps because it is the hoopoe and not the Athenians speaking), giving the sense of technical, rarefied language use, consistent with the poet's, though different from it.[111]

Aristophanes' incorporation of a kind of learned code into *Birds* ought to be seen in the context of this broader interest in knowledge and its abuses. The hoopoe's solo, invoking a series of bird species, comprises one of several interesting catalogues in the play. Catalogues contribute significantly, here and elsewhere, to the feeling that Aristophanes is intent on bamboozling his audience with a certain amount of scholarly prattle, providing he can do so in a graceful way. The catalogue offered by the hoopoe in *Birds* is carefully arranged according to the concepts that Aristophanes develops using the marvellous and rare compounds we have been considering. Dunbar's analysis of the catalogue as a whole clearly foregrounds the conceptual complexity of the passage.[112] This catalogue 'covers pretty well the actual habitat-range in and around Athens', but more importantly it has a clear, methodical approach to conveying this information.[113] The logic of this solo, with its hierarchical concepts and nestled subdivisions, adds to the already powerful impression of a concise and comprehensive survey of the birds of the area, and allows the individual terms Aristophanes employs, some of which he perhaps coins himself, to emerge as concepts of scientific precision. Dunbar goes so far as to suggest that the several poetic metres employed in this song – impressively 'exhibiting every attic meter except choriambic' – function in a basically pictorial fashion here.[114] The set piece thus offers a wonderful poetic equivalent to modern ornithological taxonomies, detailing the habitat, sound, and conceivably even the movement and appearance of the birds it names. Tereus describes familiar Greek birds in a way that would allow his audience to identify them for themselves based on these criteria. The capacity of Aristophanes' dexterous prosody to act as a primitive musical notation adds to the scope of such a compendium in a way that prose ethnologists could only accomplish with much more prolixity and much less precision.

But Aristophanes does much more than set down an ornithology. By setting up a storehouse of classical metres he essentially devises a handbook of Greek prosody, comparable in scope to Ovid's compendium of Greek and Latin myth in *The Metamorphoses*. Parker has remarked the utility of the play in this regard: surely no single episode is comparable to the hoopoe's solo as 'a practical introduction to Greek lyric meter'.[115] Indeed, poets have set about teaching their art to acolytes in this manner for a very long time; T. S. Eliot famously suggests that *The Cantos of Ezra Pound* serve in a similar way, as 'an inexhaustible reference book of verse form' for twentieth-century poets.[116] The hoopoe is given recourse to so many metres in part because he is, after all, the birds' tutor in the language of the symposium; his command of the full range of poetic metre amounts to a poetic lingua franca capable of mediating between birds of all species, and even between bird and simian. He is the original poetic Dr Doolittle.

* * *

When Aristophanes explicitly addresses the matter of poetics, in the passage dealing with the Pindaric Poet for example, he relies pronouncedly upon this extended bird symbolism. This could not easily escape the notice of the audience since, in the first place, the poet 'comes in singing, and generally talks in song. And even when he condescends to speak in prose (that is, in iambics), there is a rhythmical singsong in the lines.'[117] The poet himself then explains:

> O I'm a warbler, caroling sweet lays
> An eager meager servant of the muses,
> As Homer says.[118]

His credentials as a 'warbler' are confirmed by a quick allusion to Homer, implying that allusion is a key component in any verse that would approach the condition of birdsong.[119] Aristophanes suggests that the poets quite literally learned their art from birds and that poetic technique is merely an extension of the qualities already incipient in the song of birds. This idea is, of course, the crucial one in the play, and it is powerfully echoed later on by the Bird-Chorus:

> Tri-tri-trii, tri-tri-trii, tri-tri-trii!
> Our calls were borrowed by Phrynichos,
> Extracting nectar like a bee
> From our ambrosial melodies
> To make his lovely music.
> Twee-twee-twee, twee-twee-twee![120]

The metaphor is striking. Phrynichos, who was Aristophanes' elder contemporary, is credited with surveying, gathering and extracting the beautiful essence of birdsong, and the connotations make the process seem natural and inevitable. Sweetness, the most celebrated quality of Prokne's song, here becomes the common denominator between birdsong and poetry. The poet's bee-like activity is, however, not merely 'the farming of a verse', to use Auden's famous phrase, but also a kind of imitative improvisation. Nature itself conspires to teach the poet his or her lesson and provides an opportunity for the poet to equal or surpass the tutor.

The idea that poets owe a particular rather than general debt to birds for their art is not originally of Aristophanes' invention and has precedent in a couple of passages by Alkman,[121] as well as an anthropological fragment of the fifth century BCE philosopher, Democritus.[122] The latter is quite as direct as Aristophanes, and recommends our keen attention to animals in several more or less specialised disciplines, including singing. 'In some of the most important skills men have been pupils of animals', Democritus tells us: 'of the spider in weaving and healing, of the swallow in house-building, and of song-birds, swan and nightingale, in singing, by imitation.'[123] Though we cannot be sure that Aristophanes knew these works, the idea appears to be consistent with contemporary interest in the 'origins and development of civilization' and indicates the extent and scope of the broader interrelatedness between poetry and birdsong posited here.[124] It is also worth remarking that this is not the reciprocal lyrical education and competition that emerges in the Renaissance (in Crashaw's 'Musik's Duel', for example): the direction of influence and deference is clear and unambiguous for the Greeks. Though little is known about Phrynichos, Aristophanes' interest in the poet and his original poetic jargon points to a particular and *technical* debt to birdsong, such as we have been considering here. This is in addition to the general qualities such as the 'sweetness' that he hopes his verse might share with birdsong, and which have received much more critical attention.

His Phrynichian ideal of achieving a birdlike poetry inspires Aristophanes to break with convention, producing a problem play that defies generic expectation in several important ways. Many critics, for instance, have been uncomfortable with the lack of direct social commentary in *Birds*, and hence its supposed lack of serious comedic intentions. But in the context of Aristophanes' aesthetic aims and achievements in the play, and of his all-pervasive jargoning, such arguments miss the aesthetic point rather comically. Aristophanes is interested in exploring the imperatives of the imagination and sonic invention in this play, and his style is often calculated to avoid discursiveness per se. One should not be surprised, in such circumstances, to find it difficult to pin down the moral of the story because the verse insists, above all, on providing alternatives to expository human discourse. The play's triumph in these terms is not a social but a poetic one, and it does not lessen the comedic impact one iota.

If Aristophanes' lyric predecessors established a precedent for thinking about poetry in terms of birdsong, Aristophanes transforms this general affinity into a systematic poetics of jargon. The strategies he develops and the devices he employs have, as Leonard Lutwack observes, become 'standard practice' in subsequent poetic treatments of birds, and they also suggest a practical means by which poetry can more thoroughly aspire to the condition of natural music, regardless of subject matter.[125] They are also quite elementary: 'he describes the song in words arranged in rhythmic patterns that imitate the musical pattern of the song itself, and he also supplies phonetic equivalents of the sounds made by the bird'.[126] To these devices may be added an array of complementary strategies that admit various degrees and sources of obscurity: literary conventions and habits, allusive and inter-textual strategies, strange lexical borrowings. With sufficient concentration these devices may frustrate the ability of human language to make direct, predicative, unambiguous, prose sense; focus attention and meaning on the sound and rhythm; transform it into poetry.

Notes

1. Cf. Osborne, *Greece in the Making*, pp. 70–136.
2. Long, *Barbarians*, p. 4.
3. Long includes, for example, Aristeas's 'fantastic, ethnographic epic on the Arimaspi'; in Herodotus's *Logoi*, 'substantial and systematized reports on the country and manners of the Lydians, Babylonians, Egyptians, and Scythians, with more selected information about the Carians, Caunians, Lycians, Massegetei, Thracians, and Indians'; Ctesias's writings on the Persians; Xanthus of Lydia's writing about Lydia; Charon of Lampsacus' *Persica*; Xenophon's ethnographic descriptions in his *Anabasis*; and Theocritus of Cheos's *Lybyaca* (*Barbarians*, pp. 3–4). The list goes on. Among dramatists who directly incorporated this information in their writings were Aeschylus, Sophocles, Euripides, Epicharmus (*Persians*), Magnes (*Lydians*), Aristophanes (*Babylonians*), Apollophanes (*Cretans*), Pherecrates (*Persians*), Antiphanes (*Scythotaurians* and *Carians*), Eubulus (*Mysians*), Xenarchus (*Sythians*), Timocles (*Egyptians*) and Strattis (*Macedonians or Pausanias*).
4. Thucydides, *Peloponnesian War*, p. 14; I.1.
5. Homer, *Iliad*, 2, l. 867.
6. Strabo, *Geography*, 14.2.28.
7. The fact that the word *barbaros* continues to be employed onomatopoeically – as in Eubulus, where a boiling pot is described as a 'barbarian babble' – lends some incidental support for Strabo's inference (qtd in Long, *Barbarians*, p. 133).
8. Long, *Barbarians*, p. 130.
9. Ibid. p. 137.
10. Ibid. pp. 7–8.
11. Thucydides provides ample testimony to the practice. Cf. 'After the battle the Corcyreans put up a trophy on Leukimme, a headland of Corcyra. They then put all the prisoners to death, with the exceptions of the Corinthians, whom they still kept in custody' (Thucydides, *Peloponnesian War*, p. 53; I.2).
12. Aeschylus, *Agamemnon*, p. 139; ll. 948–54.
13. Ibid. p. 139; ll. 952–3.
14. Peacocks become quite prominent in Greek drama (cf. *Birds*, p. 18; l. 102).

By Aristophanes' time (448–380 BCE), they were 'still a recent import from Persia'; a generation earlier, at the time of *The Agamemnon*, they were still more remarkable and, of course, more exotic (Aristophanes, *Aristophanes Birds*, trans. Halliwell, p. 255, n. 102).

15. Aeschylus, *Agamemnon*, p. 146; ll. 1097–8. This is true neither of Argos nor the play. Both Agamemnon and Clytaemnestra have only just led us to infer the contrary:

> CLYTAEMNESTRA: Would you have sworn this act to god in a time of terror?
> AGAMEMNON: Yes, if a prophet called for a last drastic rite. (Ibid. p. 138; ll. 929–30)
> Or: CLYTAEMNESTRA: I would have sworn to tread on legacies of robes at one command from an oracle. (Ibid. p. 140; ll. 964–5)

16. Ibid. pp. 143–4; ll. 1037–68. This silence profoundly unsettles Clytaemnestra – she is presumably wary of Cassandra's prophetic talents from her dress and her reputation, and anxious to dispose of her. The impasse that the two women reach in the short scene when both are on-stage is one of the dramatic highlights of the play: Aeschylus communicates rather a lot between the lines. Clytaemnestra's injunction is, after all, not simply that Cassandra should speak, but rather that she should cooperate and be made to acknowledge Clytaemnestra's command. She responds combatively to the silence, proposing to make her instructions known even if they have to resort to 'one of her exotic handsigns' (ibid. p. 144; l. 1060), but finally leaves it to the Chorus Leader to compel her as best he can, knowing that she will not have to waste any more effort or time persuading her (ibid. p. 144; l. 1068). For both Clytaemnestra and the audience, Cassandra's silence at this point in the play speaks volumes: it articulates her passive resistance to the doom Clytaemnestra intends more effectively than mere words, which, however incomprehensible, would at least indicate a willingness to communicate and recognition of her obligation to respond to her masters. Her silence is, as Michel Foucault and James Joyce realise quite independently, not separate from but a part of discourse. For Foucault, 'Silence itself—the thing one declines to say, or is forbidden to name, the discretion that is required between speakers—is less the absolute limit of discourse, the other side from which it is separated by a strict boundary, than an element that functions alongside the things said, with them and in relation to them' (Foucault, *History of Sexuality*, p. 27).

17. Aeschylus, *Agamemnon*, p. 143; ll. 1046–51.

18. Aeschylus, *Agamemnon*, p. 144; ll. 1063–4.

19. Agamemnon protests that her anthropolatry *is* quite sufficient to damn them all (ibid. pp. 137–8; ll. 914–20). The terms of this description, however, seem commonplace rather than blasphemous; in fact they closely parallel and conceivably allude to a fragment attributed to Anacreon: 'Zeus, put to sleep solecian speech / lest you babble barbarously' (Fragment 423a and b, Fowler, *Archaic Greek Poetry*, p. 189).

20. Aeschylus, *Agamemnon*, p. 143; l. 1046; p. 146; l. 1106; p. 147; l. 1113.

21. Aeschylus, *Agamemnon*, p. 144; ll. 1061–2.

22. Aeschylus, *Agamemnon*, p. 146; l. 1106; p. 147; ll. 1114–15.
23. Ibid. p. 148; ll. 1134–7.
24. Ibid. p. 150; ll. 1204–8.
25. Ibid. p. 147; ll. 1132–3.
26. Ezra Pound evokes this gruesome story in its Provençal retelling in Canto IV.
27. Aeschylus, *Agamemnon*, p. 149.
28. Aeschylus, *Agamemnon*, p. 149; ll. 1164–8; ll. 1175–9.
29. Aeschylus, *Agamemnon*, p. 145; l. 1077.
30. Lutwack, *Birds in Literature*, p. 116.
31. Qtd in Flacelière, *Greek Oracles*, pp. 7–8.
32. Qtd in ibid. p. 14.
33. According to Dunbar, 'the distinction was maintained in classical Latin with added particularity: *oscen* came to designate a bird whose song (as distinct from its flight) was used for augury, thus emphasizing the directness of antiquity's identification of augury and song, and hence poetry. The term was for the Romans a technical one, and it subsequently entered modern science as a taxonomic term in the 19th century from this usage' ('Oscine', *Oxford English Dictionary*. Qtd in *Aristophanes Birds*, ed. Dunbar, p. 222, n. 254).
34. Flacelière, *Greek Oracles*, pp. 8–9.
35. Aristophanes, *Birds*, p. 42; ll. 719–21; p. 259, n. 719.
36. Flacelière, *Greek Oracles*, p. 11.
37. Ibid. p. 9. Flacelière derives his understanding of cledomancy from Bouché-leclercq, who explains it thus: 'Everything that is said … a phrase, an isolated word or exclamation, if heard by a man preoccupied with some idea unfamiliar to the man who utters it, could become for the hearer the kind of prophetic sign that the Greeks used to call a cledon. An unforeseen connection, fortuitous consonance, might contain a providential warning. Presages of this kind were all the more reliable when they were uttered by those least capable of calculating their effect, by children for example' (Flacelière, *Greek Oracles*, p. 11). Hence, perhaps, the Chorus Leader's earlier ejaculation, 'a child could see the truth' (Aeschylus, *Agamemnon*, p. 149; l. 1176).
38. Aeschylus, *Agamemnon*, pp. 107–8; ll. 118–39.
39. Cf. 'There appeared another faulty and barbarian-like pronunciation in our language, whenever any person speaking Greek did not pronounce it correctly, but pronounced the words like barbarians who are only just beginning to learn Greek and are unable to speak it accurately, as is also the case with us speaking in their languages' (Strabo, *Geography*, 14.2.28).
40. Slavoj Žižek offers a précis of the same epistemological impasse in more contemporary terms echoing the Kantian sublime: 'far from signaling the failure of our thought to grasp reality, the inherent inconsistency of our notional apparatus is the ultimate proof that our thought is not merely a logical game we play, but is able to reach reality itself, expressing its inherent structuring principle' (Žižek, *Ticklish Subject*, p. 99). The fact that human language can only grasp *logos* in a partial and fleeting sense, far from undermining *logos*, only emphasises that it exists to be apprehended.

41. Flacelière, *Greek Oracles*, p. 6.
42. Hubbard, *Mask of Comedy*, p. 170.
43. Aristophanes, *Birds*, p. 21; ll. 199–200.
44. Cf. *Thesmophoriazusae*, ll. 1070–175.
45. Aristophanes, *Birds*, p. 22; l. 210; l. 211; l. 214; l. 213.
46. Ibid. p. 72; ll. 1573–4. This barbarian, like the birds, is also designated as such by his attire, but the comparison with their lavish costumes is not in the Triballian's favour. Poseidon asks: 'What *are* you up to there? Your cloak's all skew / Adjust it, so it's properly draped like mine. / What a vagabond! A right old Laispodias!' – the Triballian appears to be struggling with a Greek cloak that is unfamiliar to him (Aristophanes, *Birds*, p. 72; ll. 1567–9).
47. *Aristophanes Birds*, ed. Dunbar, p. 725. Friedrich first articulated this argument noting, however, that there is insufficient extant Triballic to be certain (qtd in Long, *Barbarians*, p. 135, n. 11).
48. Long, *Barbarians*, p. 135.
49. Aristophanes, *Birds*, p. 76; ll. 1677–82.
50. Though enormously popular and influential, augury nonetheless attracts some scepticism in Greek literature; its most outspoken critic is perhaps Jocasta in *Oedipus Rex*. Only Xenophanes of the ancient philosophers repudiates divination outright, according to Cicero (Flacelière, *Greek Oracles*, p. 74). But even to those who were convinced of augury's truth, it was conceivable that some signs could be rendered meaningless or misinterpreted, as the so-called 'Homeric Hymn to Hermes' suggests:

> Whoever shall come
> In answer to the cries and flight of birds of sure omen,
> He shall have joy of my voice, and I will not deceive him.
> But whoever puts his trust in birds that chatter idly
> And seeks to enquire of my prophetic powers against my will,
> And so to apprehend more than the immortal gods,
> I say his journey shall be fruitless. (Qtd in Pollard, *Seers, Shrines and Sirens*, pp. 22–3)

51. Long, *Barbarians*, p. 135.
52. Aristophanes, *Birds*, p. 76; l. 1696.
53. Consigny, *Sophist and Artist*, p. 36.
54. Qtd in ibid. p. 45.
55. Aristophanes, *Birds*, p. 76; ll. 1697–9.
56. This is consistent with Aristophanes' portrayal of the philosopher elsewhere. Hubbard notes for example that throughout *Clouds* 'Socrates has been connected with . . . social and moral disintegration, whether in his skywalking indifference to practical human affairs or in his active debunking of belief in the Olympian gods' (Hubbard, *Mask of Comedy*, p. 111).
57. Aristophanes, *Birds*, p. 31; ll. 429–30.
58. Ibid. p. 7.
59. Ibid. p. 8.
60. Consigny, *Sophist and Artist*, p. 44.
61. Ibid. p. 47.

62. Aristophanes, *Birds*, p. 22; ll. 209–22.
63. The presence of the piper sets up a correlation and a tension between music and verse in the play by alternately *augmenting* the play's verse and *directly transposing* the bird's song. Dunbar supposes 'both Procne, who accompanies the Parabasis (667–800), and the Raven, who accompanies the choral songs at 851–7 ~ 895–902, were probably mutes, mimed piping in fact being done by the official αυλητης' (*Aristophanes Birds*, ed. Dunbar, p. 15). The piper probably 'regularly played in full view of the audience, who simply accepted his dramatically irrelevant presence' (ibid. p. 203).
64. The emphasis on harmony in this passage is entirely consistent with other Greek texts that involve both human and avian singers: despite the competitive nature of the Symposia, the idea of a mortal competition between lutanist and songbird appears to be a much later development, possibly beginning with Pliny the Elder.
65. Aristophanes, *Birds*, p. 40; ll. 659–60.
66. Ibid. p. 22; ll. 222–3.
67. Ibid. p. 41; l. 681. The Greek expression, κρέκιν, is revealing: 'in the oldest occurrence, in Sappho 102, it governs . . . *web* or *loom*, and [means] (1), weave . . . But it is also found in music making contexts, where it means either (2), as here, play an instrument, for which the only classical parallel seems to be a fragment of the late-5th-c. Athenian tragedian Diogenes . . . or (3), sing to an instrumental accompaniment, which it seems to mean at 771–2' (*Aristophanes Birds*, ed. Dunbar, p. 427). The notion of weaving sounds together, or of weaving sound and sense, seems to be as old as this.
68. Lutwack, *Birds in Literature*, p. 8.
69. *Aristophanes Birds*, ed. Dunbar, p. 297.
70. Ibid. p. 297.
71. Parker, *Songs*, p. 4.
72. Aristophanes, *Birds*, pp. 22–3; ll. 227–62.
73. The Greek name for the bird, ἐποποι, is an onomatopoeic derivation from its typical call, 'a low, far-carrying poo-poo-poo', but this call may easily be mistaken for that of other birds, for example the cuckoo (Petersen et al., *Field Guide to the Birds of Britain and Europe*, p. 141, qtd in *Aristophanes Birds*, ed. Dunbar, p. 154).
74. Powers, *BirdTalk*, pp. 49–51.
75. Ibid. p. 64.
76. Cf. *Aristophanes Birds*, ed. Dunbar, pp. 243–56.
77. Dunbar indicates that Tereus calls to those 'who live in well-sown farmers' fields' in dochmaics; he invokes 'the barley-eaters, / Seed-peckers' in hemiepes; he summons those who 'twitter round the crumbling clods' in trochees; he appeals to birds of hill and plain in cretics, etc. (l. 230; ll. 231–2; l. 235). This careful distinction between bird-rhythms is also maintained inversely, by conspicuous silences and abrupt changes of metre (*Aristophanes Birds*, ed. Dunbar, p. 210).
78. Another fine example of characterisation by strategic metrical differentiation may be found in the iambic scenes that introduce a series of supplicants to the new city of Cloud-cuckoo-land. As Dunbar again observes, this sequence 'matches the detailed treatment of the Chorus

in their entry scene' (*Aristophanes Birds*, ed. Dunbar, p. 520). The first character to enter is the destitute 'Pindaric Poet' of lines 903–57, who pleads successfully for the patronage of Cloud-cuckoo-land. His lines are 'probably best interpreted as dacto-epitrite', according to Dunbar, which 'is particularly apt for these "Pindaric" passages ... and had already been adopted by Aristophanes for Pindaric parody' (ibid. p. 522). These lines feature several other complementary prosodic effects that would remind the audience of Pindar in local passages, for example 'the mixing of iambic and aeolic cola' (l. 524); 'reduced hemiepes' (l. 525); 'initial resolved cretic(s)' (l. 525; cf. ibid. pp. 522–8 for a systematic appraisal of these details). The oracle-monger is the next character to appear, and is treated even less favourably, perhaps because his pronouncements do not deviate from 'oracular-style hexameters' regardless of whether he speaks in an official capacity, or in his own voice; the scientist Meton uses an unlikely combination of solemn and tragic prosodic effects and paradoxes and absurdities; the inspector from Athens speaks casually and assuredly in anapestic rhythms, but his confidence is no more winning than that of the other supplicants; the rough merchant's prose of the decree-seller also falls flat (ibid. p. 541; pp. 552–7; p. 568). The distinction between the successful Pindaric Poet and the Dithyrambic poet Kinesias, who enters somewhat later in the play, is even more pointed and dramatically effective than these. In the latter case, 'Aristophanes is clearly parodying both the polymetry and the artificiality of the New Dithyramb', and signals his intent by scripting the Dithyrambic poet's part in heterogeneous lines with heavy syncopation, mid-sentence changes in metre and a general sense of exoticism (ibid. pp. 662–3). Since the play was initially performed at the Dionysia, we perhaps ought to see this rivalry between proponents of heterogeneous poetic styles as part of what Hubbard calls the prevailing 'atmosphere of developed agonistic competition and intense literary allusion, wherein the poets sought and created for themselves visible public identities' of the festival (Hubbard, *Mask of Comedy*, p. 33).

79. See p. 169.
80. Powers, *BirdTalk*, p. 49.
81. Qtd in Parker, *Songs*, p. 116.
82. In discussing the sung exchange between Chorus and Chorus Leader at ll. 406–34, Parker notes that 'the dochmaics of the strophe could fitly express the distress and sense of betrayal of the Birds, and the cretics of the antistrophe their aggressive firmness and resolution. This would be entirely consistent with the use of the two meters elsewhere', though she concludes by wondering why, given the promising scope of this device, Aristophanes did not use it more often (Parker, *Songs*, p. 307). Parker does note that this strategy *is* adopted by the Chorus on other occasions, as, for example, when it 'comes to touch on the subject of the good faith of their human ally, the rhythm shows signs of heightened emotion: dochmaics in the MS text, resolution in the emended version' (ibid. p. 317).
83. Parker provides an overview of some of these sanctified emotional associations in her 'Introduction' to *The Songs of Aristophanes*. Dochmaics, for instance (the most consistently expressive of Greek metres), are regarded as having the virtually habitual function of 'expressing violent

excitement' (Parker, *Songs*, p. 336). They are, for the Greeks, 'the meter of violent emotion: anger, grief, fear, even, in later tragedy, tumultuous joy' (ibid. p. 67). This makes them particularly suitable to the Bird-Chorus in this comedy, which is 'generally excitable and, both literally and figuratively, twittery' (ibid. pp. 67–8). Similarly, iambic metres are associated with invective and burlesque, and in the scenes in the second half of the play where we meet the catalogue of intruders, both associations are instrumental in Aristophanes' parody of the inflated rhetoric of each of these characters (ibid. pp. 28–9). Trochaic metres are regarded by classical authorities as being fast-moving and undignified; cretic metres as virile and vehement, and particularly associated with dance; dactylic metres are more ornate and connote dignity, etc. (ibid. p. 35; p. 45; p. 48). Aristophanes utilises each of these associations in a limited and localised fashion in *Birds*.

84. Aristophanes, *Birds*, p. 22; ll. 227; *Aristophanes Birds*, ed. Dunbar, p. 214.
85. As Dunbar advises editors and scholars, 'the accentuation of ἰτω is uncertain, but it seems best to have a bird-call ἰτώ (cf. 211–12n) four times, leading by a change of accent to the verb ἴτω' (*Aristophanes Birds*, ed. Dunbar, p. 215).
86. Ibid. p. 215.
87. Line 237, for instance, approximates trilling with its sequence of τιο eight times; line 242 'probably represents [a] "general assortment of bird-calls"', says Dunbar, citing several other uses of its constituent phrases to denote a variety of avian sounds; she observes, moreover, that the passage is certainly non-discursive, since 'no real Greek word ends in "k"' (*Aristophanes Birds*, ed. Dunbar, pp. 218–19). Line 249 provides a similarly onomatopoeic appeal to the francolin or black partridge: its repeated ἀτταγας, 'securely identified as the Black Francolin or Black Partridge . . . seems intended to suggest a bird call' (ibid. p. 220). Finally, the hoopoe's solo lyric ends as it began: with a neat segue between pure sound and discursive chatter, this time the other way round. Line 259, with its 'repeated δευρο, unlike the repeated τορο of 260, 262, reinforces the summons simultaneously in Greek and bird language', since it is both a real word and a highly onomatopoeic one, before transitioning 'to the similar sounding τορο, so that pure bird-call ends the song as it began it' (ibid. p. 223).
88. Cf. Aristophanes, *The Birds: An English Version*, l. 259; l. 310; l. 314; l. 857.
89. Ibid. p. 19; l. 119.
90. Descartes, *Discourse on Method*, p. 116.
91. Chomsky, *Cartesian Linguistics*, p. 15.
92. Aristotle, *Poetics*, p. 1478; §22.
93. Ibid. p. 1478; §22.
94. *Aristophanes Birds*, ed. Dunbar, p. 206.
95. Qtd in *Aristophanes Birds*, ed. Dunbar, p. 206. A word may become an iconym for several reasons. As Silk notes, 'in a literate, but not bookish community before the advent of dictionaries', the meaning of a word, in the proper sense, 'is guaranteed *only* by communal usage' (qtd in ibid.

p. 311). If a word is borrowed from a foreign tongue, if it has fallen long out of use and memory, if those who know the word are few for whatever reason, the word ceases to possess meaning in the conventional sense at all. The word 'may still survive passively', in religious formulae or poetry for example, but it can no longer be said to *mean* in a direct, unambiguous way.

96. Qtd in ibid. p. 311.
97. Silk's point that the use of iconyms establish membership of a certain class of antiquarian authors is also relevant since an important aspect of Aristophanes' art is to estrange and impress the audience with an avian and poetic arcana ('LSJ', p. 328).
98. *Aristophanes Birds*, ed. Dunbar, p. 222.
99. Long, *Barbarians*, p. 135.
100. Dover, *Aristophanic Comedy*, p. 147ff.
101. Dunbar fully considers thirty-three instances in her comprehensive notes to the play, many of which involve jokes; see her 'General Index', which identifies 'Puns and Double Meanings' in ll. 142, 145, 149, 172, 182, 185, 202, 233–4, 239, 246, 261, 289, 295, 346, 362, 379, 417, 422–3, 489–90, 530, 533, 535–6, 540, 590–1, 617, 618–19, 628, 638–9, 690–1, 698, 703 and 740–2.
102. Parker, *Songs*, pp. 13–14.
103. Looking just in the vicinity of the hoopoe's solo one finds: 'much-wept-over' (l. 221), 'my fellow birds' (l. 229), 'well-sown farmer's fields' (l. 230), 'barley-eaters' (l. 231), 'seed-peckers' (l. 232), 'both oleaster-eaters and arbutus-eaters' (l. 240), 'dew-soaked plains' (l. 248), 'long-necked' (l. 254), etc.
104. Most are, however, almost otherwise unknown, and would most probably have been 'unknown in common life', like the poetic obscurities Aristotle defends in Homer. See below.
105. This view, manifest in Aristophanes' practice in *Birds*, anticipates Nietzsche's famous view of poetic language as essentially metaphoric: 'metaphor, for the authentic poet, is not a figure of rhetoric but a representative image standing concretely before him in lieu of a concept' (Nietzsche, *Birth of Tragedy*, p. 55).
106. There is some critical debate about the effect of such a high concentration of compound words, especially on a passage's tone. For Dunbar, the hoopoe's solo is something of an anomaly: 'it neither closely follows a high tragic model with incongruous deviations . . . nor shows stylistic exaggeration including parody' (*Aristophanes Birds*, ed. Dunbar, p. 212). Compound adjectives are indeed a prominent feature of 'dithyrambic' style, but in this instance they seem to lack the usual 'florid extravagance' that might alert the audience to a parodic intent (ibid. p. 213). Nor are they obviously indecorous, and instead seem 'designed to charm the audience by . . . strangeness, gracefulness, and ingenuity rather than make them laugh' (ibid. p. 213). In some instances, these qualities are arguably supplied by a scientific lexicon rather than a more narrowly poetic one. Several of the most choice compounds in the hoopoe's solo ('well-sown farmer's fields' [l. 230], 'barley-eaters' [l. 231], 'both oleaster-eaters and arbutus-eaters' [l. 240]) seem closer to *scientific* language than poetic

language. These compounds function as particularising concepts rather than epithets or poetic descriptions. In utilising language in this way, Aristophanes gestures towards the more esoteric usage of the philosophers, and effectively produces a poetry that includes jargon not only in the original but also in the modern sense. His poetry defers to 'the language of scholars or philosophers, the terminology of a science or art, or the cant of a class, sect, trade, or profession' as needed ('Jargon', *Oxford English Dictionary*).

107. Aristotle, *Poetics*, p. 1479; §22.
108. Ibid. p. 1479; §22.
109. Andreas Willi defines technical language as 'the sum of all the linguistic features (a) which are necessary for the formulation and labeling of concepts, ideas, and phenomena in what a given society perceives as a specialized area, but (b) whose active and passive handling does not form part of what that society acknowledges as the general linguistic knowledge and competence which every adult member is expected to have acquired in the process of his or her education' (Willi, *Languages of Aristophanes*, p. 56). The distinction on which Willi's definition rests remains Aristotle's 'expressions unknown in the language of common life', with the emphasis placed on the role of specialists in determining what is or is not universal (Aristotle, *Poetics*, p. 1479; §22).
110. Silk, 'LSJ', p. 303.
111. Aristophanes' interest in a scientific tone and in scientific terminology in *Birds* is also reflected in his treatment of the philosophers Socrates and Gorgias, mentioned towards the climax of the comedy. He envisions these 'nasty beasts who live by tongue work' (l. 1696), in terms of Plato's critique of Gorgias, as 'mere jugglers of words rather than true philosophers intent on finding truth', to use Scott Consigny's suggestive paraphrase (*Sophist and Artist*, p. 36). One thing at least ought to be evident from the foregoing: Aristophanes is no less of a word-juggler than the rhetoricians and philosophers his Chorus denounces. This special critique of his learned fellows, who dally with words but neglect the supposedly more substantial things they designate, might well have been directed at Aristophanes' own art (John Ruskin for instance charges that he goes too far in the direction of pure music, remaining insensitive to Procne's plight and the anguish she forever laments as a nightingale [*Love's Meinie*, §38]).
112. *Aristophanes Birds*, ed. Dunbar, p. 209.
113. Ibid. p. 210.
114. 'The heavy beat of unresolved dochmaics (230) perhaps suggest a bird poking and prodding around, and the lighter hemiepes (231–2) its flying off; the trochees of 235 (perhaps also 237) give a hint of hopping, and the many resolved feet (esp. 233, 237, 240–1) a hint of rapid flight, while the ponderous cretics of 243–7 may suggest waders prodding with their beaks, as the dactyls of 250–1 admirably suggest the skimming movements of seabirds' (*Aristophanes Birds*, ed. Dunbar, p. 210).
115. Parker, *Songs*, p. vii.
116. Eliot, 'Introduction' to Pound, *Selected Poems*, p. x. Notable Anglophone examples include Coleridge's short epigrams describing and illustrating

various classical metres, or John Hollander's more recent introduction to English prosody, *Rhyme's Reason*.

117. Aristophanes, *The Birds of Aristophanes*, trans. Rogers, p. 124.

118. Ibid. p. 124, ll. 908–10.

119. I have hinted at the allusive concentration of the play, but it is far too extensive to document here. Aristophanes' original audience would have been well enough acquainted with a corpus of literary material aside from Homer from performances at Symposia and would be comfortable with the emergence of complex and fully inter-textual meaning in very much the manner we finally assume, many years later, in *The Waste Land* or the initial *Cantos*. By requiring the audience to recognise the sources of his many borrowed forms, or at the very least the disparity between his 'Pindaric utterances' and this present dramatic context, verbal allusion establishes a 'community of knowledge' and produces secondary associations and further meanings that operate within that community ('Allusion', *Princeton Encyclopedia of Poetry and Poetics*). Because these associations are often indirect, allusions 'suggest a substantive interpretive response which enriches the play in which the allusion has been placed' (Garner, *From Homer to Tragedy*, p. 183). They are, in effect, esoteric hermeneutical exercises that can be completed only by trained exegetes, in this instance, the seasoned Athenian playgoer, very much the same kind of chicanery that Pound discovered in Villon (and that he rejected as a datum of interpretation in Cavalcanti).

120. Aristophanes, *Birds*, p. 43; ll. 747–52.

121. Fragment 39: 'Alkman found lyric / and song by noting / the tongued trill / of Partridges'; Fragment 40: 'I know the songs / of all the birds' (Fowler, *Archaic Greek Poetry*, p. 103). The latter might well have been sung by the hoopoe.

122. *Aristophanes Birds*, ed. Dunbar, pp. 465–6.

123. Qtd in *Aristophanes Birds*, ed. Dunbar, p. 466.

124. *Aristophanes Birds*, ed. Dunbar, p. 466.

125. Lutwack, *Birds in Literature*, p. 8.

126. Ibid. p. 8.

References

Adams, Stephen J. 'The Metrical Contract of *The Cantos*'. *Journal of Modern Literature* 15.1 (Summer 1988): 55–72.

Aeschylus. *The Oresteia*. Trans. Robert Fagles. New York: Penguin, 1979.

Agamben, Giorgio. *Potentialities: Collected Essays in Philosophy*. Ed. and trans. Daniel Heller-Roazen. Stanford: Stanford University Press, 1999.

Agard, John. *Mangoes and Bullets: Selected and New Poems, 1972–84*. London: Pluto, 1985.

Albright, Daniel. *Quantum Poetics: Yeats, Pound, Eliot, and the Science of Modernism*. Cambridge: Cambridge University Press, 1997.

Altieri, Charles. *Painterly Abstraction in Modern American Poetry: The Contemporaneity of Modernism*. Ed. Walter Sutton. Gainsville: University Presses of Florida, 1995.

Amirkhanian, Charles. 'Lost and Found Pound'. Accompanying notes to *Ego Scriptor Cantilenae: The Music of Ezra Pound*. CD. Cond. Robert Hughes. Other Minds, 2003.

Anderson, David. *Pound's Cavalcanti: An Edition of the Translations, Notes, and Essays*. Princeton: Princeton University Press, 1983.

Aristophanes. *The Birds of Aristophanes, Acted at Athens at the Great Dionysia B.C. 414*. Trans. and commentary Benjamin Bickley Rogers. London: Bell, 1906.

—. *The Birds: An English Version*. Trans. Dudley Fitts. New York: Harcourt, Brace and World, 1957.

—. *Aristophanes Birds, Lysistrata, Assembly-women, Wealth: A New Verse Translation*. Trans. Stephen Halliwell. Oxford: Clarendon, 1997.

—. *Aristophanes Birds*. Ed. with commentary Nan Dunbar. Oxford: Clarendon, 1998.

Aristotle. *Poetics*. *The Basic Works of Aristotle*. Ed. Richard McKeon. New York: Random House, 1942.

Arnold, Matthew. *Culture and Anarchy: An Essay in Political and Social Criticism* and *Friendship's Garland*. New York: Macmillan, 1883.

Aviram, Amittai F. *Telling Rhythm: Body and Meaning in Poetry*. Ann Arbor: University of Michigan Press, 1994.

Barton, John. *Playing Shakespeare*. New York: Methuen, 1984.

Bately, Janet. 'Time and the Passing of Time in "The Wanderer" and Related OE Texts'. *Essays and Studies* 37 (1984): 1–15.

Beckson, Karl. *London in the 1890's: A Cultural History.* London: Norton, 1992.

Berryman, John. *Collected Poems, 1937–1971.* Ed. Charles Thornbury. New York: FSG, 1991.

—. *Berryman's Shakespeare.* Ed. John Haffenden. New York: FSG, 1999.

Booth, Wayne. *The Rhetoric of Fiction.* 2nd edn. Chicago: University of Chicago Press, 1983.

Bridges, Robert. *Milton's Prosody with a Chapter on Accentual Verse & Notes.* Revised edn. Oxford: Oxford University Press, 1921.

Browning, Robert. *The Works of Robert Browning.* 10 vols. Ed. F. G. Kenyon. New York: AMS, 1966.

Burke, Kenneth. *The Philosophy of Literary Form: Studies in Symbolic Action.* Baton Rouge: Louisiana State University Press, 1941.

Burns, Robert. *Poems and Songs.* Ed. James Kingsley. Oxford: Oxford University Press, 1969.

Campbell, Jackson J. 'Oral Poetry in *The Seafarer*'. *Speculum: A Journal of Medieval Studies* 35.1 (1960): 87–96.

Carne-Ross, D. S. 'New Metres for Old: A Note on Pound's Metric'. *Arion* 6 (1967): 216–32.

Carpenter, Humphrey. *A Serious Character: The Life of Ezra Pound.* Boston: Houghton Mifflin, 1988.

Carr, Helen. 'Imagism and Empire'. *Modernism and Empire: Writing and British Coloniality, 1890–1940.* Ed. Howard J. Booth and Nigel Rigby. Manchester: Manchester University Press, 2000.

Ch'ien, Evelyn Nien-Ming. *Weird English.* Cambridge, MA: Harvard University Press, 2004.

Chomsky, Noam. *Cartesian Linguistics.* New York: Harper and Row, 1966.

Coleridge, Samuel Taylor. *Coleridge's Poetry and Prose.* Ed. Nicholas Halmi, Paul Magnuson and Raimonda Modiano. New York: Norton, 2004.

Columbia Granger's World of Poetry.<http://www.columbiagrangers.org> (accessed 20 October 2006).

Consigny, Scott. *Gorgias, Sophist and Artist.* Columbia: University of South Carolina, 2001.

Cornell, Julian. *The Trial of Ezra Pound.* New York: John Day, 1966.

D'Agapeyeff, Alexander. *Codes and Ciphers.* London: Oxford University Press, 1939.

Daniel, Arnaut. *The Poetry of Arnaut Daniel.* Trans. James J. Wilhelm. New York: Garland, 1981.

Dante Aligheri. *Inferno.* Trans. Henry W. Longfellow and Matthew Pearl. New York: Modern Library, 2003.

Davie, Donald. *Studies in Ezra Pound.* Manchester: Carcanet, 1991.

Deleuze, Gilles. *Essays Critical and Clinical.* Trans. Daniel W. Smith and Michael A Greco. Minneapolis: University of Minnesota Press, 1997.

De Nagy, N. Christoph. *The Poetry of Ezra Pound: The Pre-Imagist Stage.* Basel: Francke Verlag Bern, 1960.

Descartes, Rene. *Discourse on Method* and the Meditations. Trans. F. E. Sutcliffe. London: Penguin, 1968.

Dickey, Marcus. *The Maturity of James Whitcomb Riley.* Indianapolis: Bobbs-Merril, 1922.

Diepeveen, Leonard. *The Difficulties of Modernism*. New York: Routledge, 2003.

Douglas, Gavin. *Poetical Works*. 4 vols. Edinburgh: s.n., 1874.

Dover, Kenneth. *Aristophanic Comedy*. Berkeley and Los Angeles: University of California Press, 1972.

Dowson, Ernest. *The Letters of Ernest Dowson*. Ed. Desmond Flower and Henry Maas. Cranbury, NJ: Associated University Presses, 1967.

Edwards, Barry S. '"The Subtler Music": Ezra Pound's Prosody'. *Paideuma* 27.1 (Spring 1998): 31–5.

Edwards, Dannah. 'Addendum to the Preliminary Catalog of Ezra Pound's Library'. *Paideuma* 24.2–3 (1995 Fall/Winter): 51–5.

Eliot, T. S. 'Ulysses, Order, and Myth'. *Dial* (November 1923): 480–3.

—. *The Use of Poetry and the Use of Criticism: Studies in the Relation of Criticism to Poetry in England*. London: Faber, 1933.

—. *On Poetry and Poets*. New York: Farrar, Straus and Cudahy, 1957.

—. *The Letters of T. S. Eliot*. San Diego: Harcourt Brace Jovanovich, 1988.

—. *The Sacred Wood, and Major Early Essays*. New York: Dover, 1998.

Ellmann, Richard. *James Joyce*. Revised edn. New York: Oxford University Press, 1982.

Fein, David. *François Villon and His Reader*. Detroit: Wayne State University Press, 1989.

—. *François Villon Revisited*. New York: Twayne, 1997.

Fielder, Leslie A. *The Stranger in Shakespeare*. New York: Stein and Day, 1972.

Fisher, Margaret. *Ezra Pound's Radio Operas: The BBC Experiments, 1931–1933*. Cambridge, MA: MIT Press, 2002.

—. 'Ezra Pound: Composer'. Accompanying notes to *Ego Scriptor Cantilenae: The Music of Ezra Pound*. CD. Cond. Robert Hughes. Other Minds, 2003.

Flacelière, Robert. *Greek Oracles*. Trans. Douglas Garman. New York: Norton, 1966.

Foley, John Miles. 'Genre(s) in the Making: *The Seafarer*'. *Poetics Today* 4.4 (1983): 683–706.

Forster, E. M. *Aspects of the Novel*. New York: Harcourt, 1927.

Forster, R. F. *W. B. Yeats: A Life, vol. 1. The Apprentice Mage*. Oxford: Oxford University Press, 1997.

Foucault, Michel. *The History of Sexuality, Volume One: An Introduction*. Trans. Robert Hurley. New York: Vintage, 1990.

Fowler, Barbara Hughes. *Archaic Greek Poetry: An Anthology*. Madison: University of Wisconsin, 1992.

Froula, Christine. *A Guide to Ezra Pound's* Selected Poems. New York: New Directions, 1983.

Garner, Richard. *From Homer to Tragedy: The Art of Allusion in Greek Poetry*. London: Routledge, 1990.

Gautier, Théophile. *The Works of Théophile Gautier*. Trans and ed. F. C. De Sumichrast. Vol. 23. New York: George Sproul, 1908.

—. *Mademoiselle de Maupin*. Trans. Helen Constantine. London: Penguin, 2005.

Gibson, Mary Ellis. *Epic Reinvented: Ezra Pound and the Victorians*. Ithaca: Cornell University Press, 1995.

Goldsmith, Margaret E. 'The Seafarer and the Birds'. *Review of English Studies* 5.19 (July 1954): 225–35.

Gower, John. *Confessio Amantis*. Ed. Russell A. Peck. Trans. Andrew Galloway. Vol. 3. Kalamazoo, MI: Medieval Institute Publications, 2004.

Graves, Robert. *The White Goddess: A Historical Grammar of Poetic Myth*. 1948. Enlarged edn. New York: FSG, 2001.

Grieve, Thomas F. *Ezra Pound's Early Poetry and Poetics*. Columbia: University of Missouri Press, 1997.

Gugelberger, Georg M. *Ezra Pound's Medievalism*. Las Vegas: Lang, 1978.

Heaney, Seamus. 'Burns's Art Speech'. *Robert Burns and Cultural Authority*. Ed. Robert Crawford. Edinburgh: Edinburgh University Press, 1997.

Hegel, G. W. F. *Phenomenology of Spirit*. Trans. A. V. Miller. Oxford: Oxford University Press, 1977.

Hollander, John. *Rhyme's Reason*. New Haven: Yale University Press, 1989.

Homer. *Iliad*. Trans. Robert Fagles. New York: Penguin, 1998.

Hubbard, Thomas K. *The Mask of Comedy: Aristophanes and the Intertextual Parabasis*. Ithaca: Cornell University Press, 1991.

Jackson, Thomas H. *The Early Poetry of Ezra Pound*. Cambridge, MA: Harvard University Press, 1968.

Johnson, Samuel. *Dictionary of the English Language*. 2nd edn. London: Knapton et al., 1760.

Joyce, James. *Finnegans Wake*. London: Penguin, 2000.

Kahn, David. *Codebreakers: The Story of Secret Writing*. London: Weidenfeld and Nicolson, 1966.

Keats, John, and Percy Bysshe Shelley. *Complete Poetical Works*. New York: Random House, n.d.

Kenner, Hugh. *The Pound Era*. Berkeley: UCLA, 1971.

King, Michael. 'Go, Little Book: Ezra Pound, Hilda Doolittle, and "Hilda's Book"'. *Paideuma* 10.2 (Fall 1981): 337–60.

Kinghorn, Alexander M., and Alexander Law (eds). *Poems by Allan Ramsay and Robert Ferguson*. Edinburgh: Scottish Academic Press, 1974.

Lawrence, D. H. 'Birds'. *The Complete Poems of D. H. Lawrence*. Ed. Vivian De Sola Pinto and F. Warren Roberts. New York: Viking Penguin, 1971.

Lewis, Wyndham. *Men Without Art*. London: Cassell, 1934.

Locke, John. *An Essay Concerning Human Understanding*. Ed. Roger Woolhouse. London: Penguin, 1997.

Long, Timothy. *Barbarians in Greek Comedy*. Carbondale, IL: Southern Illinois University Press, 1986.

Longinus. *Longinus On The Sublime: The Greek Text Edited After the Paris Manuscript*. Trans. W. Rhys Roberts. Cambridge: Cambridge University Press, 1899.

Lutwack, Leonard. *Birds in Literature*. Gainesville: University of Florida Press, 1994.

McDougal, Stuart Y. *Ezra Pound and the Troubadour Tradition*. Princeton: Princeton University Press, 1972.

McGann, Jerome J. *Swinburne: An Experiment in Criticism*. Chicago: University of Chicago Press, 1972.

Martz, Louis L. 'Pound's Early Poems'. *Ezra Pound*. Ed. Harold Bloom. New York: Chelsea House, 1987.

Matthew, H. C. G. *The Oxford History of Britain, Volume Five: The Modern Age*. Ed. Kenneth O. Morgan. Oxford: Oxford University Press, 1992.

Moody, A. David. *Ezra Pound: Poet, A Portrait of the Man and his Work. I: The Young Genius, 1885–1920*. New York: Oxford University Press, 2007.

Morgan, Edwin. *The Second Life*. Edinburgh: Edinburgh University Press, 1968.

Morris, William. *The Collected Letters of William Morris, vol. 2*. Ed. Norman Kelvin. Princeton: Princeton University Press, 1987.

Nash, Walter. *Jargon: Its Uses and Abuses*. Oxford: Blackwell, 1993.

New Catholic Encyclopedia. 17 vols. Ed. Catholic University of America Staff. New York: McGraw Hill, 1967–79.

Nietzsche, Friedrich. *The Birth of Tragedy* and *The Genealogy of Morals*. Trans. Francis Golffing. New York: Doubleday, 1956.

—. *The Gay Science*. Trans. Walter Kaufmann. New York: Random House-Vintage, 1974.

North, Michael. *The Dialect of Modernism: Race, Language, and Twentieth-Century Literature*. Oxford: Oxford University Press, 1994.

Opland, Jeff. 'Beowulf on the Poet'. *Mediaeval Studies* 38 (1976): 442–67.

Osborne, Robin. *Greece in the Making*. London: Routledge, 1996.

Ovid. *Metamorphosis*. Trans. Allen Mandelbaum. New York: Harcourt Brace, 1993.

Oxford Dictionary of English Etymology. Ed. C. T. Onions. Oxford: Oxford University Press, 1966.

Oxford Dictionary of Philosophy. Ed. Simon Blackburn. Oxford: Oxford University Press, 1996.

Oxford English Dictionary, 2nd edn. 1989.<http://dictionary.oed.com> (acessed 20 October 2006).

Parker, L. P. E. *The Songs of Aristophanes*. Oxford: Clarendon, 1997.

Pater, Walter. *The Renaissance. Walter Pater: Three Major Texts*. Ed. William E. Buckler. New York: New York University Press, 1986.

Petersen, R., G. Mountfort and P. A. D. Hollom. *A Field Guide to the Birds of Britain and Europe*. Boston: Houghton Mifflin, 1966.

Plarr, Victor. *Ernest Dowson 1888–1897: Reminiscences, Unpublished Letters and Marginalia*. London: Elkin Mathews, 1914.

Poe, Edgar Allan. *Spirits of the Dead: Tales and Poems*. London: Penguin, 1997.

Pollard, John. *Seers, Shrines and Sirens: The Greek Religious Revolution in the Sixth Century B.C.* London: Allen and Unwin, 1965.

Pope, Alexander. *The Poems of Alexander Pope, Esq. In three volumes*. Ed. Samuel Johnston. Wittingham: Chiswick, 1822.

—. *Alexander Pope*. Ed. Pat Rogers. Oxford: Oxford University Press, 1993.

Pope, John C. 'Second Thoughts on the Interpretation of "The Seafarer"'. *Anglo-Saxon England* 3 (1974): 45–86.

Pound, Ezra. *Spirit of Romance*. London: Dent, 1910.

—. *Cathay*. London: Elkin Mathews, 1915.

—. 'Chinese Poetry'. *To-day* 3 (April–May 1918): 54–7; 93–5.

—. *The Instigations of Ezra Pound, together with An Essay on the Chinese Written Character, by Ernest Fenollosa*. New York: Boni and Liveright, 1920.

—. *ABC of Reading*. New York: New Directions, 1934.

—. *Literary Essays of Ezra Pound*. Ed. T. S. Eliot. London: Faber, 1954.

—. *The Selected Poems of Ezra Pound*. New York: New Directions, 1957.

—. *Selected Cantos of Ezra Pound*. New York: New Directions, 1968.

—. *Gaudier Brzeska: A Memoir*. New York: New Directions, 1970.

—. *Guide to Kulchur*. New York: New Directions, 1970.

—. *Selected Letters of Ezra Pound, 1907–1941*. Ed. D. D. Paige. New York: New Directions, 1971.

—. *The Cantos of Ezra Pound*. New York: New Directions, 1972.

—. *Selected Prose, 1909–1965*. Ed. William Cookson. New York: New Directions, 1973.

—. *Ezra Pound Speaking: Radio Speeches of World War II*. Ed. Leonard W. Doob. Westport, CT: Greenwood, 1978.

—. *Ego Scriptor Cantilenae: The Music of Ezra Pound*. CD. Cond. Robert Hughes. Other Minds, 2003.

—. *Poems and Translations*. Ed. Richard Sieburth. New York: Library of America, 2003.

Pound, Omar, and Robert Spoo (eds). *Ezra and Dorothy Pound: Letters in Captivity, 1945–1946*. New York: Oxford University Press, 1999.

Powell, Barry. 'Who Invented the Alphabet: The Semites or the Greeks?' *Archaeology Odyssey* 1.1 (1998): 44–53.

Powers, Alan. *BirdTalk: Conversations with Birds*. Berkeley: Frog, 2003.

Princeton Encyclopedia of Poetry and Poetics. Ed Alex Preminger. 1965. Enlarged edn. Princeton: Princeton University Press, 1975.

Ramsay, Allan. *The Works of Allan Ramsay*. 6 vols. Ed. Burns Martin, John W. Oliver, Alexander M. Kinghorn and Alexander Law. Edinburgh: Blackwood, 1951–74.

—, and Robert Fergusson. *Poems by Allan Ramsay and Robert Fergusson*. Ed. Alexander M. Kinghorn and Alexander Law. Edinburgh: Scottish Academic Press, 1974.

Redman, Tim. 'Pound's Library: A Preliminary Catalog', *Paideuma* 15.2–3 (Fall/Winter 1986): 213–37.

Riley, James Whitcomb. *Complete Poetical Works*. New York: Grosset and Dunlap, 1937.

Robinson, Fred C. '"The Might of the North": Pound's Anglo-Saxon Studies and "The Seafarer"'. *Yale Review* 71.2 (Winter 1982): 199–224.

Ruskin, John. *Love's Meinie. Lectures on Greek and English Birds. The Works of John Ruskin*, Ed. E. T. Cook and Alexander Wedderburn. Vol. 25. London: George Allen, 1906.

Santayana, George. *Interpretations of Poetry and Religion*. Ed. William G. Holzberger and Herman J. Saatkamp, Jr. Cambridge, MA: MIT Press, 1989.

Shakespeare, William. *The Tempest*. Ed. Virginia Mason Vaughan and Alden T. Vaughan. London: Thomson, 1999.

Silk, M. S. 'LSJ and the Problem of Poetic Archaism: From Meanings to Iconyms'. *Classical Quarterly* 33.2 (1983): 303–30.

Stark, Robert. '"Keep[ing] Up the Fire": Elizabeth Barrett Browning's Victorian Versification'. *Journal of Browning Studies* 1.1 (Spring 2010): 49–69.

Stauder, Ellen Keck. 'Towards a Grammar of Relationships: The Rhetoric of Music in Pound and Rousseau'. *Paideuma* 17.1 (1988): 45–57.

—. '"Beyond the Synopsis of Vision": The Conception of Art in Ezra Pound and Mina Loy'. *Paideuma* 24 (1995): 195–227.

—. '"Crystal Waves Weaving Together": Visual Notation and the Phrasal Music of the *Rock-Drill Cantos*'. *Paideuma* 26 (1997): 93–110.

—. '"Without an Ear of his Own": Pound's Janequin in Canto 75'. *Quaderni di Palazzo Serra* 15 (2008): 257–77.

Stevens, Wallace. *Collected Poetry and Prose*. Ed. Frank Kermode and Joan Richardson. New York: Library of America, 1997.

—. *Selected Poems*. Ed. John N. Serio. New York: Knopf, 2011.

Stevenson, Robert Louis. *Familiar Studies of Men and Books*. New York: Scribner, 1914.

Stock, Noel. *Life of Ezra Pound*. San Francisco: North Point, 1982.

Strabo. *Geography*. Trans. Horace Leonard Jones. Cambridge, MA: Harvard University Press, 1933.

Sullivan, J. P. Ed. *Ezra Pound: A Critical Anthology*. Harmondsworth: Penguin, 1970.

Surette, Leon. '"Dantescan Light": Ezra Pound and Eccentric Dante Scholars'. *Dante and the Unorthodox: The Aesthetics of Transgression*. Ed. James Miller. Ontario: Wilfred Laurier University Press, 2005.

Sutton, Walter. *Pound, Thayer, Watson and The Dial: A Story in Letters*. Gainsville: University Presses of Florida, 1994.

Swift, Jonathan. *Major Works*. Ed. Angus Ross and David Woolley. London: Oxford University Press, 1984.

Swinburne, Algernon Charles. *Poems and Ballads, Second Series*. New York: R. Worthington, 1878.

—. *Selected Poems*. Ed. L. M. Findlay. New York: Routledge, 2002.

Tate, Allen. *Collected Essays*. Denver: Swallow, 1959.

Terrell, Carroll F. *A Companion to* The Cantos of Ezra Pound. Berkeley: UCLA, 1980.

Thornton, R. K. R. *The Decadent Dilemma*. London: E. Arnold, 1983.

Thucydides. *The Peloponnesian War*. Trans. Rex Warner. London: Penguin, 1954.

Tiffany, Daniel. *Radio Corpse: Imagism and the Cryptaesthetic of Ezra Pound*. Cambridge, MA: Harvard University Press, 1995.

Tolstoy, Leo. *Anna Karenina*. Trans. Richard Pevear and Larissa Volokhonsky. New York: Penguin, 2000.

Van Allen, Elizabeth J. *James Whitcomb Riley: A Life*. Bloomington: Indiana University Press, 1999.

Vico, Giambattista. *The New Science of Giambattista Vico, Unabridged Translation of the Third Edition (1744)*. Trans. Thomas Goddard Bergin and Max Harold Fisch. New York: Cornell, 1968.

Villon, François. *The Jargon of Master François Villon*. Trans. Jordan Herbert Stabler. Cambridge, MA: Houghton Mifflin, 1918.

Whitman, Walt. *Whitman: Poetry and Prose*. New York: Library of America, 1996.

Wilhelm, James J. *American Roots of Ezra Pound*. New York: Garland, 1985.

Willi, Andreas. *The Languages of Aristophanes: Aspects of Linguistic Variation in Classical Attic Greek*. Oxford: Oxford University Press, 2003.

Williams, Raymond. *The Politics of Modernism: Against the New Conformists*. New York: Verso, 1989.

Witemeyer, Hugh. *The Poetry of Ezra Pound, 1908–1920*. Berkeley: University of California Press, 1969.

Wordsworth, William. *William Wordsworth: The Major Works*. Ed. Stephen Gill. Oxford: Oxford University Press, 2000.

Yeats, W. B. *Essays and Introductions*. New York: Macmillan, 1961.

—. *Memoirs*. Ed. Denis Donoghue. New York: Macmillan, 1972.

—. *A Vision*. New York: Collier, 1972.

—. *The Poems*. Ed. Daniel Albright. London: Everyman, 1992.

Žižek, Slavoj. *The Ticklish Subject: The Absent Centre of Political Ontology*. New York: Verso, 2000.

Index